DHARMAKĪRTI'S THEORY OF HETU-CENTRICITY OF ANUMĀNA

BUDDHIST TRADITION

Edited by
ALEX WAYMAN

VOLUME V

DHARMAKĪRTI'S THEORY OF HETU-CENTRICITY OF ANUMĀNA

MANGALA R. CHINCHORE

MOTILAL BANARSIDASS PUBLISHERS
PRIVATE LIMITED
Delhi

First Edition: Delhi, 1989

ISBN: 81-208-0623-9

Also available at :

MOTILAL BANARSIDASS
Bungalow Road, Jawahar Nagar, Delhi 110 007
Chowk, Varanasi 221 001
Ashok Rajpath, Patna 800 004
24 Race Course Road, Bangalore 560 001
120 Royapettah High Road, Mylapore, Madras 600 004

PRINTED IN INDIA
BY JAINENDRA PRAKASH JAIN AT SHRI JAINENDRA PRESS, A-45 NARAINA INDUSTRIAL AREA, PHASE I, NEW DELHI 110 028 AND PUBLISHED BY NARENDRA PRAKASH JAIN FOR MOTILAL BANARSIDASS PUBLISHERS PVT. LTD., BUNGALOW ROAD, JAWAHAR NAGAR, DELHI 110 007

FOREWORD

Mangala Chinchore's philosophical exposition of Buddhist logic is a remarkable rationalization of the system, taking *hetu* (the "reason") as the guiding thread of *anumāna* ("inference"). Her procedure is to use the numerous technical terms in the manner of names or titles. These are not translated, but are the subjects of the philosophical propositions. For example, when she insists that Dharmakīrti did indeed clearly distinguish between Svārthānumāna and Parārthānumāna and in a novel way, her method does not require rendering the first as "inference for oneself", the second one as "inference for others". She takes it for granted that the reader knows what these terms mean in a purely lexical manner. The author is a mediator between the extensive literature, especially of Sanskrit texts and associated scholarship, abundantly accessible to her at Pune, India. Her bibliographical notes establish this mediation. For the purpose she does not actually cite Sanskrit passages.

Thus Chinchore's exposition is acutely philosophical; and since some comparisons are stipulated, she carries on such comparisons within the Indic context, expectedly involving the Nyāya of Hindu logic. Her *tour-de-force* is probably unique in modern writing. That it is possible to expose the system of Buddhist logic in such a manner, betokens a kind of maturity of philosophical discourse. She uses all these texts and scholarly aids as a kind of platform, one's address or where one lives; and it is there she stands and speaks. There is no point to doubting that Chinchore's procedure is feasible, because she has done it.

A. WAYMAN

ACKNOWLEDGEMENTS

Right from the time I was working on my doctoral dissertation on Dharmakīrti's *Vādanyāya*, and especially after completing it, I began faintly to see the need and necessity of working on his theory of *Anumāna*. My repeated and prolonged discussions with Prof. M. P. Marathe not only enkindled my interest in this sort of investigation but also considerably helped to deepen it. I also began to see that this kind of inquiry would be very significant especially in the context of the marked contrast of Dharmakīrti's theory of *Anumāna* with that of his *Nyāya* or Buddhist predecessors.

With a view to make a humble beginning in this direction, I undertook to study Dharmakīrti's *Hetu-bindu*, as a Research Associate of the University Grants Commission. I am thankful to the Commission for making this opportunity available to me. Although I relinquished the Research Associateship after a short period and joined the Department as a Faculty Member, my continued and sustained interest in the inquiry of this sort got deepened and widened with the march of time. I began to pursue the problem of Dharmakīrti's theory of *Anumāna* with renewed zest and enthusiasm. In this respect, too, I am immensely indebted to Prof. Marathe.

After I began working on Dharmakīrti's theory of *Anumāna*, two prominent features of it started becoming progressively clearer: (a) Dharmakīrti's theory of *Hetu*-centrality of *Anumāna* and (b) various aspects of the theory of *Anumāna* as they surfaced through two channels: (i) prolonged debates between adherents of (*Prācīna*) *Nyāya* and Buddhism and (ii) refinements introduced by the later Buddhist philosophers into the views of their predecessors concerning *Anumāna* and their respective rationales. My prolonged discussions with Prof. Marathe and Pt. Dr. Baliram Shukla of our Department helped me considerably in segregating these two aspects of the theory of *Anumāna* and concentrate basically on Dharmakīrti's theory of *Hetu*-centrality of

Anumāna in the present work, postponing the consideration of the latter two aspects to some later time.

I am grateful to the Department of Philosophy, Poona University, for a small grant made available to me for typing out the first draft of some parts of the present work.

It is also a matter of great pleasure to express my deep sense of gratitude and indebtedness to Profs. S. S. Barlingay, V. V. Gokhale, P. V. Bapat, R. D. Vadekar, the late Prof. Jagannath Upadhyaya and Dr. Pratap Chandra for constant encouragement and support I have been privileged to receive from them from time to time in my endeavour. I am, likewise, thankful to those scholars who favoured the first draft of the present work with their helpful suggestions. However, I am alone responsible for whatever shortcomings still remain in it.

I am also thankful to my colleagues and friends in the Department, conversation and dialogue with whom helped me sustain my interest in the area of investigation. I am likewise grateful to Prof. D.N. Govilkar, who, in spite of indifferent health, helped me by editing the present work. In the same way I am thankful to Mr. Futoshi Omea for his kind help in making available to me xeroxed copies of some articles, which were not otherwise easily accessible.

It would be a matter of ungratefulness on my part if I do not acknowledge my indebtedness to the secretarial staff of the Department, as also to the staff of the Departmental Library. Likewise, I am grateful to the authorities of the Bhandarkar Oriental Research Institute Library, Deccan College Library, the Library of the Centre of Advanced Study in Sanskrit and Jaykar Library, Poona University, for constant and never-failing help I received in getting the necessary reading and reference material.

My sincere thanks are also due to Shri S.B. Bhave for his perseverance and patience in neatly typing out the entire work in a comparatively very short span of time.

I am also immensely grateful to M/s Motilal Banarsidass and especially to Shri N.P. Jain for *suo moto* volunteering to publish the work and thus bringing it to the attention of the concerned for careful scrutiny and assessment of its worth.

Mangala Chinchore

ABBREVIATIONS

H.B.	*Hetu-bindu* of Dharmakīrti
H.B.T.	*Hetu-bindu-ṭīkā* of Arcata
H.B.T.A.	*Hetu-bindu-ṭīkā-āloka* of Durveka Miśra.
M.N. Vṛtti	*Manorathanandi-vṛtti* (on *Pramāṇa-vārtika*)
N.B.	*Nyāya-bindu* of Dharmakīrti
P.V.	*Pramāṇa-vārtika* of Dharmakīrti
P.V.A.	*Pramāṇa-vārtikālaṅkāra* of Prajñākara Gupta
P.V.T.	*Pramāṇa-vārtika-ṭīkā* of Karṇakagomin
Svārthānumāna-pariccheda	Pramāṇa-vārtikāntargata Svārthānumāna-pariccheda-Sva-vṛtti of Dharmakīrti

CONTENTS

INTRODUCTION

Motif:

It is a well-known fact that Buddhism occupies a very important position in the history of Indian philosophical thought. Many attempts have been made in the direction of understanding the contribution of Buddhist philosophical thoughts to the history, growth and development of Indian philosophy. However, till recently, one finds that one trend was predominant in the studies of Indian philosophy, viz., to treat a particular school as a homogeneous whole. Buddhism has not been an exception to it. Naturally, the various stages of the development of a particular philosophical trend of thought appear to have been glossed over, and as a result, the different historical stages through which such a trend of thought passed, the various problems it considered, the way it interpreted various issues and responses to them were all held to have been handed down from its inception. In the process, contributions of various philosophers to its furtherance and growth were either ignored or were held unimportant. It would seem that the same trend of thought perpetuated itself generation after generation.

Instead of looking merely at the superficially considered common points and agreed upon views accepted by adherents of the same trend of thought, an inquiry into growth and development of it seeks to look more for differences and investigation into various issues considered hopes to highlight contributions of prominent philosophers of a particular trend of thought. By merely emphasising the points of similarity one cannot hope to point out and evaluate the significant contribution each one of the philosophers belonging to that particular school has made with reference to that particular thought. Such a kind of in-depth study into the thought of different prominent philosophers of various trends of Indian philosophical thought needs to be undertaken. The need for this kind of study is in order not only in the philosophy of Dharmakīrti but also of other prominent philosophers owing their allegiance to other trends of Indian philosophical thought as well. Our present interest lies, however, in Buddhism in general and in Dharmakīrti in particular.

In the case of Buddhism, *Anumāna* is accepted as one of the important *Pramāṇas*. If one is interested in studying the theory of *Anumāna*, from the point of view of history of Buddhist philosophical thought, one has to raise an important question: whether the theory of *Anumāna* as put forward by different philosophers at different stages is the same or is different. And if it is different, what are the reasons behind its being so changed? An answer to this and number of other related questions will, no doubt, pave a way to understand the history of Buddhist philosophical thoughts. However, to embark upon such a vast and complicated task, it is essential to gather different threads connected with it. And at present, instead of engaging ourselves into such a difficult task we prefer and propose to delimit our attention to and concentrate only on Dharmakīrti's theory of *Anumāna*, he being one of the most prominent philosophers from the Buddhist camp. Although in this work an attempt is made to briefly indicate Dharmakīrti's unique position in the Indian philosophical thought, especially with reference to the theory of *Anumāna*, a detailed inquiry of this kind is not the principal task of the present work.

The present work deals with only one important problem, viz., Dharmakīrti's theory of *Anumāna* as it is outlined in his various works. In order to articulate it and present its salient features, it is essential to take into account a number of his well-known treatises, like *Pramāṇa-vārtika*, *Nyāya-bindu*, *Hetu-bindu*, *Vāda-nyāya*, etc. Nonetheless, his *Hetu-bindu* plays a very important role with regard to Dharmakīrti's theory of *Anumāna*, as some of the major contours of the theory are presented with sufficient clarity in it. Hence, roughly speaking, the present work is directed at articulating and assessing the worth of Dharmakīrti's theory of *Anumāna* as presented in his *Hetu-bindu*, although references to his other works, wherever necessary and to the extent desirable, are not neglected.

Method:

While presenting Dharmakīrti's theory of *Anumāna* it is necessary to ensure that it does not turn out to be inconsistent at least with his epistemological, general philosophical or conceptual framework. At the same time, it is essential to take care to see that such a presentation will neither deviate from nor compromise with crucial methodological considerations about it nor ignore its retionale. To be able to gather and interconnect various aspects of his theory of *Anumāna* we have drawn upon, as stated above, his various treatises. Consequently, the present work is not delimited merely to a critical study of a particular treatise of Dharmākīrti, i.e., *Hetu-bindu*. Rather, taking into account his different important works, an attempt is made to articulate and present Dharmakīrti's theory of *Anumāna* from a methodological perspective and highlight its salient features. Hence, as it should be obvious, methodological considerations are held to be more influential as compared with epistemological, or philosophical, although the bearing of his theory of *Anumāna* on his epistemology and philosophy is neither neglected nor circumvented. With this end in view, the theory of *Hetu*-centrality of *Anumāna*, as put forth by Dharmakīrti, is presented and articulated here in such a way that major methodological aspects of it are not suppressed and yet, at the same time, it is shown to be coherent and consistent not only with Dharmakīrti's epistemology, philosophy and its conceptual framework, but also with prominent aspects of Buddhist philosophy in general. Further, its various implications are spelt out.

Resume:

As said earlier, the presentation of the theory of *Anumāna* here is governed by methodological considerations. This kind of methodological orientation would be discernible, it is hoped, in the arrangement of various chapters and the various issues discussed in them.

As presenting the theory of *Anumāna* of Dharmakīrti is our aim and since such a presentation should be consistent with the epistemological, conceptual and general philosophical framework of Dharmakīrti's thoughts, it is essential to present such a framework in which such a theory is to be fitted. Hence, the first chapter is devoted to briefly outlining conceptual framework of Dharmakīrti's philosophy.

On the background of the conceptual framework of Dharmakīrti's philosophy presented in the first chapter we proceed from the second chapter to outline and articulate various aspects of his theory of *Hetu*-centrality of *Anumāna*. In order to outline such a theory and spell out its prominent implications it is necessary to bring out the epistemic, structural and regulative conditions of *Anumāna* according to Dharmakīrti. Accordingly, the second, third and the fourth chapters are respectively directed at accomplishing this task. For, unless the epistemic conditions of *Anumāna* are articulated, it is meaningless to talk about its structural and regulative conditions, as *Anumāna* is basically designed to give us *Parokṣa-jñāna*. But similarly, unless structural conditions of *Anumāna* are formulated and considered, the very form of *Anumāna* would not be articulated, and unless it is done it is pointless to discuss the regulative conditions of *Anumāna*. For, it is the structure that is regulated by the regulative conditions. Hence, discussion of structural conditions is the point of concentration in the third chapter. Such a structure needs to be regulated and hence fourth chapter aims at presenting the regulative conditions of *Anumāna*.

It is only after the general format of *Anumāna* is articulated clearly that the question of its being valid or invalid, sound or unsound arises. Hence, after considering the epistemic, structural and regulative conditions of *Anumāna*, in the fifth chapter, conditions of validity and/or soundness are discussed. Likewise, Dharmakīrti's approach concerning classification of *Anumāna* is also considered in it.

Hetvābhāsas, as is well-known, arise out of violation of or disregard to validity determining conditions. The sixth chapter is devoted to the discussion of *Hetvābhāsas* according to Dharmakīrti and spelling out its rationale. It also seeks to discuss its implications especially in contrast to the rationale of *Hetvābhāsas* provided by (*Prācīna*) *Nyāya*.

However, merely articulating and presenting the theory of *Anumāna* according to Dharmakīrti is not enough. Over and above this, its important implications not only with reference to Dharmakīrti's philosophy and its important aspects need to be spelt out but also those which are significant with regard to

Buddhist philosophy in general. The last chapter of the present work is directed towards accomplishment of this task.

Although, in this way, Dharmakīrti's theory of *Hetu*-centrality of *Anumāna* is articulated and presented in its various aspects for the first time, assessment of the worth and significance of the exercise is a matter of expert opinion and critical judgement which competent and knowledgeable persons alone would be legitimately entitled to express. Hence, in humility, we prefer to place all the cards of our limited comprehension before them for careful scrutiny, considered opinion and expert judgement, and request their valued indulgence and seek their ameliorative counsel and sympathetic advice with a view to making desirable improvements in the subsequent editions of the work.

CHAPTER I

GENERAL PERSPECTIVE REGARDING HETU-CENTRICITY OF ANUMĀNA

I *Prefatory Remarks About Dharmakīrti's Philosophy*

Human beings have curiosity and an ability to know. In the task of knowing things one may succeed, fail or else may misunderstand them. Knowing could be said to be directed at discovering truth, uncovering of reality. The truth one may discover may not be final and irrevocable. Search after truth is, however, incessant and interminable. In such a process of search after truth one may chance upon more and more refined truth, although the final truth may continue to elude us. It is possible there is no such thing as *final* truth at all. But man's curiosity and inquisitiveness will go on endlessly.

This sort of inquisitiveness is not restricted to any single direction or a solitary knowable. Man tries to know different things in a number of ways. He tries to know himself, things and organisms belonging to the world or, in general, the world around him. Thus understood, inquisitiveness makes man embark upon an epistemological enterprise. Inquisitiveness and inquiry in any domain are epistemological in character. A philosophical inquiry into knowledge, too, is not an exception to this. There is, however, a difference. Embarking upon an epistemological enterprise is one thing and an inquiry into epistemic enterprise itself quite another. The question: What philosophy means has been attempted to be answered variously, although there is no unanimity among the answers. One way of answering this question, perhaps, is that philosophical inquiry is a *critical investigation* into our experiences of ourselves, of others and of the world at large, our knowledge about ourselves, of someone else or about the world, and their tenable interpretations. In other words, it is concerned with understanding and interpreting our experiences of different things and modes of their interconnections. While doing this, one has to respond to different issues in a number of ways, and that, too, in obviously different contexts and situations. Thus, a gateway to different kinds of problems is opened as soon as one starts inquiring philosophically.

It needs, nevertheless, to be pointed out that philosophical inquiry does not mean thinking in any direction and in any way. It is not unpurposive, unsystematic and inconsistent. Otherwise any kind of thinking, however unsatisfactory intellectually, would have to be held to be philosophically worthwhile. Hence, an appropriate perspective regarding philosophical inquiry needs to be adopted. For, it is in the light of such a perspective and approach that one can hope to solve, resolve and even dissolve certain problems one is confronted with. Although an approach and a perspective do matter in philosophical inquiry, it cannot be said solely to be determined by them. Accordingly, one may have to think of something else as well. That is, just as there are the external and regulative determinants of one's philosophy, there are also internal determinants regulating the very texture and mosaic of it. We hope to give a sketchy outline of them in the sequel.

Generally, when one is confronted with a problem, one starts philosophising. The problem, one responds to, is anchored in a particular frame of reference from which it cannot be isolated. May be, it is related to the form of knowledge at issue, the mode of cognition of the knowledge-claim concerned, its warrantable certification or its communication. Similarly, the problem may be resoluble contextually or context-freely. Either way, while reacting to an issue, a philosopher employs certain notions, concepts, ideas that are either introduced by him for the first time or else are borrowed from his contemporaries or predecessors, although not always without modifications. Just by taking note of such concepts one cannot hope to penetrate deeper into the philosophy of the philosopher concerned. For the philosophy of a philosopher is not merely a taxanomy of ideas and concepts that he happens to employ. The concepts and ideas under consideration need to be studied and their implications and interconnections comprehended in such a way that it will present a systematic, consistent, coherent and, possibly, an organic whole of his philosophy. But the way the concepts are interconnected and the way their implications become available in the philosophy of a given philosopher is determined by the conceptual framework the philosopher adopts in his philosophy. The conceptual framework a philosopher adopts is prior to and determinative of the philosophical stance he develops. A student of his philosophy, however, gets first exposed to his philosophical stance and the concepts he employs. He is, however, required to analyse it carefully and reach his conceptual framework. Thus, the discovery of conceptual framework is the end-point of his inquiry. Whereas for the philosopher concerned the conceptual framework of his philosophy is both congnitively and certificatorily—both for formulation and justification of knowledge-claims he advances—epistemologically prior to his own thought, to the student of his philosophy the ideas and concepts he employs are epistemologically prior to the intellectual framework he has inherited, while the philosopher's conceptual framework is epistemologically posterior to his own thought. In this reversal of epistemological priorities one needs to work carefully in order not to miss the conceptual framework of the concerned philosopher's philosophy. Otherwise, one is likely to end up in superficiality. Further, while for the philosopher concerned determinants of the conceptual framework of his philosophy are both logically and epistemologically prior to his own philosophy, to the student of his philosophy they are epistemologically posterior to his thought, although they continue to be logically prior.

Naturally, a question arises: how to comprehend the philosophy of the philosopher under consideration? It is obvious that we ourselves are not responding to those problems which the concerned philosopher was confronted with. Rather, we are trying to analyse, interpret and understand his reactions to them, i.e. we are studying someone else's philosophy. To do this, his extant works would have to be studied. But by merely going through such material at hand one may not comprehend his philosophy properly. Moreover, all the works of the philosopher concerned may not also be available. Nonetheless, the possibility of understanding his philosophy cannot be ruled out. Assuming that some or all the works of the philosopher are available, one may yet fail to comprehend his philosophy properly. Hence, in order to analyse correctly the thoughts of the philosopher concerned, one is required to have a certain peep-hole to grasp the conceptual framework of his philosophy. It needs to be made clear, however, that understanding conceptual framework is not the aim of our inquiry into the philosophy of the philosopher concerned. Rather, it is understanding his philosophy. And conceptual framework, as it were, is an instrument of it. Unfortunately, the conceptual framework, about which we are talking, does not become easily available. We have to search for it and discover it. For discovering and capturing the appropriate conceptual framework of a philosopher, exposure to his philosophy is essential, which one can gain by going through his treatise/s. This way, one can get at least a descriptive clue to the problems that he has discussed, the concepts he has employed, modes of their interconnections, the domain in which they are brought in, the perspective with which they are incorporated, etc. This does not guarantee, however, that one would succeed in capturing the appropriate conceptual framework under consideration as also its rationale. But without it, an investigation into the philosophy of the concerned philosopher is likely to remain blind. With a view to capturing the appropriate conceptual framework of the philosophy of a philosopher like Dharmakīrti, and its rationale, one would have to commence one's search with the important concepts employed and exploited in his philosophy. Starting with this, in the present work, we wish to study the *Hetu*-centricity of *Anumāna*, as one important aspect of Dharmakīrti's conceptual framework, and find out a clue to understand its rationale. This would enable us to comprehend at least some of the promises and failures of his philosophy in bolder relief.

Dharmakīrti, as is well-known, belongs to the systematic period of Buddhism wherein Buddhist philosophers formulated their philosophical views systematically in Sanskrit. It would be instructive to note some of the dominant traits of the period, the tradition to which he was indebted and in which he grew, and also to which he made a significant contribution.

Although, it seems, Aśvaghoṣa attempted to lay the path of systematic Buddhism,[1] it is Nāgārjuna who is generally credited with laying its secure foundations.[2] A systematic attempt to analyse, interpret, understand and represent Buddha's philosophy in the then prevalent intellectual atmosphere started with Nāgārjuna. From Nāgārjuna onwards every Buddhist philosopher in the systematic period, while interpreting Buddha's thoughts seems to be trying to avoid the two extremes—one, the so-called literal nihilism (*Śūnyavāda*) and the other the strongest mode of realism, what now-a-days we call 'Platonic realism' (*Sarvāstivāda*). Since the Buddha did not commit himself to anything in writing, it was quite possible for anybody to interpret his non-commitment and silence in either of the ways.[3] That the Buddha was silent on many matters did not mean he was disinclined to accept any reality. But neither did he accept indiscriminately anything and everything to be real. In interpreting Buddha's philosophy, avoiding the two extremes of literal nihilism (*Śūnyavāda*) and extreme realism (*Sarvāstivāda*), became an important issue in Buddhist philosophy in the systematic period. It is this engagement and orientation that is usually summarised in the expression coming down from Nāgārjuna himself: *Madhyamā-pratipad*.[4]

In spite of this general engagement, subsequent Buddhist philosophers could not work out an interpretation of Buddha's philosophy that was always equidistant from both the extremes. As a result, some Buddhist philosophers of the period unwittingly tilted the balance of interpretation in the direction of either extreme which they, of course, intended to avoid. It would be interesting and instructive to find out whether and to what extent Dharmakīrti's philosophy could be said to have adhered to this commitment, although it is not our present concern.

But how is one to know Dharmakīrti's philosophy? It is clear that one cannot comprehend his philosophy properly unless one succeeds in capturing its conceptual framework. Without such a conceptual framework, comprehension of his philosophy seems to be difficult. In its absence, one is more likely to distort his philosophy; one will, therefore, have to find out patiently those concepts and ideas which are centrally important in it. Their interconnections will have to be studied. But since our primary concern is not to find out the appropriate conceptual framework of Dharmakīrti's philosophy and justifying its tenability, we restrict ourselves presently to giving just an outline, and highlighting some of the important features, of it—insofar as they seem to have bearing on his theory of *Anumāna*.

II *A Sketch of Dharmakīrti's Conceptual Framework*

Though, perhaps, as pointed out in the previous section, the central issue before Buddhist philosophers of the systematic period was of interpreting Buddha's philosophy as the philosophy of the middle-way (*Madhyamā-pratipad*), the conceptual framework of these various interpretations was, unfortunately, not the same. We shall soon spell out some reasons of adoption of different conceptual frameworks by them. One thing, however, is clear. Their conceptual frameworks being different, a uniform and monolithic characterization of all of them seems to miss much of their individual sharpness and differences among them.

Coming to the conceptual framework of Dharmakīrti's philosophy, we hope to sketch, briefly, two aspects of it:

(i) A brief outline of his thoughts, and
(ii) An outline of the salient features of the conceptual framework of his philosophy.

For reasons to be clarified later we deal with the second point first.

We hope to probe a little deeper into the conceptual framework of his philosophy with a view to briefly highlighting some of the important problems connected with it.

As said earlier, while philosophizing one interprets one's thoughts, experiences or life in general. In the present context also, we have pointed out that Dharmakīrti, while philosophizing, is interpreting Buddha's thoughts regarding this world and various aspects of man's life in it. It was, perhaps, basically an important problem for Dharmakīrti. He may, in turn, be responding to different problems. They turn out, however, to be secondary or tertiary even in his philosophy. Or, they could be connected ultimately with the central problem. To do so, we turn to outline his conceptual framework.

While probing, however, into conceptual framework of the philosophy of a particular philosopher, one has to bear in mind certain points of seminal importance. There are two types of constraints on a conceptual framework: external and internal, regulative and structural, necessary and sufficient, methodological and intuitive. For instance, one would obviously expect the framework to be consistent and coherent. With regard to Dharmakīrti's philosophy, even if one goes through his number of works, viz. *Pramāṇa-vārtika*, *Nyāya-bindu*, *Hetu-bindu*, *Vādanyāya*, *Saṁbandha-parīkṣā*, *Pramāṇa-viniścaya*, etc., one will not, it seems, disagree that they are all consistent with one another. The views and thoughts put forth in them appear to be coherently related with one another. From this it is clear that Dharmakīrti fulfils the intuitive demand of coherence and consistency. For, inconsistent thoughts do not make coherent sense nor do they allow one to grasp any consistent conceptual framework of those thoughts. It is intuitively clear that philosophy of a philosopher anchored in incoherent conceptual framework cannot be consistent. It is further intuitively clear, in that case, that we will not be in a position to make sense of his thoughts and his philosophy. One has, therefore, to accept an intuitive demand on the conceptual framework of the philosophy of the concerned philosopher that it should be coherent and consistent.

Demand of consistent or coherent comprehension cannot, however, be restricted to a particular problem alone. It needs rather to be extended at various levels. On Dharmakīrti's philosophy, if we scrutinize all his works, we find that he has met this intuitive demand, not only with reference to the discussion of a given problem in one or different works, but also with reference to various problems discussed in his different works. His commitment to consistency in this way cannot merely be dismissed as having merely academic or entertainment significance. Even if one goes through any one of his treatises, one can hardly come across any inconsistency. Moreover, the treatises under consideration need also to be considered as philosophical, not merely because they are consistent but also because the points made in them have relevance even today. For the present, however, it is enough to note that they are at least not inconsistent.

Granted that their consistency needs to be considered, a question arises as to how this consistency is not guaranteed automatically just by putting forth different truth-claims. When one can legitimately hold two truth-claims simultaneously without giving rise to any contradiction, then alone the truth-claims under consideration could be held to be consistent with each other. In this context it is important to note that simultaneous entertainment of truth-claims is not a criterion of consistency; rather their not being inconsistent with each other is a touchstone of it. With regard to Dharmakīrti's philosophy, too, we want to assert that it is not the case that just because the various truth-claims he puts forth are acceptable and hence are coherent and worth paying attention to, but rather that it is because of their being consistent that they are held to be tenable.

Consistency in the thought of a philosopher is determined by consistent conceptual framework of his philosophy and *vice-versa*, since an inconsistent thought would be incoherent with a consistent conceptual framework, and, conversely, an inconsistent conceptual framework cannot be a legitimate basis of a consistent thought. It needs, therefore, to be seen how consistent thought of Dharmakīrti is anchored in, and determined by, corresponding coherent conceptual framework of his philosophy. Its major contours need to be mapped in order not to miss its prominent reliefs.

We observed earlier that any acceptable conceptual framework is determined by two sorts of determinants: intuitive and methodological. The conceptual framework of Dharmakīrti's philosophy is not an exception to this. An intuitive constraint or determinant could be said to be that which presents itself in any consideration of the problem—systematic or pre-systematic—and demands that its violation would be contrary to our rational resolution of the problem. A methodological constraint, on the other hand, is brought in by the methodological structure of the resolution of the problem and is relative to it, though it could be counter-intuitive. It demands that adoption of the said methodological structure and violation of the methodological constraint cannot go hand in hand. With reference to Dharmakīrti's philosophy and its conceptual framework we want briefly to show that these two major sorts of demands are satisfied.

On the methodological aspect of Dharmakīrti's conceptual framework the following distinctions he makes are of great significance:

(i) between coherent possibility/conceivability and factuality/empiricality,
(ii) between necessary and sufficient conditions, and
(iii) between context-free and contextual considerations.

These distinctions made by Dharmakīrti are not brought in as a luxury of speculation but are rather constitutive of the methodological stance he adopts, and play a vital role in his philosophical inquiry.

To start with the distinction between coherent conceivability and factuality/empiricality. A coherently conceivable thing, according to him, however, need not be actually and factually existent in the world.[5] On the contrary, a thing actually obtainable in the world we live in should always be obtainable in at least one coherently possible world. Thus, the domain of coherent conceivability is always wider than that of factuality/existentiality. That which is actual or empirical alone need not be held to be legitimately coherently conceivable. To tailor the coat of the coherently possible on the measurement of the actual seeks to obliterate the distinction between the actual and the coherently possible. It illegitimately trims the domain of the coherently possible. (*Prācīna*) *Nyāya* philosophers perhaps unwittingly accepted their co-extensivity.[6] Commonsensically, the range of the coherently possible does not extend beyond what is actual. But this is no reason why methodologically appropriate philosophical inquiry like that of Dharmakīrti's should adhere to such a commonsensical demand. A philosopher to be a philosopher need not dogmatically stick to commonsense, although mere avowed departure from commonsense does not, in itself, make one a good philosopher. We shall return to this point in the context of the discussion of the role of *Udāharaṇa* in *Anumāna* according to Dharmakīrti.

Similarly, Dharmakīrti appears to be stressing on the need of making a distinction between necessary and sufficient conditions. It is not unlikely that due to their interdefinability one may confuse one with the other. So, too, sometimes a given condition may be both necessary and sufficient for the occurrence of an event. But since every necessary condition is not a sufficient condition as well, there is a need of making a distinction between the two. A necessary condition is that in the presence of which its consequence cannot fail to occur and in the absence of which it would not occur. On the other hand, a sufficient condition is that in the presence of which its consequence may not occur, and in its absence it may occur. Contextually, sometimes necessary and sufficient conditions may overlap. But this in itself is no basis for blurring the distinction between the two. With reference to *Anumāna*, we shall show below, that Dharmakīrti makes this important distinction and seeks to draw our attention to its important consequences.

Lastly, according to Dharmakīrti, perhaps, it is essential to make a distinction between contextual and context-free considerations.[7] In a given context a particular aspect of the problem may have to be paid a serious attention to. But such an aspect of it need not be held to be such a structural feature of it that it just cannot be overlooked in any consideration of it. We shall show below that Dharmakīrti insists upon the need to make the distinction between debative and non-debative contexts of the consideration of the structure of an argument. Roughly speaking, it is nothing else but a distinction between specific and general considerations. But it is also a warning against contextual and specific considerations being elevated to the non-contextual and general considerations. Hence, there is a methodological necessity of making the distinction between the two.

Peripherally, we may note that exactly the opposite kind of considerations seem to have been upheld by the adherents of *Prācīna-Nyāya*. Due to their failure to recognise such methodologically important distinctions, they seem to have confused the domains of coherent conceivability and existentiality, blurred the distinction between necessary and sufficient conditions and obliterated the need of drawing a distinction between contextual and context-free considerations. We shall return to these points later on in proper contexts.

We turn next to the consideration of external and internal or regulative and structural determinants of Dharmakīrti's conceptual framework. Of these, the regulative determinants like consistency spell out outermost boundary of the conceptual framework of Dharmakīrti's philosophy, while internal determinants like Buddha's teaching show its mosaic and general nature. Its external determinants like consideration of *Puruṣārthas*,[8] interpretation of Buddha's teaching at the hands of Dharmakīrti's predecessors or contemporaries, various knowledge-claims advanced by his adversaries from other schools of Indian Philosophical Thought leave a legacy to Dharmakīrti and, through responding to it, the conceptual framework of his philosophy takes appropriate shape. Its structural or constitutive determinants like the distinction between *Svalakṣaṇa* and *Sāmānya-lakṣaṇa*, to be sketched below, spell out the alignment and organisation of its constituents in such a way that it gets its unique structure which marks it off from the conceptual frameworks of the philosophies of his predecessors or contemporaries, both from the camp of Buddhism or outside. Since to dwell elaborately upon the conceptual framework of Dharmakīrti's philosophy in all its aspects is not our present concern, we wish to give an outline just of that sort of determinants of it which have a direct bearing upon our present point of engagement, viz., *Hetu*-centricity of *Anumāna*.

External determinants of the conceptual framework of Dharmakīrti's philosophy enable us to place and locate it within the intellectual atmosphere in which it was presented, whereas internal determinants of it enable us to pin-point the role and significance of the discussion of the concepts and problems within it. Obviously, this does not mean that internal and external determinants are, therefore, totally unconnected with each other. But what we want to suggest is that these two sorts of determinants enable us to outline different aspects of the conceptual framework under reference. It would, further, be wrong to hold that there are no determinants of the conceptual framework of his philosophy, e.g., consistency—which are at once both regulative and constitutive of it. In the same vein, in the consideration of some determinants like the account of *Puruṣārthas* more than one aspect of the conceptual framework of his philosophy will have to be brought in and consideration of more than one kind of determinants of the conceptual framework of his philosophy would have to be invoked.

With this general background we turn to the brief discussion of external determinants of Dharmakīrti's conceptual framework.

It is natural to expect that while systematically building the system of his thoughts, Dharmakīrti should attempt to incorporate in it as many tenable aspects of Buddha's teaching as possible. This kind of attempt at greater comprehensiveness operates, naturally, as an external determinant of his conceptual framework. But he also wants that such a greater comprehensiveness should be accomplished with the least number of assumptions. Consequently, economy or simplicity operates as an internal determinant of his conceptual framework. How Dharmkīrti's conceptual framework fulfils both these demands on it and yet how his philosophy copes up with the tensions of satisfying them, would be interesting to inquire into. But since this is not our present concern we leave it for further consideration later on. As remarked earlier, the views of his predecessors and contemporaries, the teaching of the Buddha and its variant interpretations also acted as external determinants of the conceptual framework of his philosophy.

Having considered the external determinants we propose to discuss briefly the internal determinants of Dharmakīrti's conceptual framework.

As is well-known, Dharmakīrti's philosophy revolves around two basic considerations, viz. *Svalakṣaṇa* and *Sāmānya-lakṣaṇa.*[9] One may point out, however, that they are also the principal considerations of Diṅnāga's philosophy. Then, where and how do they differ? In the discussion that follows we argue that even though these basic considerations, viz. *Svalakṣaṇa* and *Sāmānya-lakṣaṇa* are the same, in the philosophy of both of them, the ways in which they are interpreted are importantly different. Not only this, but also the kind of interconnection that obtains between the two is not the same for these two thinkers. They adopt different conceptual frameworks, and the philosophical stances they subscribe to are also different. We consider below some such differences.

First turning to Diṅnāga, the predecessor of Dharmakīrti. According to Diṅnāga, it seems, *Svalakṣaṇa* is by nature unique, particular, instantial (*kṣaṇika*), e.g. the beauty of a flower in the garden or a flash of lightning. *Svalakṣaṇa* means that which cannot be defined by anything else except by itself.[10] It could be experienced just for a moment. Hence, the moment we experience it, it is obviously without any quality, name, universality, etc. i.e. it is free from all characterizations.

Sāmānya-lakṣaṇa, on the other hand, according to Diṅnāga, means that which is shareable, definable and communicable. It is not, in principle, free from all mental constructions.[11] This does not mean, however, that it is purely unreal and strictly imaginary.

Further, coming to the manner in which Diṅnāga connects them. It appears that according to him *Svalakṣaṇa* and *Sāmānya-lakṣaṇa* are diametrically opposite to each other. Whatever is applicable to *Svalakṣaṇa* cannot be relevant, even in principle, to *Sāmānya-lakṣaṇa* and *vice-versa*. So, in the world that we live in, some things are purely *Svalakṣaṇātmaka* while others *Sāmānya-lakṣaṇātmaka*, and there is no interconnection between the two, since they are fundamentally different.[12] For the present, it is enough to note that Diṅnāga accepts radical difference between *Svalakṣaṇa* and *Sāmānya-lakṣaṇa*. We shall return to this point later in proper context.

On the other hand, Dharmakīrti goes further and points out flaws in Diṅnāga's thoughts. It is not unlikely that since Dharmakīrti stands on the shoulders of Diṅnāga, he might have borrowed some of his ideas either directly from Diṅnāga himself, or indirectly from some other predecessors of his in the systematic period. This needs, however, to be conclusively established beyond reasonable doubt. However, the credit of clarity and profundity cannot be, in any sense, denied to him on the basis of his supposed borrowing.

Now, to turn to Dharmakīrti's conception of *Svalakṣaṇa* and *Sāmānya-lakṣaṇa*. According to him, Diṅnāga, while defining *Svalakṣaṇa*, did not pay enough attention to avoiding the fallacy of *Ativyāpakatva*. That is why, Dharmakīrti asserts that *Svalakṣaṇa* must fulfil two conditions: *Abhrāntatva* and *Kalpanā-apoḍhatva* (instead of mere *Kalpanā-apoḍhatva*), over and above its being unique.[13]

On closer scrutiny it becomes clear that his definition of *Svalakṣaṇa* is more refined and succeeds in circumventing all those defects Diṅnāga's definition suffers from.

At the hands of Dharmakīrti not only *Svalakṣaṇa* but *Sāmānya-lakṣaṇa* also gets a refined treatment and the way they are interconnected is also distinctive. *Sāmānya-lakṣaṇa*, in his view, is sharable, definable and communicable. It need not necessarily be a product of sheer imagination or something that is merely fictitious. Rather it has something to do with coherent ratiocinativity. It is not, accordingly, purely unreal, like *Vandhyā-putra*, *kha-puṣpa* etc. Nor does it mean that such an object of cognition must never be obtained in this world. In other words, the possibility of its being obtainable cannot be summarily dismissed. It could be real as well.[14]

From the above discussion it may be clear that both *Svalakṣaṇas* and *Sāmānya-lakṣaṇas* could enjoy the status of reality in Dharmakīrti's philosophy. In this, Dharmakīrti seems to be indebted to Diṅnāga. According to both of them these two knowables are real and irreducible to each other. But for Dharmakīrti while *Svalakṣaṇa* is *Paramārtha sat*, *Sāmānya-lakṣaṇa* is (*Loka*) *Saṁvṛtti sat*,[15] although both these knowables fall in the domain of coherent conceivability—one as actual and the other as possible. The domain of coherent conceivability is not tailored to actuality; both of them are real though irreducible to each other.

As said earlier, Dharmakīrti also spells out modes of interconnection between *Svalakṣaṇa* and *Sāmānya-lakṣaṇa* in a novel manner. He seems to relate the two through the perspective of *Madhyamā-pratipad*, the middle path. *Svalakṣaṇa* and *Sāmānya-lakṣaṇa* could be sought to be related with each other in a number of ways, although each of such modes of relating them is not acceptable to Dharmakīrti, as it is not consistent with the *Madhyamā Pratipad* which he seems to uphold.

Three possibilities of relating *Svalakṣaṇa* and *Sāmānya-lakṣaṇa* could be envisaged:

(a) Accepting preponderance of one over the other without envisaging the possibility of their convergence.
(b) Accepting them to be totally independent of each other, i.e., totally unrelated.
(c) Accepting the possibility of their convergence upon an entity.

The first of these alternatives could be worked out in two ways: (a) preponderance of *Svalakṣaṇa* over *Sāmānya-lakṣaṇa*; and (b) preponderance of *Sāmānya-lakṣaṇa* over *Svalakṣaṇa*. The latter of these alternatives has not been taken seriously by any Buddhist phliosopher to the best of our knowledge. For, taking it seriously would have meant a fundamental departure from the teaching of the Buddha. The former alternative, on the contrary, was attempted to be worked out in two alternative ways: (i) holding discrete, unique particulars externally given and having no sharable features at all to be real, and totally repudiating *Sāmānya lakṣaṇa* as philosophically unpromising. This alternative seems to have been accepted by Nāgārjuna, although the distinction between *Svalakṣaṇa* and *Sāmānya-lakṣaṇa* is not clearly drawn in his philosophy. (ii) Holding that *Svalakṣaṇa* is primarily epistemic in character, and given in our subjective experiences, *Svalakṣaṇas* were held to be preponderant, since a *Sāmānya-lakṣaṇa*, when given in our subjective experience is hardly distinguishable from *Svalakṣaṇa* in the manner of its subjectively being given. For, in our personal sensations, sensation of a unique and sharable feature can hardly be distinguished. This alternative seems to have been accepted by Asaṅga and Vasubandhu of *Vijñaptimātratāsiddhi*. In both these versions of the first alternative, however, importance of *Sāmānya-lakṣaṇa* seems either to be ignored or else is relegated to the background. For fear of digression one cannot go deeper into this question here, although in passing it is important to note that the distinction between *Svalakṣaṇa* and *Sāmānya-lakṣaṇa* does not seem to have been clearly drawn even by Asaṅga and Vasubandhu.

The second alternative seems to have been accepted by Diṅnāga. According to him *Svalakṣaṇa* and *Sāmānya-lakṣaṇa* are totally different from each other because they are, basically, objects of two different and independent modes of cognitions, i.e. of *Pratyakṣa* and *Anumāna* respectively, there being no object at all that is cognised by both the *Pramāṇas* either jointly or alternatively.

Dharmakīrti seems to favour the third alternative in which utter unrelatedness of *Svalakṣaṇa* and *Sāmānya-lakṣaṇa* is given up on the one hand and their dogmatic total convergence on the other. He seems to entertain the possibility of their convergence on a single entity,[16] although the features of it that are revealed through them cannot be the same. For, otherwise, there was no need of their being disclosed through independent *Pramāṇas*, the

Saṁplava (convergence) between which is unacceptable to Dharmakīrti, as it is to Diṅnāga. This is, in a sense, following *Madhyamā-pratipad* and making sense of Buddha's philosophy with reference to paradigmaticity of the empirical world.

Another important feature of Dharmakīrti's conceptual framework is also of great philosophical importance, viz., the conceptual geography of his philosophy. It seems to be revolving around three important notions, viz. *Anattā* (*Nairātmya*), *Anityatā* (*kṣaṇikatā*) and *Nirhetukatā*.[17] They are so important in his philosophy that without them many implications of it would not be available. We give below a brief sketch of them.

It seems, Buddhism in general and Dharmakīrti in particular believe that there is no eternal, permanent principle like *Ātman* (soul) which needs to be accepted as a structural component of the world.[18] This implies that he believes in non-eternality of anything and everything in the world.

Secondly, in Buddhism *Anityatā* (impermanence) is accepted to be a built-in feature of the world, and Dharmakīrti shares this view in full measure. According to him, since everything in the world is non-eternal, nothing can be permanent.[19] Such an impermanence could be understood in strong and weak senses of the term.[20] Generally, Dharmakīrti seems to be on the side of its weak sense, i.e., nothing is permanent in the world, although this may not necessarily mean lasting only for a moment. There can, however, be things and events lasting just for a moment. Likewise, there is a possibility that everything may change every moment,[21] although changing every moment actually is not a necessary condition of the being of a thing. Nothing, nonetheless, can be immune to the possibility of and liability to change, in principle, even for a moment. This does not mean that anything that has emerged at time 't' must vanish at time 't_1'.

The third prominent notion of his philosophy is *Nirhetukatā*.[22] Through it rationality of change is sought to be explicated, saying things change because it is in their nature to change and nothing can alienate itself from its own nature.[23] In short, whatever happens happens naturally (*svabhāva*) and there is no purpose of any kind involved in it.

As with the Buddha and Buddhism in general so too with Dharmakīrti, deliverance from pain and suffering (*Duḥkha-*

nivṛtti) remains a principal engagement. Such a deliverance is possible in this world itself.[24] *Duḥkha-nivṛtti*, however, is not the ultimate aim of our life.[25] It is not an end in itself. Rather, it is instrumental to *Puruṣārtha-siddhi*.[26] *Puruṣārtha-siddhi* is further held to be the supreme aim of human life, because it is connected with our being human, for so long as the possibility of *Puruṣārtha-siddhi* remains open in our life there is chance of our living in a characteristic human way.

Dharmakīrti, in his philosophical inquiry, also aims at *Puruṣārtha-siddhi*, without losing the sight of the paradigmaticity of the empirical world. Such a *Puruṣārtha-siddhi* is connected with our knowledge which we acquire through either *Pratyakṣa* or *Anumāna*.[27] Of them, the former has bearing on the actual, the latter on the coherently possible. *Puruṣāratha-siddhi* becomes possible through discrimination between accepting those things which are instrumental to it (*Upādeya*) and rejecting those which are not so (*Heya*).[28] Such a kind of discriminatory knowledge emerges through both the modes of comprehension, viz. *Pratyakṣa* and *Anumāna*, and over and above these two modes of comprehension there is none.[29] In addition, through discrimination between *Heya* and *Upādeya*, Dharmakīrti also perhaps wants to emphasise the need of discrimination between objects of perceptual and inferential cognition, as unwitting confusion between them gives rise to number of philosophical muddles.

With this brief sketch of the salient features of Dharmakīrti's conceptual framework, we move to outlining primordiality of epistemic considerations in his philosophy and bringing out its significance to *Hetu*-centricity of *Anumāna*, our primary concern in the present work.

III *Primordiality of Epistemological Considerations*

It may scarcely be doubted that epistemological considerations in their broad sense play a decisive role in determining the conceptual framework, which, in turn, shapes the philosophy of a philosopher. This being the case, in this section we intend to study, in outline, epistemological aspects of Dharmakīrti's philosophy and locate the point of our present study in it with a view to preparing the necessary background for its proper treatment in its different aspects from the next chapter.

Dharmakīrti, following the line of Nāgārjuna, holds that there are two sorts of reals, viz. *Paramārtha-sat* and (*Loka*) *Saṁvṛtti-sat.*[30] The first of these is the object of perceptual knowledge, while the latter is that of *Anumāna.*[31] According to Dharmakīrti and Diṅnāga, both *Paramārtha-sat* and *Saṁvṛtti-sat* are on par with each other as knowables.[32] They are not, however, known with the help of the same *Pramāṇa.* As pointed out earlier, of the two sorts of knowables, *Svalakṣaṇa* is unique, particular, instantial and yet experiential. It is momentary.[33] It is not necessarily a physical object.[34] For instance, the particular and unique crying of a child could be recognised from a distance or even in a crowd. This does not, however, mean that *Svalakṣaṇa* cannot be a physical object. On the contrary, it could have spacio-temporal extension. Being experienced is the mark of *Svalakṣaṇa*[35] and it can be experienced in the world we live in.

On the other hand, communicability is the mark of *Sāmānya-lakṣaṇa.* It is sharable, inter-personal, general and at least coherently conceivable.[36]

Svalakṣaṇas and *Sāmānya-lakṣaṇas* could either be heterogeneous features of an object or they could themselves be different sorts of objects. In the former view, objects are nothing else but collections of features. Such features could be either unique and/or general. Since Buddhists reject *Dravya-guṇa* model or are opposed to *Āśraya-Āśrayī* or *Ādhāra-Ādheya* model of explaining the nature of object (*Padārtha*)[37] accepted by *Nyāya*, the features or objects under consideration cannot be graded. But, if one accepts Diṅnāgian view that objects are only of two kinds and they are necessarily diametrically opposed to each other, the world, it seems, will be compartmentalised.[38] If an object is nothing else but a bundle of characteristics then there are two possibilities: either there are objects with diametrically opposite characteristics or that the two sorts of characteristics are unrelated with each other. Either way, there would be unsurmountable troubles. On the former alternative, inconsistency would be let loose, while on the latter there would be no connection between *Svalakṣaṇas* and *Sāmānya-lakṣaṇas,* and correspondingly *Paramārtha-sat* and *Saṁvṛtti sat* will be compartmentalized. This would entail a very heavy price to be paid. On the epistemological side, consequently, it would mean that the cognition acquired through *Pratyakṣa* and *Anumāna* (inferential cognition) would have to be segregated from each other. On the other hand, if one holds Dharmakīrti's position, which methodologically appears to be more reasonable, then difference between *Svalakṣaṇa* and *Sāmānya-lakṣaṇa* need not be compromised. But, at the same time, the possibility of their convergence on the same object not being ruled out, one will still be able to comprehend the object or the features of the homogeneous object.[39] The possibility of connecting them opens a gateway to their being simultaneously available, although through different modes of comprehension. Demarcation between *Pratyakṣa* and *Anumāna* would not force us to compartmentalise the world into two distinct sorts of objects. Likewise, the two truths around which Buddha's teaching revolves, viz. *Paramārtha-sat* and *Saṁvṛtti-sat* could be coherently related to each other.

Concerning knowledge, two questions are important: (i) how do we cognise whatever knowledge we have, and (ii) how and on what basis shall we justify our knowledge-claims, if and when we are called upon to do so? The former of these is concerned with origination of knowledge, the latter with its justification, certification or vindication. Cognition of knowledge naturally presupposes a certain tool or means of cognition (*Pramāṇa*), while certification presupposes an appropriate procedure on the basis of which we would be able to justify our knowledge-claims. In Indian thought quite a few vexing problems in epistemology revolve around these two important issues. We wish to outline the response of the Buddhists in general and of Dharmakīrti in particular to them in what follows.

Let us take up the problem of cognition first. For, the question of certification of a knowledge-claim comes up only after it has been advanced and when either its justification is solicited or an already advanced certification of it is contested. Advancing a knowledge-claim presupposes having knowledge. Hence, cognitive-epistemological issues are epistemologically prior, while certificatory epistemic issues are logically posterior, for there is no point in advancing a knowledge-claim that cannot even in principle be justified. Concerning cognition, a question can be asked: how many distinct and mutually irreducible kinds of cognitions do we have? Buddhist philosophers starting with Diṅnāga, and including Dharmakīrti, hold that we have two basic sorts of cognitions: perceptual and inferential which are independent of and irreducible to each other.[40]

Of them, perceptual cognition enables us to cognise *Svalakṣaṇātmaka* features while inferential cognition enables us to cognise *Sāmānya-lakṣaṇātmaka* features of objects and there are no features of any object which are neither *Svalakṣaṇātmaka* nor *Sāmānya-lakṣaṇātmaka*. Since there are only these two principal kinds of knowables, viz. *Svalakṣaṇa* and *Sāmānya-lakṣaṇa*, and since they cannot be cognised with the help of a single tool, there are two kinds of means of knowing them viz. *Pratyakṣa* and *Anumāna* respectively. Correspondingly, there are two kinds of cognitions, viz. *Svalakṣaṇātmaka* (*Aparokṣa-jñāna*) and *Sāmānya-lakṣaṇātmaka* (*parokṣa-jñāna*). According to Dharmakīrti the number and nature of *Pramāṇas* is determined by the number and nature of *Prameyas*. Since the *Prameyas* are two, *Pramāṇas* are also two.[41] Some other prominent trends of Indian Philosophical Thought like *Nyāya* and *Sāṁkhya* differ with Buddhists and seek to determine kinds of knowables on the basis of kinds of cognitions we have.

The distinctness of the two cognitions under consideration seems to be reinforced on a number of counts: (a) priority of *Prameya* over *Pramāṇa* tells us that since the *Prameyas* are distinct and irreducible to each other, the *Pramāṇas* through which they are cognised, as also the cognitions made available by them, too, should be like-wise distinct and irreducible to each other. (b) Even if *Svalakṣaṇa* and *Sāmānya-lakṣaṇa* are understood as two different kinds of features rather than objects, since their cognition becomes possible through two distinct modes of cognition, the two modes of cognition as well as cognitions they make available remain distinct and irreducible to each other. (c) Thirdly, it may be held that after all we have two distinct sorts of cognitions: by acquaintance or experience and by description or discursion. The first of these is direct, the latter indirect. Since these become available through two distinct means and reveal different sorts of features of objects, they are distinct and irreducible to each other. (d) The principle of economy will reject the view that one and the same kind of cognition could be alternatively available to us through alternative means as the product of idle speculation which goes contrary to the principle under consideration. Consequently, Dharmakīrti in particular and Buddhists in general, accept what is called *Pramāṇa-vyavasthā* or *Pramāṇa-viplava*,[42] according to which one kind of cognition can be had through one and only one means of cognition, and since only two principal kinds of cognitions in all could be had, two and only two means of cognition would enable us to make sense of the cognitive side of our epistemic enterprise. As against this, *Nyāya* philosophers and perhaps other philosophers of Indian origin as well accept *Pramāṇa-saṁplava*,[43] a doctrine according to which one and the same kind of cognition can be had through more than one means of cognition. For fear of digression we need not go here into the details of this aspect of the *Nyāya*-Buddhist controversy. However, we remark in passing that the *Nyāya* doctrine of preponderance of *Pratyakṣa* over *Anumāna*, their insistence that *Anumāna* must have an anchorage in *Pratyakṣa*, that *bhūyo-darśana* is the cognitive basis of our comprehension of *Vyāpti*, or their assignment of significant role to *Udāharaṇa* in *Anumāna* seem to originate, in one way or the other, from their subscription to the doctrine of *Pramāṇasaṁplava*. We would return to some of them later in proper context.

We observed above that while cognition presupposes tool/s, certification of knowledge-claim presupposes procedure. When it comes to certification of knowledge-claim already advanced, various problems crop up and we give an outline below of some of them especially insofar as they bear upon Dharmakīrti's philosophy and *Hetu*-centricity of *Anumāna*, the main point of our present consideration.

It was noticed above that according to Dharmakīrti we gain two distinct sorts of cognitions through *Pratyakṣa* and *Anumāna* respectively. Any knowledge-claim would obviously come to be advanced on the basis of knowledge gained through these means of cognition. But the problem is: on what basis are we entitled to justify a knowledge-claim we have advanced, if and when we are called upon to do so? The uniform answer with regard to certifiable knowledge-claim given by both *Nyāya* and Buddhism is that it is done on the basis of some other knowledge-claim (*Parataḥ Prāmāṇya vāda*). It is obvious that this kind of transitivity of knowledge-claims is brought in with reference to certification to avoid the defect of circularity in attempting to justify a knowledge-claim on its own basis. They also accept similar procedure of justification, viz. of justifying one justifiable knowledge-claim on the basis of another, relying on which it could be justified. This is acceptable as far as it goes.

There, however, arises a vexing problem: on what sort of other knowledge-claim can we hope to justify a knowledge-claim advanced by us, when we are called upon to do so? Here the Buddhist and the *Nyāya* approaches differ markedly. In answer to the above question it cannot be said: on the basis of *any* other knowledge-claim relying on which it could be justified, no matter how it becomes available to us. For, according to Buddhists like Dharmakīrti, different and mutually irreducible features of knowable are cognised by perceptual and inferential cognitions, and perceptually cognised features cannot be inferentially cognised. If any knowledge-claim that is advanced is put forth on the basis of appropriate cognition, then its vindication would also be possible only on the basis of the appropriate cognition. Now, if a knowledge-claim advanced concerns cognition made available perceptually then its vindication should also rest upon another cognition made available perceptually. The same thing applies to a knowledge-claim advanced on the basis of inferential cognition. Thus with regard to certification of knowledge-claims as well, Dharmakīrti upholds the doctrine of *Pramāṇa-viplava*,[44] as contrasted with *Pramāṇa-saṁplava* upheld by *Nyāya*. According to the latter, a knowledge-claim advanced on the basis of perceptual cognition can very well be defended on the basis of cognition gained with the help of a different tool of cognition as well, since various tools of cognition disclose same features of cognisable object.

Thus, while, according to Dharmakīrti, perception (*Pratyakṣa*) and discursion (*Anumāna*) play a differential role both for cognition and certification, and this is in accordance with *Pramāṇa-vyavasthā* or *Pramāṇa-viplava* to which he subscribes, according to *Nyāya* various means of knowledge (*Pramāṇas*) both for cognition as well as certification play a similar and interchangeable role. This position of *Nyāya* is in accordance with the doctrine of *Pramāṇa-saṁplava* to which they subscribe. That *Pramāṇas*, both cognitively and certificatorily, should play an interchangeable role is, according to Dharmakīrti, against the principle of economy (which he upholds), while such interchangeability which *Nyāya* philosophers uphold is in accordance with the principle of convenience and the primacy of practice (to which they subscribe). Which of these sides is backed by better methodological considerations is an interesting issue to be probed into. For fear of digression, however, we refrain from going into further details of it.

Concerning the question as to which criterion/criteria of knowledge needs to be accepted, there also is a fundamental difference between Dharmakīrti and *Nyāya* philosophers. According to Dharmakīrti, there are three criteria of knowledge, viz. *Avisaṁvādakatva*, *Avijñātārthaprakāśakatva* and *Vyavahartavyatva*,[45] while according to *Naiyāyikas* there are two principal criteria of it, viz. *Tadvati tad Prakārakatva* and *Saphalapravṛttijanakatva*.

Roughly, *Naiyāyikas* hold a view that correspondence is the test of truth. That is, the nature and features of a thing revealed by the *Pramāṇas* are true without contradiction, despite all variations in space, time etc., insofar as they tally with each other. To know a thing is to judge it as having such and such properties (*Tadvati tad prakārakatva*). This knowledge of a thing will be true if the thing concerned has those properties. If a thing lacks these qualities, our knowledge of it is false. Further such a knowledge must induce a successful action—practice (*saphala-pravṛtti janakatva*) on our part, as various actions we undertake in our life are instrumental to our realising legitimate goals of our life through *Upādāna* (acquisition of that which is worthy of being acquired) or *Hāna*[46] (rejection of that which is unworthy of being acquired).

Of the three criteria accepted by Dharmakīrti *Avisaṁvādakatva* means that the information we gather must not be inconsistent with already acquired information[47] perceptually and/or inferentially.[48] Thus, consistency as a criterion and regulative feature applies to both the kinds of cognitions, viz. *Pratyakṣa* and *Anumāna*. The criterion, further, applies to these domains of cognition both distributively as well as collectively. As it is not our present concern, we need not go into the details of the further implications of the criterion.

The criterion of *Avijñātārtha-prakāśakatva* emphasises that our (additional) knowledge must have the characteristic of novelty.[49] This criterion not only makes growth and development of knowledge possible but also enables avoidance of circularity as well as inflexibility which otherwise are likely to crop up in our knowledge. It emphasises that in the process of cognition or certification our epistemic enterprise must not close the possibility of disclosing hitherto unknown features of things or of our knowledge of them.

Thirdly, *Vyavahartavyatva* also is an important criterion of knowledge. This guarantees the application of our knowledge-claims.[50] It implies its reliability and acceptability. If our knowledge is not serviceable it is useless and, hence, redundant to have it. Such a knowledge would be deceptive and so it would be pointless to have it at all. This criterion also is uniformly applicable to both the kinds of cognitions—perceptual as well as inferential.

The above mentioned three criteria of acceptability of knowledge suggested by Dharmakīrti are supposed to be applicable jointly and not alternatively. But over and above the consideration of their general applicability, knowledge gained through perceptual cognition (*Pratyakṣa*) brings in an additional question, viz. that of truth, since it has a bearing on the realm of actuality, *Svalakṣana*, while knowledge gained through inferential cognition (*Anumāna*) has a special bearing on the realm of coherent possibility. Hence, with reference to perceptual cognition Dharmakīrti brings in *Arthakriyāsāmarthya* as a mark of the real.[51] By *Arthakriyāsāmarthya* he means that anything cognised through veridical perception could be taken to be real provided it has a disposition to induce an action on our part which would terminate in our being able to discover it.[52] Thus, *Arthakriyāsāmarthya* is a connecting link between our perceptual knowledge and the reality of an object in the external world of which we have knowledge. If on discovery of the object we find that the object in fact is as we had cognised it, then this kind of *Tad rūpatva* (correspondence) is decisive of the reality of the object concerned.[53] Thus understood, *Arthakriyāsāmarthya* operates as an additional necessary condition in the case of *Svalakṣaṇātmaka* kind of knowledge, over and above the three criteria already noted, while in case of *Sāmānyalakṣaṇātmaka* kind of knowledge, it will give us its limiting range.

It needs hardly to be stated that both these kinds of cognitions, according to Dharmakīrti, have a bearing upon *Puruṣārthasiddhi* in accordance with Buddha's teaching and proper interpretation of it. It is needless for our present purpose to probe deeper into this aspect of Dharmakīrti's Philosophy and its conceptual framework.

IV *Inferential Cognition: a Clue to Puruṣārthasiddhi*

We saw in the preceding section that according to Dharmakīrti there are two main kinds of knowables: *Svalakṣaṇa* and *Sāmānya-lakṣaṇa*; that they lead to two distinct sorts of cognitions: *Pratyakṣa* (*Aparokṣa*) and *Anumāna* (*Parokṣa*), and that they are connected with two sorts of truths: *Paramārtha sat* and (*Loka*) *Saṁvṛtti sat*. We also noticed the general criteria of knowledge accepted by him and considered in outline how the two sorts of cognitions fit into the framework of the criteria so suggested.

Starting with this it may be held that Dharmakīrti's acceptance of two distinct and mutually irreducible sorts of knowables is alright. Likewise, alright is his view that the two resultant sorts of cognitions too are distinct and mutually irreducible to each other. But does this mean that the world is inhabited by two distinct sorts of reals? If so, it would mean to compartmentalise the world in such a way that its two halves as it were would not only be distinct and independent but unconnected as well. With this sort of dichotomization of the world the fate of Dharmakīrti's upholding of *Madhyamā-pratipad* would be doomed to failure. In this connection, it was briefly agreed that the two distinct sorts of knowables Dharmakīrti talks of need not be construed as two different sorts of objects, but rather as two distinct sorts of features they may disclose through two different sorts of cognitions. Given this, it could be suggested that *Paramārtha sat* and *Lokasaṁvṛtti sat* are two different kinds of truths corelative to the features disclosed respectively by *pratykṣa* and *anumāna*. Exclusive emphasis on one or the other sort of feature would bring in aberrations which Dharmakīrti wants to steer clear of so that his adherence to *Madhyamā-pratipad* does not turn out to be lopsided.

Nonetheless, it may be held that even if *Svalakṣaṇa* and *Sāmānya-lakṣaṇa* are held to be two different sorts of features rather than two distinct sorts of objects, two problems would still continue to haunt our head, one of which would be ontological and another epistemological. The ontological problem would be this: Granted that *Svalakṣaṇa* and *Sāmānya-lakṣaṇa* are two different sorts of features, are they envisaged to be features of two different sorts of objects, or are they two different sorts of features not necessarily of two different sorts of object? If the first, then the world would continue to be compartmentalised. We saw that Dharmakīrti does not favour this alternative. If the second, then the possibility of their being simultaneously of the two sorts of features of the same object cannot be ruled out in advance. We observed that Dharmakīrti favours this alternative and thus marks his principal shift from Diṅnāga who perhaps ruled out the second alternative and favoured the first instead. Thus, it was shown briefly that at least ontologically Dharmakīrti does not depart from the tacit subscription to *Madhyamā-pratipad.*

But if epistemologically the two sorts of cognitions are distinct and mutually irreducible to each other then at least our knowledge of the world, if not the world itself, would be compartmentalised, such that between the two halves of it there would be no connection. Thus understood, Dharmakīrti would be said to have avoided ontological dichotomization of the world, but he, nonetheless, continues to subscribe to epistemic dichotomization. This would mean that according to him *Aparokṣa* and *Parokṣa* kinds of cognitions stand asunder and insofar as this is so at least epistemically he could be said to be unable to uphold *Madhyamā-pratipad.* If this be the case, then according to him it would be pointless to inquire into *Hetu*-centricity of *Anumāna*, for in that case (*Loka*) *Saṁvṛtti sat*, the domain of inferential cognition, would stand severed from *Paramārtha sat*, the domain of perceptual cognition.

To start with, in this section we intend to show that Dharmakīrti does not subscribe to epistemic dichotomization even though perceptual and inferential cognitions are, according to him, of different kinds and that epistemically also he continues to uphold *Madhyamā-pratipad* to be a trait of his philosophy.

Given that in principle objects may have two principal sorts of features—*Svalakṣaṇa* and *Sāmānya-lakṣaṇa*, respectively unique and sharable—disclosed through two kinds of knowledges, viz. *Aparokṣa* and *Parokṣa*, there could be in all three classes of objects: (a) those which have only unique features (particularity), (b) those which have only sharable features (generality), and (c) those which have unique as well as sharable features (individuality). Perhaps the class of third sort of objects is the biggest, although the first two sorts of classes cannot be empty. Given this, it is perfectly possible to have knowledge of one and the same object from two different perspectives—that of *Aparokṣa* and *Parokṣa jñāna.*[54] True, that these two modes of cognition do not disclose the same features and hence are distinct. But there is a possibility of their convergence on the same object, which has two distinct sorts of features. If Dharmakīrti rejects such a convergence, then its consequences would be disastrous to his philosophy and its conceptual framework. We take a brief note of them below: (i) Suppose, *Aparokṣa* and *Parokṣa* kinds of knowledge are totally separate and unconnected from each other, then, as mentioned earlier, perhaps, as Diṅnāga seems to hold, our knowledge would be compartmentalized. Likewise, our experiences and our discursive thoughts would be difficult to be related to our life, and that would be contrary to the teaching of the Buddha.

(ii) Dichotomization of knowledge, viz. *Aparokṣa* and *Parokṣa* to the extent that they are unconnected with each other would also make likewise *Paramārtha-sat* and *Saṁvṛtti-sat* unconnected.

(iii) As *Svalakṣaṇas* are particular, *Aparokṣa jñāna* (*Pratyakṣa*) is anchored in particularity, whereas *Sāmānya-lakṣaṇa* by nature is general hence the knowledge emerging from it is bound to be general. In other words, *Parokṣa-jñāna* (*Anumāna*) consists of generality. Through keeping them unconnected, particularity and generality aspects of our knowledge would also likewise remain unconnected, and in consequence, individuality would remain unaccounted for.

(iv) Separating these two sorts of knowledge to the fullest extent is tantamount to saying that the domain of the actual and the factual on the one hand and that of the coherently conceivable and the possible on the other are unconnected, a move which is methodologically untenable.

(v) If *Svalakṣaṇātmaka jñāna* i.e. *Aparokṣa/Pratyakṣa jñāna* and *Sāmānya-lakṣaṇātmaka-jñāna* i.e. *Parokṣa/Anumāna* are held to be incapable of being related with each other then it is pointless and deceptive as well to accept common criteria of their acceptability or certification as is done by Dharmakīrti.

Hence it becomes philosophically necessary on the part of Dharmakīrti to accept coherent possibility of connection between thoughts, experiences and life in accordance with the teaching of the Buddha. This becomes possible only through the coherent possibility of convergence between *Aparokṣa* and *Parokṣa jñāna*. To reduce life, experience or thought into any one of them is one untenable alternative, while to keep them unconnected is another such alternative, and Dharmakīrti manages to avoid both these dangers.

Given that *Parokṣa jñāna* cannot be reduced to *Aparokṣa jñāna*, problems characteristic to the former need to be considered separately and in greater detail. As observed earlier, the domain of *Parokṣa jñāna* is that of sharable, communicable, general, intersubjective or the objective. It is the domain of coherent conceivability or possibility. This domain has its characteristic epistemic problems which need a separate and full-scale treatment. Further, the domain of coherently conceivable and general is far too larger than that of actual and particular. Nothing that is actual and particular can transgress the domain of the coherently possible and general, and yet many things held to be perfectly coherently possible are hardly experienced. *Anumāna* or the domain of *Parokṣa jñāna*, therefore, merits a separate and full-scale treatment to discuss at length its characteristic aspects.[55] This is what Dharmakīrti undertakes to do in his celebrated work *Hetu-bindu*, in which, it will be argued in the sequel, he establishes *Hetu*-centricity of *Anumāna*.

The *Hetu*-centricity of *Anumāna* needs to be understood generically, i.e. not only with regard to inferences or with regard to coherently possible objects, but also with regard to actual and existent objects, provided and insofar as, of course, they have sharable features. *Parokṣa* or discursive knowledge of both coherently possible and actual objects could be had, and since the domain of the actual falls within the domain of the coherently possible, what holds with regard to *Hetu*-centric *Anumāna* concerning coherently possible objects must also hold *mutatis mutandis* with regard to *Anumāna* concerning existent objects.[56] As it would be argued later, this would give us some of the minimal conditions—regulative as well as constitutive—concerning acceptability of *Anumāna*.

Granted that the problem of establishing *Hetu*-centricity of *Anumāna* arises in the domain of *Parokṣa-jñāna*, which is distinct from *Aparokṣa-jñāna* and yet they are not strictly unconnected, it becomes essential to give a brief sketch of the range of applicability of *Anumāna*. It is to this that we now proceed.

First, as observed above, the range of *Anumānātmaka jñāna* is coextensive with that of *Parokṣa jñāna*. Nonetheless, it will be argued that just as it is correct to say that there cannot be a classification of *Pratyakṣa* into two kinds, viz. *Laukika* and *A-laukika* or *Savikalpaka* and *Nirvikalpaka*,[57] as accepted by *Naiyāyikas*, so too it is incorrect to hold that *Svārthānumāna* and *Parārthānumāna* are two different kinds of *Anumānas*. Both of these classifications—of *Pratyakṣa* and *Anumāna* — are counter-intuitive.

Secondly, to have inferential cognition, all characteristic features of an object need not be sharable. Likewise, for perceptual cognition non-sharability of all the features of an object is not essential. On the contrary, a thing (an individual) could have some sharable and some non-sharable features. To say that a thing must have at least one non-sharable feature for its being experienced, is the lowermost limit with regard to *Pratyakṣa* (perception), while having at least one sharable feature is enough for its being inferentially cognised. The upper most limit of inferential cognition would obviously be that where every feature is a sharable feature. Accordingly, the range of applicability of *Anumāna* would vary from an object having purely *Sāmānya-lakṣaṇātmaka* kind of features to an object having at least one *Sāmānya-lakṣaṇātmaka* kind of feature. Hence, the framework and theory of *Anumāna* that Dharmakīrti intends to explain in *Hetubindu* is of such a wide range. In the case of objects, each feature of which is sharable, *Anumāna* makes their cognition available only as coherently possible objects, while in the case of those objects each feature of which is unique and hence non-sharable, perceptual cognition alone is available. In the case of cognition of all other objects *Pratyakṣa* as well as *Anumāna*, *Aparokṣa* as well as *Parokṣa*. *Svalakṣaṇa* as well as *Sāmānya-lakṣaṇa* have a respective role to play.

If we restrict ourselves only to those objects which have *Sāmānya-lakṣaṇātmaka* features while deciding the framework of *Anumāna*, then the resultant framework of *Anumāna* would be too restrictive. But similar would be the case if we stick to the view that applicability of *Anumāna* should be restricted only to the objects which could only be experienced, as on Dharmakīrti's view nothing can be experienced unless it has at least one non-sharable feature.

Obviously, in such a framework of *Anumāna* necessary and/or sufficient conditions of the formulation and certification of it would be determined by its applicability. We shall have an occasion later on to take into account more details of the problem.

Peripherally, it is interesting to look into the different frameworks of *Anumāna* held by *Naiyāyikas* and the Buddhists, especially by Dharmakīrti. For it is generally claimed that they hold the same frameworks of *Anumāna*. It is well known that *Naiyāyikas* advocate the co-extensivity of the domain of ontology, epistemology and logic and/or language, i.e. anything that we know and comprehend must be capable of being disclosed via experience or, to be precise, by perception. Buddhists, on the contrary, believe that whatever we know or cognise need not necessarily be anchored in experience. Cognition is possible without experience. For the certification of knowledge we need not depend upon its being experienced, although for factual truth/reality experience is essential. One need not stick to a view that whatever we know must be capable of being given to us in experience. A piece of information, which is false, could be entertained as a piece of knowledge. Thus, experience is not a pre-condition of knowledge in the view of Buddhists. Unfortunately, not seeing the point behind the methodological contention of Buddhists, *Naiyāyikas* are bent upon accepting experience as a pre-condition of knowledge. Naturally, their framework could be labelled less flexible and philosophically less promising.

Just as what we know must be experienced is a principle with *Naiyāyikas*, so too is communicability a pre-condition of knowledge for them. According to them, whatever we know must be communicable. To subscribe to such a view, according to Buddhists, appears to be submitting ourselves to the dictates of commonsense. Buddhists, especially Dharmakīrti, seem to be correct in refusing to subscribe to such a condition of knowledge, which is not backed by an appropriate philosophical promise. He states that whatever we know/cognise need not necessarily be communicable, as in case of *Pratyakṣa*. To tailor the domain of comprehension to the domain of communication is narrowing the scope of our knowledge field.

This does not, however, mean that whatever we cognise must be made available to us in experience. Nor does it mean that whatever we cognise cannot be communicated. Although there is a possibility of what we know to be experienced or communicated, this need not be a pre-condition of cognising something. This is a point worth taking serious note of. To give due justice to the dictates of both common-sense and methodology, middle-path seems to have been followed by Dharmakīrti, by accepting mere coherent knowability as a pre-condition of knowledge. We shall have an occasion later on to return to some of these points in different context.

Thus, in the treatment of *Anumāna* or *Parokṣa jñāna* many epistemological and methodological questions are involved. We have given above a brief sketch of the sort of epistemic questions which are involved. In the next section we propose to outline some of the methodological issues involved in the treatment of *Anumāna*.

V *Methodological Treatment of Anumāna*

In the preceding four sections, we have explained, in fairly great details, Dharmakīrti's philosophy, the salient features of his conceptual framework, his epistemological perspective and his views regarding inferential cognition, etc. On this background, we highlight below some salient features of Dharmakīrti's methodological treatment of *Anumāna*.

Earlier, in the second section, it was pointed out that although Diṅnāga and Dharmakīrti belong to the same school and there is a considerable similarity between their responses to a number of questions, their philosophical and conceptual frameworks are not identical. It could be held legitimately that since Dharmakīrti is the successor of Diṅnāga, he owes a great deal to him. At the same time, at the hands of Dharmakīrti great many sophistications have been introduced in the treatment of *Anumāna*, the methodological considerations have been clearly articulated and differences from the *Nyāya* tradition have been precisely formulated. As a result, treatment of *Anumāna* at his hands has gained greater profundity and depth. It is this aspect of his treatment of *Anumāna* that is designed to be probed into in considerable details.

In the process, we would have to take into account his differences with Diṅnāga on the one hand and with the adherents of the *Prācīna-Nyāya* tradition on the other. Going this way, characteristic features of his treatment of *Anumāna* could be brought out in bolder relief and clearer contrast.

Similarly, we pointed out earlier that he is not an extremist with regard to any issue or problem he has dealt with. He is a follower of the middle-way (*Madhyamā-pratipad*). Hence, while analysing his consideration and treatment of various issues concerning *Anumāna*, one has also to endeavour to show that this note of his philosophy keeps on ringing here as well. Similarly, sufficient care would also have to be taken to ensure that either his thoughts are not confused with those of someone else, or that they are not misinterpreted to give an impression that he held some views contrary to the dictates of the conceptual framework of his philosophy.

One vexing question is: Why was Dharmakīrti required to establish *Hetu*-centricity of *Anumāna* and how does his treatment of *Anumāna* methodologically differ from that of others from within the camp of Buddhism or otherwise. We briefly consider below this question.

In the treatment of *Anumāna*, various kinds of issues are likely to be taken up for consideration. First, its role as a tool of *Parokṣa jñāna* could be dealt with in sufficient details and its significance in our epistemic enterprise could be brought out. Or else, secondly, the role of *Anumāna* in debates, controversies could be examined either as an instrument of gaining victory over an adversary in a debate or as a powerful instrument of clarification and persuasion. Thirdly, one may take up the role of *Anumāna* as a tool of communication for a detailed consideration and analyse its promises or hazards. Lastly, one may inquire and investigate into the nature, structure and function of *Anumāna*, its epistemic, constitutive and normative conditions, its form, validity, etc. irrespective of the purpose for which *Anumāna* is sought to be employed. Here methodological and logical issues concerning *Anumāna* are taken up for detailed treatment.

Dharmakīrti takes up various issues concerning *Anumāna* for treatment in his different works like *Pramāṇa-vārtika*, *Nyāya-bindu*, *Pramāṇa-viniścaya Svārthānumāna-pariccheda*, *Vādanyāya*, *Hetu-bindu*, etc. Although, superficially, *Anumāna* is considered in these treatises, it is not the same aspect of it or the same problem concerning it that is taken up for treatment. Otherwise, these works would have lapsed into pointless repetition of the same points over and over again. Fortunately, such is not the case. This means Dharmakīrti seems to be aware of the need of treating different problems concerning *Anumāna* differently. Such a treatment of *Anumāna* at his hands does not also become fragmented and compartmentalized. This is so for the following reasons: (i) First, all these different aspects of *Anumāna* are considered within the compass of the same philosophical position and with reference to a uniform conceptual framework of it. (ii) Secondly, through cross-references to his other treatises he exhibits his keen awareness as to which problem is dealt with in which of his treatises and from which point of view. (iii) Thirdly, Dharmakīrti is simultaneously working on three fronts: (a) putting forth his own philosophical position, (b) registering his differences with such worthy predecessors from the Buddhist camp as Diṅnāga, and (c) holding detailed and prolonged debates over various issues of philosophical interest with his principal adversaries—adherents of *Prācīna-Nyāya* tradition. In his different works, accordingly, he deals with different aspects and problems, say, concerning *Anumāna* and it is only by piecing them coherently together that one can get a glimpse of his full-scale treatment of

Anumāna. We do not propose to write here such a compendium on Dharmakīrti's treatment of *Anumāna* in its different aspects. Instead, we wish to restrict ourselves to the methodological and epistemic considerations of *Anumāna* at the hands of Dharmakīrti in his *Hetu-bindu* and argue that therein he seeks to establish *Hetu*-centricity of *Anumāna* as its primary epistemic and methodological aspect.

Apart from such comprehensive treatises like *Pramāṇa-viniścaya* and *Pramāṇa-vārtika*, or introductory works like *Nyāya-bindu*, Dharmakīrti wrote at least four works devoted to the specialised themes or topics, and *Hetu-bindu* is one of them. In the *Vādanyāya*, the main issue is to consider what sort of debate is philosophically worthwhile, what are the determinants of the forfeiture of one's right to continue to debate and on what ground *Nigrahasthānas* accepted by *Nyāya* are unacceptable.

In the *Hetu-bindu*, as stated above, methodological problems concerning nature, structure and kinds of *Anumāna*, apart from the purpose for which it is sought to be employed, are considered. We shall investigate into this sort of treatment of *Anumāna* at the hands of Dharmakīrti from the second chapter onwards in detail.

In his *Santānāntarasiddhi* Dharmakīrti is concerned with the methodological defence of the possibility of plurality of *Santānas*, while in his *Sambandhaparīkṣā* the nature and philosophical significance of relations is taken up for a detailed specialised treatment.

The framework within which various methodological issues concerning *Anumāna* are discussed in the *Hetu-bindu* has certain readily discernible prominent aspects which have wielded considerable influence on the discussion. We wish to mention them at this juncture, the fuller implications of which would be clear as we proceed. They are: (i) *Hetu-centricity* of *Anumāna* remains the principal shaft around which discussion of various aspects of *Anumāna* revolves.

(ii) Principle of economy is not allowed to be compromised, no matter which methodological problem concerning *Anumāna* is considered.

(iii) Distinction between formal and material (non-formal)

considerations concerning *Anumāna* is never allowed to be either obliterated or compromised.

(iv) The framework so explicated is not allowed to be discordant with either principal tenets of Buddha's philosophy and its acceptable important implications or with the main issues of it dealt with by the predecessors of Dharmakīrti and their warrantable treatment at their hands.

(v) The distinction between two aspects of epistemology—cognitive and certificatory—is not allowed to be overlooked and issues connected with them are not allowed to be confused with one another.

(vi) The framework is not allowed to force us to embrace, or admit, even by back door, untenable implications of (*Prācīna*) *Nyāya* treatment of *Anumāna* into it in order not to sacrifice its coherenee, orientation and focus.

Before we end this chapter a brief discussion of the proximate and remote aims of the *Hetu-bindu* is in order. It is to this that we now turn.

First we consider its long-term or remote aim and then turn to its proximate aim. This would enable us to connect them with Dharmakīrti's philosophy and its conceptual framework.

As said earlier, there are two truths, viz. *Paramārtha-sat* and (*Loka*) *Saṁvṛti-sat*. *Paramārtha-sat*, the truth concerning *Svalakṣaṇa*, is cognisable through *Pratyakṣa*. On the other hand, it is *Anumāna* which enables us to comprehend (*Loka*) *Saṁvṛti-sat*, the truth concerning *Sāmānya-lakṣaṇa*. In the frame of *Saṁvṛti-sat* with *Santāna* as its locus, it is a fact that we experience *Duḥkha*. It could be got rid of with the help of the central tenet of the teaching of the Buddha, viz. *Nairātmya-darśana*, provided we adopt, the focus or perspective of *Nirvāṇa* and use procedural device of *Śūnyatā*. Given this, the gates to *Puruṣārthasiddhi*, which is a goal of our life in general, could be opened. The cognitions made available by *Pratyakṣa* and *Anumāna* have bearing on our knowledge of *Puruṣārthas*, and hence an inquiry into the methodological and epistemic aspects of *Anumāna*, the theme of *Hetu-bindu*, has bearing on *Puruṣārthasiddhi*.

Secondly, to justify that Buddha's philosophy could be interpreted without taking divorce either from the warrantable contentions about it at the hands of Dharmakīrti's predecessors or without giving up our commitment to middle-path (*Madhyamā-pratipad*). For doing this, one neither needs to lose sight of common sense nor exclusively take recourse to experience alone. One's acceptance of the paradigmaticity of empirical world too does not force one to eliminate or neglect *Anumāna*, which has an important role to play in our effort to make sense of the teaching of the Buddha and to study its continued relevance.

Dharmakīrti's criticism of the views of the adherents of *Nyāya*, *Mīmāṁsā*, etc. cannot be held to be a principal issue in any of his treatises, and *Hetu-bindu* is not an exception to it. There the aim is two-fold: on the one hand to reinforce and strengthen one's own position, and on the other to expose points of weakness and vulnerability in their treatment of *Anumāna*.

Coming to the proximate or immediate aims. They seem to be as follows:

(1) First and foremost, to establish *Hetu*-centricity of *Anumāna*.

(2) To consider methodological defence of the possibility of convergence of *Parokṣa* and *Aparokṣa jñāna* on an object of normal cognition.

(3) To outline the methodological framework of *Anumāna* and articulate its constitutive, epistemic and methodological conditions.

(4) To demarcate the necessary and/or sufficient conditions of its validity and/or soundness, and

(5) To study the consequences of non-fulfilment of such necessary and/or sufficient conditions of *Anumāna*. That is, to outline *Hetvābhāsas* and their rationale.

There is an interconnection between proximate and remote aims of the *Hetu-bindu*. Remote aims of the work have so close a connection with Dharmakīrti's philosophy and the salient features of its conceptual framework that no proximate aim is ever allowed to have supercedence over remote aims in such a way that a remote aim is brushed aside or neglected. Thus, proximate aims are sought to be accomplished not independently of, or in contravention with, remote aims, but rather within the compass of the possibility of their accomplishment.

Lastly, a word about the title of the work *Hetu-bindu* is in order. '*Hetu-bindu*' literally means centrality of *Hetu*. *Hetu* is not, however, considered to be central to *Anumāna* simply because it is indispensable. For, that which is indispensable need not necessarily be central. That is, indispensability is not the sole determinant of centrality. For example, *Sādhya*, in case of *Anumāna*, is also indispensable, but it is not central to it. The details of the reasons and rationale of the *Hetu*-centrality of *Anumāna* would be presented in the next and succeeding chapters.

For the present, it is enough to note that through *Hetu*-centrality what is intended to be argued is that consideration of every methodologically worthwhile aspect of *Anumāna* revolves around taking into account some or the other aspect of *Hetu.*

In the sequel, we hope to inquire into various aspects of the *Hetu*-centrality of *Anumāna*. The domain of *Anumāna* is that of *Parokṣa-jñāna*. It needs, therefore, to be shown that *Parokṣa-jñāna* is *Hetu*-centric in character. For, if *Parokṣa-jñāna* itself is not *Hetu*-centric then *Anumāna* cannot be *Hetu*-centric, because *Anumāna* always gives us *Parokṣa-jñāna*. Thus, we shall have to begin our investigation with an inquiry into epistemic aspect of *Anumāna*. For methodological considerations concerning *Anumāna*, however important they may be, cannot transgress the requirements of the epistemic aspect of *Anumāna*, no matter whether it is sought to be employed in cognition or certification. Hence, in the next chapter we turn to the discussion of epistemic condition of *Anumāna*.

Notes and References

1. Winternitz, M.; *A History of Indian Literature*; Vol. II; pp. 256-270.
2. Vidyābhūṣaṇa, Satīś Chandra; *History of Indian Logic*; pp. 251-261.
3. Murti, T.R.V.; *The Central Philosophy of Buddhism*; pp. 1-9.
4. Nāgārjuna; *Madhyamaka-Śāstra*; 24.18; p. 219.
5. Dharmakīrti; *P.V.*; II. 7-11, M.N. *Vṛtti*; pp. 102-104. and *P.V.*; II. 54, M.N. *Vṛtti*; p. 117.
6. Vātsyāyana; *Nyāya-Bhāṣya*; I. i.4, p. 198.
7. Dharmakīrti; *H.B.*; p. 66. and *N.B.* (with Dharmottara's *Ṭīkā*); pp. 103-104.
8. Dharmakīrti; *N.B.*; (with Dharmottara's *Ṭīkā*); p. 1. also Prajñākara Gupta; *P.V.A*; p. 7.
9. Dharmakīrti; *P.V.*; II.1, M.N. *Vṛtti*; pp. 98-99.
10. That is why, perhaps, one does not find in Diṅnāga's *Pramāṇa-samu-*

ccaya any definition of *Svalakṣaṇa*, nor does one find any definite description of it. But in the discussions relating to the nature of *Pratyakṣa* one does indirectly come across his views about *svalakṣaṇa*.

11. Diṅnāga; *Pramāṇa-samuccaya*; I.2, *Sva-vṛtti*; pp. 6-7.
12. *Ibid*; pp. 4-9.
13. Dharmakīrti; *N.B.*; (with Dharmottara's *Ṭīkā*); pp. 16-17.
14. Dharmakīrti; *P.V.*; III. 39, M.N. *Vṛtti*; p. 271 and Dharmakīrti; *Svārthānumāna-pariccheda*; pp. 15-16.
15. Dharmakīrti; *P.V.*; II. 3, M.N. *Vṛtti*; p. 100.
16. Dharmakīrti; *P.V.*; II. 3, M.N. *Vṛtti*; p. 117.
17. Chinchore, M.R.; "Some Epistemological and Social Implications of *Kṣaṇikatā*", *Annals of the Bhandarkar Oriental Research Institute*, Poona, LXVII (1986), pp. 57-76.
18. Dharmakīrti; *P.V.*; I. 69-74, M.N. *Vṛtti*; pp. 31-32. also, Prajñākara Gupta; *P.V.A.*; I. 253-269, pp. 157-161.
19. Dharmakīrti; *P.V.*; I. 65-70, M.N. *Vṛtti*; pp. 30-31.
20. Chinchore, M.R.; *op. cit*.
21. Dharmakīrti; *P.V.*; I. 69, M.N. *Vṛtti*; p. 31.
22. Dharmakīrti; *H.B.*; pp. 56-57, Arcaṭa *H.B.T.*; pp. 127-145.
23. Arcaṭa; *H.B T.*; pp. 144-149.
24. Prajñākara Gupta; *P.V.A.*; p. 116.
25. Dharmakīrti; *P.V.*; I. 254-259. M.N. *Vṛtti*, pp. 86-88.
26. Prajñākara Gupta; *P.V.A.*; p. 52.
27. Dharmakīrti; *N.B.*; I.1. Dharmottara's *Ṭīkā*, pp. 1-8.
28. Arcaṭa; *H.B.T.*; p. 3. Dharmakīrti; *P.V.*; III. 218-219. M.N. *Vṛtti*, p. 324.
29. Dharmakīrti; *P.V.*; I. 63-64. M.N. *Vṛtti*, p. 120.
30. Dharmakīrti; *P.V.*; II.3. M.N. *Vṛtti*, p. 100.
31. Dharmakīrti; *N.B.*; and Dharmottara's *Ṭikā*; pp. 16-18.
32. Dharmakīrti; *P.V.*; II. 1-3, 10, p. 104. M.N. *Vṛtti*, pp. 98-100.
33. Arcaṭa; *H.B.T.*; pp. 117-118.
34. Dharmakīrti; *P.V.*; II. 503-508. M.N. *Vṛtti*, pp. 245-246.
35. Dharmakīrti; *P.V.*; II. 66-67, 78-80, 341-342, 345-346. M.N. *Vṛtti*, pp. 121, 125, 202, 203.
36. Dharmakīrti; *P.V.*; II. 49-50, 102-104. M.N. *Vṛtti*, pp. 116; 132.
37. Dharmakīrti; *P.V.*; IV. 138-142. M.N. *Vṛtti*, pp. 406-407.
38. Dharmakīrti; *P.V.*; II. 51-77. M.N. *Vṛtti*, pp. 116-124.
39. Dharmakīrti; *P.V.*; II. 41, 58-65, 68-80. M.N. *Vṛtti*, pp. 113, 119-121, 122-125.
40. Dharmakīrti; *N.B.* (with Dharmottara's *Ṭīkā*), pp. 7-10.
41. Dharmakīrti; *P.V.*; II. 1-3. M.N. *Vṛtti*; pp. 98-100.
42. Arcaṭa; *H.B.T.*; Section 24, pp. 34-35.
43. Prajñākara Gupta; *P.V.A.*; II. 2, pp. 169-175. or Uddyotakara; *Nyāya-vārtika*; I.i.1; pp. 8-10.
44. Prajñākara Gupta; *P.V.A*; II. 63-83, pp. 223-229.
45. Dharmakīrti; *P.V.*; I. 3-8, M.N. *Vṛtti*; pp. 3-9.

46. There is a difference between Naiyāyikas' and Dharmakīrti's interpretation of *Hāna* and *Upādāna*; for the purpose behind bringing in these terms is different.
47. Dharmakīrti; *P.V.*; I.3, M.N. *Vṛtti*, pp. 3-4. also Prajñākara Gupta; *P.V.A.*; I.1, pp. 3-7.
48. Dharmakīrti; *P.V.*; I. 3, II.100. M.N. *Vṛtti*, pp. 3-4, 131.
49. Dharmakīrti; *P.V.*; I. 7-8, M.N. *Vṛtti*, pp. 8-9.
50. Dharmakīrti; *P.V.*; I. 3-6, M.N. *Vṛtti*, pp. 4-7.
51. Dharmakīrti; *P.V.*; II.3, M.N. *Vṛtti*, pp. 100-101.
52. Prajñākara Gupta; *P.V.A.*; II. 1-4, pp. 169-183.
53. Dharmakīrti; *P.V.*; II.10-11, 50-54. M.N. *Vṛtti*, pp. 104-105, 116-117.
54. Dharmakīrti; *P.V.*; II.50-54, M.N. *Vṛtti*, pp. 116-117.
55. Arcaṭa; *H.B.T.*; pp. 3-5, Seetion 28, pp. 39-41.
56. *Ibid*; Section 18, pp. 28-30.
57. Dharmakīrti; *P.V.*; II. 123-130; M.N. *Vṛtti*, pp. 138-139. also Arcaṭa; *H.B.T.*; Section 25, p. 36.

CHAPTER II

EPISTEMIC CONDITION OF ANUMĀNA

In the preceding chapter, we explained, in considerable details, some important points concerning Dharmakīrti's philosophical position and its conceptual framework. It was pointed out there that there are two important kinds of knowledge, viz. direct (*Aparokṣa*) and indirect (*Parokṣa*). We get them through *Pratyakṣa* (perception) and *Anumāna* (inference) respectively. Taken together, both of them exhaust the totality of knowledge. Although *Parokṣa* and *Aparokṣa jñānas* are of different kinds yet the possibility of their being complementary cannot be ruled out. Their *Avisaṁvādakatva* (non-inconsistency) ensures mutual coherence while their *Avijñātārthaprakāśakatva* (disclosure of hitherto unknown feature) keeps the doors of the possibility of growth and development of knowledge open.

In this chapter, we wish to point out that (a) *Svārthānumāna* stipulates epistemic condition of *Anumāna*, (b) although, as pointed out earlier, *Parokṣa* and *Aparokṣa jñānas* are complementary to each other, they are nonetheless of distinct kinds. Accordingly, certain fundamental differences between them would have to be maintained uniformly and that they cannot be glossed over or neglected without engendering serious epistemic and methodological consequences. (c) Even with regard to the epistemic condition of *Anumāna*, *Hetu*-centricity of *Anumāna* is such a methodological feature of it that it cannot be allowed to be ignored without paving a way for unsurmountable difficulties. Of these three points, the first and the third have a direct bearing on *Hetu*-centricity of *Anumāna* while the second has only indirect bearing on it. We take up, first, the second point for consideration, and then we proceed to the first, and lastly turn to the third point. The rationale of this sort of treatment of them would be clear as we proceed.

Aparokṣa and Parokṣa Jñāna

As stated earlier, the distinction between *Aparokṣa* and *Parokṣa jñāna* is connected with the distinction between *Svalakṣaṇa* and *Sāmānya-lakṣaṇa* on the one hand and that between *Pratyakṣa* and *Anumāna* on the other. There are some points and issues which are connected with both of them. For example, the general criteria of acceptability of them are common. On this ground, they could be held to be similar to each other. Further, they are also complementary to each other. This does not, however, mean that they are the same. Their complementarity can neither make them similar nor make them the same. It is on account of confusion of this kind that it is sometimes held that the rationale behind making the distinction between *Svārthānumāna* and *Parārthānumāna*, and that between *Savikalpaka* and *Nirvikalpaka Pratyakṣa* appears to be the same, viz. priority of knowing over communicating. But this is a mistake. For, while in the case of the *Svārthānumāna* and *Parārthānumāna* distinction, it is, we shall see, the priority of cognition over communication that is involved,[1] in the case of the distinction between *Savikalpaka* and *Nirvikalpaka Pratyakṣa* it is the priority of being over knowing[2] that is at stake. That is, while in the first distinction epistemic priority is involved, in the second distinction ontological priority is involved. Since, however, both these distinctions are made in epistemic domain it could be surmised that a similar issue could be posed concerning *Pratyakṣa* and *Anumāna*, viz. the minimum conditions that need to be fulfilled if one is to cognise respective objects of perceptual and inferential cognition. Though the problem is the same, answers to it with reference to perception and inference are bound to be different because they are two distinct sorts of cognitions. The domains in which these distinctions (i.e. between *Svārtha* and *Parārtha Anumāna* or between *Savikalpaka* and *Nirvikalpaka Pratyakṣa*) are made have different contexts and the issues connected with them are different. Hence, one should not tackle problems connected with both of them in a similar or the same way. The necessary and/or sufficient conditions of *Aparokṣa* and *Parokṣa jñānas* being different, it is important to treat them differently. Further, it is also important to understand that in the case of

Aparoksa jñāna our cognition is always non-discursive in nature. The *Parokṣa jñāna,* on the other hand, is always discursive in character, and to the extent to which discursiveness as a distinguishing feature of it comes to be neglected or relegated to the background, the dividing line between *Parokṣa* and *Aparokṣa jñāna* comes to be blurred. In consequence, the very purpose and rationale of distinguishing between them turns out to be philosophically unrewarding. Accordingly, it would be a mistake of a serious kind to foist the distinction between *Nirvikalpaka* and *Savikalpaka Pratyakṣa* on that between *Aparokṣa* and *Parokṣa jñāna.*

In this context, it may be noted that *Naiyāyikas* also appear to be making the distinction between *Savikalpaka-Nirvikalpaka Pratyakṣa* and also between *Svārthānumāna* and *Parārthānumāna.* However, it is essential to note that their rationale of making these distinctions is quite different from that of the Buddhists. Accordingly, it would be a folly to confuse between these distinctions made by the Buddhists and by the *Naiyāyikas.* Going by the superficially similar fact that both of them make these distinctions, some persons, unfortunately, are led to confuse, misinterpret and misunderstand them. It is further doubtful whether the kind of conceptual sophistication that one is required to have in order to make these distinctions free from ambiguity, was available to Dharmakīrti's predecessors from the camp of *Prācīna-Nyāya.* Going perhaps by the distinction in the historical context between *Savikalpaka* and *Nirvikalpaka Pratyakṣa* on the one hand, and that between *Svārtha* and *Parārtha Anumāna* on the other, it could possibly be surmised that adherents of *Prācīna Nyāya* came to incorporate them within its framework under the influence of Buddhists philosophers. They seem, nonetheless, to have confused between the rationale behind these distinctions.

It becomes, therefore, necessary to throw some light on the need to make the distinction between *Svārthānumāna* and *Parārthānumāna* at the hands of Buddhists. Since the establishment of the *Hetu*-centricity of *Anumāna* is the major point of our interest, it is all the more necessary to show that with regard to both *Svārthānumāna* and *Parārthānumāna*, *Hetu*-centricity holds good. Rather, *Hetu*-centricity has an important role to play in *Parokṣa-jñāna*, of which *Svārthānumāna* is an epistemic condition. We turn our attention, therefore, to understanding the rationale behind making the distinction between *Svārthānumāna* and *Parārthānumāna*.

I *The Need to Distinguish*

As pointed out earlier, though both *Parokṣa* and *Aparokṣa jñānas* are categorised as two kinds of knowledges, their necessary and sufficient conditions are different.[3] For acquiring and/or certifying *Parokṣa* kind of knowledge, *Anumāna* is enough, whereas *Pratyakṣa* is instrumental to the cognition and/or certification of *Aparokṣa jñāna*. *Sāmānya-lakṣaṇa* being object of *Anumāna*, coherent conceivability seems to be the minimum necessary condition that is required to be satisfied by inferential cognition. On the other hand, *Svalakṣaṇa* being the object of *Pratyakṣa*, its being experienced is the minimum necessary condition of perceptual cognition. And since its being experienced does not lie outside the domain of the coherently conceivable, the former would determine the sufficient condition of inferential cognition. This is suggested by the possibility of their convergence. Thus, to say, therefore, that knowledge gained through inference must also, in principle, be available through perception, is too stringent a demand to be made on inferential cognition, and hence needs to be avoided.[4] That is what, perhaps, Dharmakīrti wishes to advocate when he says that perceptual cognition is not a precondition of inferential cognition and that it could be certified without any recourse to perceptual cognition.[5] Thus, although the possibility of convergence of perceptual and inferential cognitions on the same object of knowledge is not ruled out, it is consistently insisted that necessary and sufficient conditions of the occurrence of perceptual and inferential cognitions respectively need to be differently formulated and stipulated, so that the necessary and sufficient conditions of one sort of cognition do not turn out to be identical with those of the other and the very distinction between *Aparokṣa* and *Parokṣa jñāna* does not come to be obliterated.

In order to formulate the necessary and sufficient conditions of *Anumāna*, it must be made clear what inferential cognition means. Hence, we turn to the meaning of inferential cognition itself. According to Dharmakīrti, it seems, inferential cognition is that which is determined by the knowledge of the general features (*Sāmānya-lakṣaṇa*) of an object.[6] It is acquired through *Trairūpya* (of *Hetu*).[7] Obviously, it should be capable of being made available to us at least in the domain of coherent conceivability, for the nature of *Sāmānya-lakṣaṇa* itself determines the nature of *Anumāna*. In *Anumāna* we acquire the knowledge of something (*Gamya*) with the help of something else (*Gamaka*).[8] Such a thing which we come to know newly, need not be given to us in experience and hence need not exist factually. Its being given to us merely as coherently conceivable would also suffice for its being cognised. Likewise, the *Gamaka* could also be given to us merely as coherently conceivable and yet this in itself should not mark the impossibility of inferential cognition. Since there is a close similarity between what we intend to know (*Sādhya*) and that on the basis of which we know (*Sādhana*),[9] it is the *Sādhana* that determines the nature of *Sādhya*. Since inferential cognition is concerned with *Sāmānya-lakṣaṇa* alone, which cannot be perceptually cognised, and since the *Sādhya* or *Gamya* that is inferentially cognised need not be existent or factual, *Hetu*, *Sādhana* or *Gamaka*, too, need not be existent.[10] The only thing one has to ensure is that the relation between *Gamya* and *Gamaka* or *Hetu* (*Sādhana*) and *Sādhya* is governed by *Avinābhāva-niyama*.[11] For the present, however, it suffices to note that the object of inferential cognition need not necessarily be existent, though the possibility of its being instantiated cannot be ruled out in advance.[12]

From this, we hope, it should be clear that the object we succeed in cognising inferentially is given to us, at least coherently conceivably, and need not necessarily be obtainable factually and actually in the world we live in.[13] Correspondingly, the *Parokṣa-jñāna* is also of general, common, sharable features.[14] Generality and commonness of features of things are enough as a basis of *Parokṣa-jñāna*. The nature of *Parokṣa jñāna* is governed by *Anumāna* on the one hand and *Sāmānya-lakṣaṇa* on the other. But since *Anumāna*, too, is govered by the nature of *Sāmānya-lakṣaṇa*, it is *Sāmānya-lakṣaṇa* which has the decisive role to play in the characterization of *Parokṣa-jñāna*,[15] while the possibility of convergence of *Svalakṣaṇa* and *Sāmānya-lakṣaṇa* not being ruled out, it would operate as a sufficient condition of *Anumāna* and *Parokṣa jñāna* as well.[16]

In this context, it is important to note that just as one can cognise a perceptual object by himself alone, so too for getting inferential cognition there is no need of other person. In other words, for perceptual or inferential cognition presence of some other person is not a necessary condition. A single individual is enough for cognising inferentially. When one is formulating the necessary and/or sufficient conditions one should think of minimum conditions that need to be satisfied and the other possible cases of it will determine the sufficient conditions. In the case of *Anumāna*, to be precise, *Svārthānumāna* is a necessary condition for an inferential cognition, whereas *Parārthānumāna* indicates its possible range of application. And, as said earlier, necessary and sufficient conditions are and must be related to each other, although they are not the same. But, at the same time, we should not confuse between them. Hence, there is a need to make a distinction between *Svārthānumāna* and *Parārthānumāna*; i.e. fashioning and formulating an argument and its articulation and communication.[17]

Likewise, one could think about communicability. According to Dharmakīrti, it appears, communicability is not a pre-condition of cognition—perceptual and/or inferential. For knowing anything through either perception or inference we do not require linguistic ability. Without articulation and communication we can cognise. But, so too, the presence of words is not a barrier in our cognitive process. This amounts to saying that communicability functions and operates as a sufficient condition of cognition—inferential or otherwise.[18]

Having made these two important points, we can now look to the distinction between *Svārthānumāna* and *Parārthānmāna* a bit more closely.

To start with, it needs to be mentioned that *Svārthānumāna* has something to do with cognitive aspect of *Anumāna*, while *Parārthānumāna* revolves around its being communicated. The former is concerned with fashioning and formulating an argument,[19] the latter with its being articulated and communicated.[20] Within the context of *Anumāna*, the first is prior, the other, obviously, is posterior. The necessary and sufficient conditions of each one of them differ, since the domains and the contexts in which they figure also differ. To discuss these points in detail it is interesting and important to turn to the need of making the distinction between *Svārthānumāna* and *Parārthānumāna*.

(1) The distinction between *Svārthānumāna* and *Parāthānumāna* needs to be made because certain priorities are involved in it, viz. priority of cognition over that of communication. In the context of *Anumāna*, obviously, *Svārthānumāna* comes first in order of knowing and *Parārthānumāna* comes later. Whatever we communicate is already known—cognised and comprehended—by us. Hence, one cannot reverse their priority nor can they be treated on par with each other. To do so will be logically as well as methodologically illegitimate.[21]

(2) Just as *Svārthānumāna - Parārthānumāna* distinction needs to be made within the domain of cognitive epistemology, so too it is essential to distinguish between them in justificatory epistemology. In other words, it is not only pertinent in the field of cognitive epistemology but also with regards to justificatory one as well.[22]

We cannot confuse between a cognition of something and its certification. When we employ *Anumāna* to cognise and/or comprehend something we are not certifying our knowledge-claim made with the help of *Anumāna*. On the contrary, when a demand for certification of a knowledge-claim is made, the claim under consideration is required to be advanced first, and for its being advanced it is required to be cognised.

In other words, even when *Anumāna* is to be employed for justification, such a justification must first be 'seen' or comprehended—which is cognitive (inferentially) in character. After cognising and comprehending it alone could *Anumāna* be employed as a justification in a communicative situation and not otherwise.

To illustrate the point. We first acquire a piece of information, advance a knowledge-claim about it, and then attempt to justify or certify it if we are called upon to do so. It is methodologically incorrect to say that we first justify or certify certain claim and then cognise and comprehend it. Certificatory epistemology presupposes cognitive one and not *vice-versa*.

(3) Unless we cognise something we cannot put it in linguistic garb. To put the linguistic garb on something we must have cognised it first and then alone can we articulate it. Cognition is a pre-condition of communication, and not the other way round. If we do not have cognition, the question of its communication will just not arise, i.e. communication presupposes cognition. So too, *Parāthānumāna* presupposes *Svārthānumāna* in the context of *Anumāna*. Thus understood, *Svārthānumāna* is prior, *Parārthānumāna* is posterior.

(4) For employment of *Anumāna*—either in cognition or in justification—communication is not necessarily required. For inferential cognition or for its justification, we do not necessarily require more than one person. This is, however, not to rule out in advance the very possibility of interpersonal cognition or justification. Nonetheless, to hold that being interpersonal is a minimum necessary precondition of cognition or certification is to lay down too stringent a condition on either of them. For each of them, what is minimally required is that there should at least be one individual to cognise or to certify.

Hence communicative-situation is not a necessary condition for *Anumāna*. This is what is sought to be stipulated by making the distinction between *Svārthānumāna* and *Parārthānumāna*, where *Svārthānumāna* is a minimum condition for the employment of *Anumāna*—in cognition or in justification.[23]

(5) The necessary and sufficient conditions of *Svārthānumāna* and *Parārthānumāna* are not the same and hence they need to be distinguished. For *Svārthānumāna* fulfilment of the condition of cognition is a must, whereas in case of *Parārthānumāna* inferential cognition of something is not enough; we have to fulfil the additional condition of its articulation also. However, *Svārthānumāna* and *Parārthānumāna* are not totally discordant with each other. The latter accommodates the first, or rather the former is the heart which throbs in the latter. Inferential cognition does not necessarily mean systematically articulated cognition concerning *Sāmānya-lakṣaṇa* (*Parārthānumāna*). It could be reckoned to be *Anumāna* even if it is merely fashioned and formulated (but is not articulated—*Svārthānumāna*). That is, *Svārthānumāna* stipulates the necessary condition of *Anumāna*,

whereas *Parārthānumāna* is its sufficient condition. And hence they need to be clearly distinguished.

(6) If one is giving priority to *Nirvikalpaka Pratyakṣa* in the field of *Pratyakṣa*, then correspondingly one also needs necessarily to give priority to *Svārthānumāna* in the field of *Anumāna*. For, the two distinctions are parallel, although they are governed by different kinds of priority-considerations at stake. As *Svārthānumāna* stipulates minimal condition of inferential cognition, so too *Nirvikalpaka Pratyakṣa* stipulates minimal necessary condition of perceptual cognition.[24]

From the above discussion it should, we hope, be clear that there is a need to make a distinction between *Svārthānumāna* and *Parārthānumāna*. That is, they should not be confused with each other and treated on par with each other. Granting that there is a need to distinguish between the two, it is important to consider the way Dharmakīrti draws a distinction between them. It is to this that we move in the next section.

II The Distinction Between Svārthānumāna and Parārthānumāna:

In the last section, we have seen the reasons which necessitate a distinction between *Svārthānumāna* and *Parārthānumāna*. However, the way this distinction is drawn by Dharmakīrti and some of the prominent implications of this distinction, need to be looked into a bit closely. This is what we take up in this section.

To begin with, the two separate chapters given to the treatment of *Svārthānumāna* and *Parārthānumāna* in Dharmakīrti's *Pramāṇa-vārtika* and *Nyāya-bindu* form no basis for treating them as two distinct kinds, or two independent or separate aspects, of *Anumāna*. In *Vādanyāya* as well as in *Hetu-bindu*, such a treatment of them is not available. The distinction under consideration needs to be understood as based on the consideration of priority. The constitutive conditions, viz. *Pakṣa*, *Sādhya* and *Hetu*, and the regulative conditions, viz. *Vyāpti* and *Pakṣadharmatā*, of both of them (*Svārthānumāna* and *Parārthānumāna*) are, and must be the same.[25] We shall have an occasion to look into some implications of this in the next section. For the present, however, it suffices to note that the distinction between them revolves round the issue of priority, and not that of classification.

In fact, it will be argued later that *Svārthānumāna* and *Parārthānumāna* are not and cannot be prominent classes of *Anumāna* and treating them as such serves no worthwhile methodological purpose. The order in which they are discussed cannot, however, be reversed. For, unless one cognises, one cannot communicate. To think about the possibility of communication without cognition is meaningless, and hence absurd.

Naturally, a question arises as to what kind of priority is this. As mentioned earlier, it is the epistemological, i.e. the cognitive priority. Further, the necessary conditions need to be formulated and fulfilled. It is the fulfilment of necessary conditions which opens the gateway, whereas sufficient conditions disclose its possible instances. Unless the necessary conditions are fulfilled, possibility of the emergence of consequence cannot be guaranteed. Accepting this, epistemic condition of *Anumāna*, i.e. *Svārthānumāna*, being a necessary condition of *Parokṣa jñāna*, will enjoy the status of priority, whereas *Parārthānumāna* will and must come later.

For generating inferential cognition or entertaining a knowledge-claim based on inferential cognition, we require understanding and/or comprehension of *Sāmānya-lakṣaṇa*. That could be made available to us only through *Svārthānumāna*. Such an inferential knowledge-claim could be communicated through language. But communicating a knowledge-claim verbally is not a necessary condition of its being occasioned.

Knowledge of both the kinds, viz. *Parokṣa* and *Aparokṣa*, is subjective in its occurrence. But it does not preclude its being communicable. All knowledge that we have, is given to us subjectively. In other words, communication is not a determinant factor in knowledge. Otherwise, we would have to accept the claim that we can have an experience of *Svalakṣaṇa*, but just because it has not fulfilled the condition of communication, it is not knowledge worth the name. Accepting communicablity as the minimum condition of knowledge in general—regardless of the distinction between *Pratyakṣa* and *Anumāna*—requires *Pratyakṣa* to satisfy too strong a condition, while satisfaction of the *Udāharaṇa* requirement requires *Anumāna* to satisfy too stringent a condition. We shall have an occasion to return to this point later.

From the above discussion, we hope, one point is clear that one could have knowledge without its being communicated and/or justified. The possibility of unarticulated cognition cannot be ruled out. This does not, however, mean that such a cognition cannot, later on, be communicated. The contrast is between the communicable but yet not communicated and already communicated knowledge-claim. This does not, in any sense, mean that *Pratyakṣa* must be prior to *Anumāna*. To subscribe to this is, again, to lay down too stringent a condition for inferential cognition to satisfy. But it also paves a way for obliteration of the distinction between *Svalakṣaṇa* and *Sāmānya-lakṣaṇa*, the objects respectively of perceptual and inferential cognitions.

The contrast between *Svārthānumāna* and *Parārthānumāna* is not so much between coherently conceivable and communicable or sharable as between cognisable and communicable. For, something could be cognised without satisfying the condition of its being communicated, while something else could be cognised because and insofar as it is communicated.[26]

Hence, *Svārthānumāna* could be interpreted, perhaps, as that kind of comprehension of a thing which is communicable but yet not communicated. On the other hand, *Parārthānumāna* means communicated comprehension of a thing. In other words, *Svārthānumāna* is an inferential cognition without communication, whereas *Parārthānumāna* is an inferential cognition which is communicated.

Further, communicable knowledge need not arise in a communication-situation, though when such a situation presents itself, it cannot fail to be communicated. In other words, inferential knowledge is and must be communicable in nature, since communicability is a distinguishing mark of it. This does not, however, mean that whatever is communicable must be communicated, and unless it is communicated it cannot be cognised.[27] There could be a degenerate case of communication, i.e. *Svārthānumāna*, too. Further, without communication there could be inferential cognition. Hence communication is not necessary for having an inferential cognition.

Further, as direct cognition (*Pratyakṣa*) is necessarily non-interpersonal in its occurrence, so too indirect cognition (*Anumāna*) could likewise be non-interpersonal in its occurrence. However, interpersonal sharability of the latter kind of cognition cannot be ruled out. This does not in any sense mean that it is a pre-condition of both the kinds of cognitions.

It would be interesting to see, on this background, the consequences which would have followed from failure on the part of Dharmakīrti to make the distinction under consideration. It is to this that we now turn:

(i) Priority of *Svārthānumāna* enables him to avoid explaining the nature of *Anumāna* counter-intuitively as well as counter-methodologically. Accepting communicability as a pre-condition of cognition goes against the intuitive consideration. For the possibility of cognition, minimum condition that needs to be fulfilled needs to be taken into account. A consideration contrary to this would also endanger the principle of economy.

(ii) Secondly, if *Svārthānumāna* is not considered as prior to *Parārthānumāna*, it would mean that cognition is not a pre-condition of communication, explanation and/or justification. This would entail the possibility of communication without cognition, and perhaps also of explanation/justification without understanding and interpretation. In the case of *Pratyakṣa*, *Nirvikalpaka*, and in the case of *Anumāna*, *Svārthānumāna* would be required to satisfy the same condition of cognition, viz. communicability. Consequently, one would have been forced to take recourse to upholding *Pramāṇa-saṁplava* as against *Pramāṇa-viplava*. By reversing the priority consideration concerning *Anumāna* we not only confuse between fashioning an argument and its communication, but also between cognitive and communicative aspects of it, and leave no option other than embracing blindly *Pramāṇa-saṁplava*.[28]

(iii) *Parārthānumāna* means spelling out *Pakṣa*, *Sādhya* and *Hetu*, along with the relation among them, communicatively. *Svārthānumāna* means *Pakṣa*, *Sādhya* and *Hetu*, and the cognition of their relation but it is neither articulated nor justified. If we say that *Parārthānumāna* is prior and *Svārthānumāna* is posterior, then justified inferential cognition will naturally enjoy the status of priority over unjustified inferential cognition. But to say that we have justified cognition first and then have unjustified cognition is itself a wrong assertion—intuitively speaking. Marginally, it will be interesting to note that to accept priority of *Parārthānumāna* over *Svārthānumāna*, or even of *Savikalpaka* over *Nirvikalpaka Pratyakṣa* would go against another thesis of Buddhists, viz. *Svataḥ-a-prāmāṇya*.[29] For fear of digression we refrain from going into details of this aspect.

(iv) To ignore or water-down the distinction between *Svārthānumāna* and *Parārthānumāna* will boil down to mixing the necessary and/or sufficient conditions of *Anumāna*. When we say that *Svārthānumāna* is a necessary condition (i.e. epistemic condition) of *Anumāna* and *Parārthānumāna* is a sufficient condition of *Anumāna* in general, what we mean is that *Anumāna* must satisfy at least the condition of cognition. If it does not fulfil it, it forfeits its right to be called *Anumāna*. Fulfilment of the sufficient condition is not an imperative. It is not a constitutive condition, and if *Anumāna* does not fulfil it, it does not lose its status as *Anumāna*. In addition, such a confusion between necessary and sufficient conditions of *Anumāna* would be productive of confusion in more than one way.

(v) Confusing between or rejecting the distinction between *Svārthānumāna* and *Parārthānumāna* will not merely influence our treatment of *Anumāna*. It will also correspondingly affect our treatment of *Pratyakṣa* as well. If we accept interpersonal communicability as a necessary condition of knowledge inclusive of *Anumāna* (inference), then we will have to accept *Savikalpaka Pratyakṣa* as a necessary condition of *Pratyakṣa*. To accept *Parārthānumāna* as a necessary condition of *Anumāna* and, on the other hand, to accept *Nirvikalpaka Pratyakṣa* as a necessary condition of *Pratyakṣa* would be internally inconsistent. Hence, in that case *Savikalpaka Pratyakṣa* would have to be accepted as a necessary condition of *Pratyakṣa*. But, then, the uniform refusal to uphold the distinction between cognition and communication will be the consequence which, obviously, is a mistake.

(vi) In addition to the points made so far there is another matter to consider. Refusal to accept priority of *Svārthānumāna* with regard to *Anumāna* and of *Nirvikalpaka* with regard to *Pratyakṣa* would have forced Dharmakīrti to make a compromise with the principle of economy which he upholds, and that would have led to inconsistency in his philosophy and its conceptual framework.

(vii) If he had refused priority to *Svārthānumāna* then the treatment and explanation of *Hetvābhāsas* would have been different at the hands of Dharmakīrti.[30] Instead of accepting three *Hetvābhāsas*, depending, basically, upon the inferential cognition, he would have been forced to admit two more and in turn, his treatment of *Anumāna* would have been indistinguishable from that of *Naiyāyikas*.

From the above discussion, it would, we hope, be clear that there was not only the need to make this distinction, acknowledged by Dharmakīrti, but also that if it had not been made then serious consequences would have followed. So also, many confusions would have arisen. Hence knowing all these difficulties well, it is no wonder he attempted to make such an important distinction and followed it right through in his philosophy.

Sometimes, however, it is claimed that this distinction is not originally given to us by Dharmakīrti. Prior to him it was present in the then prevalent intellectual atmosphere. He laid his hands upon it, drew our attention to some of its implications and refined our understanding of it. That is all. But if this is so, then certain questions remain unanswered. If Dharmakīrti cannot be credited with drawing this philosophically important distinction, then who pioneered it? Was it present prior to him and if it was not, what and how much influence did any of his predecessors wield on him—either from the (*Prācīna*) *Nyāya* or Buddhist camp? If any of them had anticipated it, was it in a rudimentary form or in clear sophisticated form? To answer these questions and to articulate and assess Dharmakīrti's contribution with regard to the distinction under consideration, we turn to the next section.

III Dharmakīrti's Remonstration

Our contention that Dharmakīrti made clear the distinction between *Svārthānumāna* and *Parārthānumāna*, taking into account its various implications, needs to be taken in all seriousness that it deserves. Though it has been held that such a distinction was already present before him, we shall argue in this section that such a claim is ill-founded. To prove that this distinction is Dharmakīrti's innovation, our task is two-fold, viz. to show that neither *Naiyāyikas*, before Dharmakīrti, succeeded in instituting this important distinction, nor did any Buddhist philosopher prior to him address himself to this task. This does not, however, mean that it was not there even in a rudimentary form. Not only the germ of it was present in the intellectual atmosphere, of those days—especially in the Buddhist camp, but some Buddhist philosophers attempted to make it. However, they failed to draw thc distinction clearly and articulate its implications thoroughly. The credit for this goes to Dharmakīrti. In the following discussion we will see the *Nyāya*-position first and then turn to the Buddhist predecessors of Dharmakīrti.

(a) It is often argued and claimed that the *Naiyāyikas* too have made the distinction between *Svārthānumāna* and *Parārthānumāna*. People try to claim that right from *Nyāya-Sūtras* of Gautamācārya it is indicated and at the hands of Vātsyāyana it can be clearly seen. To see to what extent this view could be considered tenable, we first give a brief outline of the *Nyāya* framework of *Anumāna* and then inquire if it could have been possible at all for *Nyāya* philosophers to institute and justify such a distinction in that framework.

Careful attention needs to be paid to the following points if we want to understand the framework of *Anumāna* given by the *Prācīna Naiyāyikas*.

(i) For the *Naiyāyikas*, the object of inference and the object of perception or, for that matter, of any other *Pramāṇa* is the same i.e. they hold that *Prameya* with reference to all the *Pramāṇas* is the same. This undoubtedly is the position of all the *Naiyāyikas*, which needs to be noted.[31] The object of knowledge (*Prameya*) being the same, the tools or instruments alone differ, and, hence, knowledge is of different kinds.

If the knowable is the same it is no wonder that for *Naiyāyikas* whatever we know has to fulfil the condition of being communicable or of being able to exist in order to be knowable.[32] *Pratyakṣa* is, indeed, a pre-condition of *Anumāna*[33] but it must also be communicable. Then, in that case *Svārthānumāna* loses its priority to *Parārthānumāna* for *Naiyāyikas*.[34] Moreover, since there is no priority of any kind involved, it does not matter for them whether former is prior or the latter.

Since they do not make a distinction between object of perception and that of inference, as both are the same for them, it is no wonder that existence and inference are, for them, on par with each other. The object of inference is also existent, or at least, its knowledge is reducible to experience.[35] For, Uddyotakara very explicitly states that the process of inference is from *Dṛṣṭa* to *Adṛṣṭa*, through *Dṛṣṭa*.[36] If so, it does not make any difference to *Naiyāyikas* whether *Svārthānumāna* is prior or *Parārthānumāna*.[37] On the contrary, one can go a step forward and argue that for *Naiyāyikas*, *Anumāna* is necessarily both *Svārthānumāna* and *Parārthānumāna*. So, if one argues that *Naiyāyikas* also make a distinction between *Svārthānumāna* and *Parārthānumāna* it will mean that communicated inference alone gives us cognition, in which case, the distinction loses its methodological importance and becomes futile.

On the contrary, the Buddhist contention is basically different. They advocate a view that being experienced is the mark of *Pratyakṣa*, whereas being coherently conceivable is the mark of *Anumāna*.[38] The knowledge which we have through inference is not necessarily based on experience (*Dṛṣṭa*). Rather, it is a cognition of an object with the help of another, although neither may be in existence.[39] That such an object is coherently conceivable is enough for inferential cognition. Further, being coherently conceivable cannot be confused with being experienced and/or perceived.[40] Hence, one could have the knowledge of *Dṛṣṭa* or *Adṛṣṭa* determined by *Dṛṣṭa* or *Adṛṣṭa*, respectively,[41] i.e. in both the directions. That is, what matters importantly is mere coherent conceivability in both cases.

Naturally, questions as to the priority of cognition over communication or their simultaneity would not be pertinent in the *Nyāya* framework of *Anumāna*. If this is the case, then there is no need for *Nyāya* philosophers to have made the distinction between *Svārthānumāna* and *Parārthānumāna*.

(ii) It is sometimes claimed that through the definition of *Anumāna* itself Vātsyāyana indicates the distinction between *Svārthānumāna* and *Parārthānumāna*. But if it were the case, then he should have made the distinction under consideration and he should also have drawn its implications. If he did not do so then it should have been done by his predecessor—Gautama—or by his successor—Uddyotakara. But to our utter surprise nobody has even mentioned the distinction earlier than Jayanta

Bhaṭṭa, and Jayanta Bhaṭṭa, too, perhaps, might have mentioned it only because of Dharmakīrti's prolonged criticism of the *Nyāya*-position.

Sometimes, again, it is held that it was indicated through the stipulation: *Liṅga-liṅginoḥ sambandha-darśanam anumānam.*[42] This claim, too, seems to be ill-founded. For, it all depends upon how the expression '*Darśanam*' is sought to be interpreted. If it means cognition of relationship between *Liṅga* and *Liṅgi* by oneself, then the distinction under consideration is needless to be drawn. If it means enabling others to cognise such a relation, then its prior cognition on our part is essential. If, however, both of these were meant, the point should have been stated clearly. In the absence of such a clear statement of the distinction under consideration and explication of its rationale, Vātsyāyana or some other predecessor of Dharmakīrti from the *Nyāya*-tradition cannot possibly be given credit for perceiving the need of the distinction under consideration. Further, since in the *Nyāya* tradition, the form of *Parārthānumāna* seems to be held primary, there was hardly any need for *Nyāya* philosophers to have drawn and instituted such a distinction. Hence the stipulation mentioned above cannot legitimately be regarded as the basis of the distinction between *Svārthānumāna* and *Parārthānumāna*, and the *Nyāya* predecessors of Dharmakīrti cannot be credited with having instituted the distinction under consideration.

(iii) We are told, off and on, that *Naiyāyikas* believe that *Anumāna* gives us the knowledge of *Kārya* emerging from *Kāraṇa*, or *Kāraṇa* giving rise to *Kārya*.[43] It is further held that the distinction between *Svārthānumāna* and *Parārthānumāna* was sought to be reinforced by adherents of *Nyāya* through their classification of *Anumāna* into *Pūrvavat*, *Śeṣavat* etc.[44] But this contention could also be shown to be misplaced. First, so far as *Anumāna* is concerned, it is *Gamya-Gamaka-bhāva* which is fundamental, not the relation of causation. Secondly, the former cannot be said to be determined by the latter. Thirdly, relation of causality cannot be said to determine *Gamya-Gamaka-bhāva*. Lastly, if the classification of *Anumāna* into *Pūrvavat* etc. is important and suggestive of the distinction between *Svārthānumāna* and *Parārthānumāna*, then it is difficult to understand why the former came altogether to be dispensed with in the later *Nyāya* tradition, although the distinction between *Svārthānumāna* and *Parārthānumāna* comes to be retained, although more from habit than out of any conviction of its rationality.

(vi) More importantly, the *Nyāya* thinkers while considering the constituents of *Anumāna*, did not comprehend for quite a long time, the epistemic condition of *Anumāna* or the constitutive or regulative conditions of it, and although *Vyāpti, Pakṣadharmatā* etc. were later incorporated under the Buddhist influence, their full rationale and implications became available in that tradition only after the advent of *Navya-Nyāya*. Under such circumstances, to say that such a distinction as that between *Svārthānumāna* and *Parārthānumāna* was available to the predecessors of Dharmakīrti from the *Nyāya* tradition amounts to reading too much into their respective treatises, when they hardly realised even the rudimentary implications of it.

(v) As pointed out earlier, communicability being a precondition of any cognition, the *Nyāya* adherents take communicable cognition alone to be worthwile. Consequently, the very basis of making the distinction on the level of *Pratyakṣa* between *Savikalpaka* and *Nirvikalpaka* or on the level of *Anumāna* between *Svārthānumāna* and *Parārthānumāna* itself seems to have been withdrawn. Similarly, there is no distinction drawn between the context of occurrence of cognition and its subsequent communication or certification. Further, one finds that for *Naiyāyikas*, an argument for communication should always be used in a debate situation, and never, as it were, in a non-debate situation. Accordingly, they could hardly have envisioned the distinction between (a) prior cognition and its subsequent communication, or (b) fashioning and formulating an argument, and articulation or communication of an already fashioned and formulated argument. Given this, it is hard to understand how the predecessors of Dharmakīrti from the tradition of the *Prācīna-Nyāya* could reasonably be credited with having made the distinction between *Svārthānumāna* and *Parārthānumāna*. They had also not attempted to demarcate the necessary and/or sufficient conditions of either of them. Given this, it is no surprise that they seem to have altogether glossed over this important distinction.

(vi) Lastly, their subscription to the doctrine of *Pramāṇa-saṁplava*, together with their view that *Pratyakṣa* is a precondition of *Anumāna*, seems to have made the predecessors of Dharmakīrti from the *Nyāya* tradition unable to see the rationale of making the distinction between *Svārthānumāna* and *Parārthānumāna*, and explore its implications. Now, since everything that we do is necessarily according to them, purposive, their not having seen the rationale of making such a distinction is strong enough a basis of their not having made it at all.

Uptil now we have seen that the claim of some of the later *Naiyāyikas* that Dharmakīrti should not be credited with having made the distinction between *Svārthānumāna* and *Parārthānumāna*, and that it was already given to us right from the *Nyāya-bhāṣya*, if not from the *Sūtras* as well, is misplaced on number of counts. Accordingly, Dharmakīrti cannot be said to have borrowed the distinction or its rationale from his predecessors from the *Nyāya* tradition. Later on, although the distinction came to be adopted in the works of Vācaspati, Jayanta, Bhāsarvajña, Varadarāja, Udayana etc. it came to be done merely as a matter of lip-sympathy, omitting altogether the consideration of the rationale of making such a distinction. In consequence, its epistemic and methodological rationale never came to be explored in that tradition.

Accepting, then, that *Naiyāyikas* cannot be credited with the origination of the distinction between *Svārthānumāna* and *Parārthānumāna*, it needs to be seen whether credit can be given for this at least to the predecessors of Dharmakīrti in the Buddhist camp. It is to the consideration of this that we must now turn.

There is, however, one important hurdle. As is well-known, all the very important original works of Nāgārjuna, Asaṅga, Vasubandhu, Diṅnāga etc. are not, unfortunately, available in Sanskrit. Their Tibetan translations, however, exist. Under such circumstance, we are forced to make do with whatever material that is extant. This obviously puts a serious limitation on this kind of exploration, and yet we cannot help running the risk.

From Asaṅga's or Vasubandhu's definition of perception it could, perhaps, be surmised that both of them are aware of the distinction between *Savikalpaka* and *Nirvikalpaka Pratyakṣa*, although it is doubtful whether they knew the rationale of it.

Further, it seems that they accept two *Pramāṇas*, viz. *Pratyakṣa* and *Anumāna*, and their respective *Prameyas* also seem to be distinct. Asaṅga and Vasubandhu, however, have difference of opinion when they come to consider the question, whether to accept these two *Pramāṇas* on par or whether to accept preponderance of one over the other. Both of them, perhaps, accept hierarchy between them, although it is certified by them differently. According to Asaṅga, it seems, inferential cognition needs to be made sense of only in terms of perceptual cognition, whereas for Vasubandhu even perceptual cognition needs to be certified with the help of inference.

In the *Vādavidhi* we are told that *Anumāna* is either implicative or applicative in character such that on the basis of previous perception of an inseparable connection between two facts a person proceeds to derive implication of such connection or apply such connection to similar facts.

This indicates that although perception is held to be precondition of inferential cognition by both of them, Vasubandhu seems also to be making communication to be a pre-condition of cognition. However, both seem to be unclear about the distinction between *Svārthānumāna* and *Parārthānumāna*. From this one should not immediately hasten to infer that they wield no influence whatsoever on Dharmakīrti.

Coming to Diṅnāga, he appears to be much influenced by both Asaṅga and Vasubandhu. In his *Pramāṇa-samuccaya* the distinction between *Svārthānumāna* and *Parārthānumāna* is made by devoting two separate chapters to their treatment. Further, regarding *Svārthānumāna* we are told: *Svārthaṁ trirūpād liṅgato' rthadṛk* and regarding *Parārthānumāna: Trirūpaliṅgākhyānam.*[45] Yet, he does not seem to be clearly aware of the methodological and epistemic rationale of the distinction between them as Dharmakīrti is. While defining *Svārthānumāna* and explaining its nature he seems to be stating that actual perception of the object is necessary. That is, perception continues to be counted as a precondition of inferential cognition and herein Vasubandhu's impact on him is noticeable. That is why for *Svārthānumāna* he uses the term *Vyākhyāṅgaṁ*, which consists of *Pakṣa* and *Hetu*, i.e. *Pakṣa* and *Hetu* are sufficient to give us cognition of an object, whereas *Parārthānumāna* is *Parapratipādanāṅga*, which consists of three constituents, viz. *Pakṣa*, *Hetu* and *Dṛṣṭānta* as well. Thus, it seems to boil down to the distinction between ground and consequence, in which case the former is cognition backed by perception, while in the latter case it is cognition plus communication of it. Dharmakīrti, however, goes further and gives us the logic and methodology of inferential cognition in general, and explicates not only the distinction under consideration but also the epistemic and methodological rationale of making it.

From this it is clear that though Dharmakīrti and Diṅnāga have used the same terms, viz. *Svārthānumāna* and *Parārthānumāna* and though both apparently at least seem to be making the distinction between the two, what they distinguish, the way they distinguish and its rationale are not the same. Further, in the discussion of *Anumāna*, in *Pramāṇa-samuccaya*, at the hands of Diṅnāga, many logical and methodological considerations brought in by Dharmakīrti, for the first time, seem to be missing. Moreover, he seems not to have clearly articulated the necessary and sufficient conditions of *Svārthānumāna* and *Parārthānumāna*. Diṅnāga also seems to usher in a confusion in stating that constitutive conditions of each of them are different. The consideration of epistemic priority that Dharmakīrti brings in with regard to the distinction under consideration is his original and unique contribution in the light of which the rationale of making the distinction becomes reasonably clear. Thus, the need to make the distinction seems to be clearly seen, along with its implications, by Dharmakīrti, which Diṅnāga seems to be unaware of. Thus, it is, perhaps, clear that it is Dharmakīrti who should be credited with making the distinction under consideration with sufficient clarity and explicating its epistemic and methodological rationale. Accordingly, he could not be said to have borrowed these considerations from his Buddhist predecessors.

With what purity these considerations brought in by Dharmakīrti were preserved, modified, refined or distorted and misinterpreted at the hands of the Buddhist successors of Dharmakīrti like Dharmottara, Durveka Miśra, Prajñākara Gupta, Arcaṭa etc. would be interesting to inquire into. Since such an inquiry falls outside the jurisdiction of our present investigation, we refrain from undertaking it.

IV Svārthānumāna: Epistemic Condition of Anumāna and Its Hetu-centricity:

In the preceding sections we saw the need to distinguish between *Svārthānumāna* and *Parārthānumāna*, and pointed out briefly Dharmakīrti's contribution to the evolvement of this distinction. As we shall argue in the sixth chapter, the role of this distinction is not classificatory in nature. Hence, *Svārthānumāna* should not be equated with a mere sub-species of *Anumāna*; its nature and significance have to be considered on their own. It was seen earlier that *Anumāna* gives us indirect cognition of *Sāmānya-lakṣaṇa*, its only legitimate object according to Buddhists in general and Dharmakīrti in particular. It was also pointed out that concerning knowledge two sorts of distinctions are of great significance: (a) cognition and certification of what is cognised, and (b) formulation of a knowledge-claim and its communication. In the case of both these distinctions there is a certain kind of priority which is at stake. In the former distinction cognition is prior to certification, while in the latter formulation of a knowledge-claim is prior to its communication. *Svārthānumāna-Parārthānumāna* distinction has nothing to do with the distinction between an argument for oneself and that for anybody else, for with regard to the two distinctions concerning knowledge such a sort of distinction does not supply any philosophically worthwhile clue. Although, therefore, it is true that the distinction between *Svārthānumāna* and *Parārthānumāna* is often explained in this way it remains sterile both epistemically as well as methodologically. Hence, leaving it aside, the role of *Svārthānumāna* would have to be brought out in a different way. At the same time the other aspect of *Anumāna*, viz. *Parārthānumāna* cannot either be neglected or reduced to *Svārthānumāna*.

As observed above, the question of certification arises only with regard to knowledge that is already cognised. Likewise, a knowledge-claim can be communicated only after it is fashioned and formulated. However, cognition or formulation of a knowledge-claim itself requires certain conditions to be satisfied, in the absence of which there would neither be cognition nor formulation of a knowledge-claim. And in the absence of cognition, certification of knowledge is meaningless, or in the absence of formulation of a knowledge-claim, the question of its communication is futile to be raised. *Svārthānumāna* on the one hand is cognitive aspect of inferential or discursive knowledge, while on the other hand it has something to do with formulation of a knowledge-claim. Since with regard to certification of knowledge its cognition is prior, and since with regard to communication of a knowledge-claim its fashioning and formulating is prior, and since *Svārthānumāna* embraces both these aspects of priorities, it is held to be prior. Primordiality of *Svārthānumāna* is thus built into its nature both epistemically as well as communicatively. And since for significant communication not only appropriate formulation but also cognition being necessary, epistemic priority of *Svārthānumāna* happens to be reinforced and strengthened. With regard to certification of an indirect knowledge-claim and its communication, *Svārthānumāna* seems to lay down certain minimum epistemic condition/s, the non-fulfilment of which would render indirect or inferential cognition impossible. If conditions of cognition are not fulfilled, certification of a knowledge-claim would be impossible, although the required conditions of certification may have been fulfilled. Likewise, one may have a good apparatus of communication, but if one has no knowledge-claim already fashioned and formulated, he would not be in a position to communicate anything which is significant.

Svārthānumāna, thus, brings to our notice what may be called an epistemic condition of indirect or inferential cognition. But since such a cognition is always indirect (*Parokṣa*) and since it is always routed through *Gamya-Gamaka-bhāva* (indicator-indicated relation) it is the role of *Gamaka*, *Liṅga* or *Hetu* which remains decisive in it. Thus understood, even on the level of epistemic condition of *Anumāna*, viz. *Svārthānumāna*, the principal considerations concerning it seem to revolve around *Hetu*. Consequently, *Hetu*-centricity of *Anumāna* comes to be firmly established. As an epistemic condition of *Anumāna*, *Svārthānumāna* seems to constitute its womb such that no feature of *Anumāna* which is not decisively significant with regard to *Svārthānumāna* cannot likewise be significant with regard to *Parārthānumāna*. For, the latter after all is nothing else but verbalised form of the former. It is perhaps for this reason that Dharmakīrti called *Svārthānumāna* to be epistemic (*Jñānātmaka*) in nature while *Parārthānumāna* to be linguistic (*Śabdātmaka*) in character.

Since in this way *Svārthānumāna*, the very womb of indirect or inferential cognition, remains *Hetu*-centric in character, and since it constitutes epistemic condition of *Anumāna*, it would not be a matter of great surprise that its conditions, too, are likewise *Hetu*-centric in nature. One may, perhaps, show that the very nature of *Anumāna* and its various kinds of conditions are so intimately and inextricably related with each other that *Hetu*-centricity of *Anumāna* would be merely a dispensable feature of it if its determinant conditions too are not likewise *Hetu*-centric. Conversely, if the latter are *Hetu*-centric in nature, it would be inconsistent to hold that *Anumāna* is nonetheless not *Hetu*-centric. Thus, *Hetu*-centricity of *Anumāna* and that of various kinds of conditions and features of it are inalienably connected with each other.

In this chapter we argued that *Svārthānumāna* constitutes an epistemic condition of *Anumāna* and that it is *Hetu*-centric in nature. To have shown this, however, is the beginning of our envisaged prolonged exercise, and we shall present the remaining aspects of it in the sequel.

The Argument to Follow:

Although we considered above the nature of *Svārthānumāna* as an epistemic condition of inferential cognition (*Parokṣa-jñāna*) such a condition is not its sole determinant. Apart from the satisfaction of epistemic condition, that is, apart from every *Anumāna* at least being *Svārthānumāna*, an *Anumāna* would be required to satisfy two sorts of additional conditions for its formulation. They are: (a) structural or constitutive conditions like, *Pakṣa*, *Sādhya*, *Hetu* and the modes of their organization or interrelationship, and (b) regulative conditions, like *Vyāpti* and *Pakṣadharmatā*. With reference to the satisfaction of epistemic condition it was argued earlier that it brings in *Hetu*-centricity of *Anumāna*. Now on the level of the fulfilment of constitutive and regulative conditions of *Anumāna*, too, it would have to be shown that from their side also it is *Hetu*-centricity of *Anumāna* that is at stake. If in this way *Hetu*-centricity of *Anumāna* is established with regard to the satisfaction of its epistemic, constitutive and regulative conditions, it would be comparatively easy to show this feature of *Anumāna* with regard to the consideration of its validity and/or soundness, as also with regard to the consideration of *Hetvābhāsas*. Doing the exercise in this way, with reference to various aspects of it, it would finally enable us to establish our principal claim that Dharmakīrti seeks to establish *Hetu*-centricity of *Anumāna* in his treatment of it in such works as *Hetu-bindu*, *Nyāya-bindu*, *Pramāṇa-vārtika*, etc.

These various points are going to occupy our attention in the subsequent chapters. Of them, consideration of constitutive and regulative conditions of *Anumāna* need to be first taken up, for without fulfilling them an argument may not come to be formulated at all. Hence, we turn to them in the next two chapters.

Notes and References

1. Dharmakīrti, *P.V.*; IV. 1, M.N. *Vṛtti*; pp. 363-364. also Prajñākara Gupta; *P.V.A.*; pp. 467-470.
2. Dharmakīrti; *P.V.*; II.174-180, M.N. *Vṛtti*; pp. 153-155. also Prajñākara Gupta; *P.V.A.*; pp. 266-272.
3. Dharmakīrti; *P.V.*; II. 1-3. M.N. *Vṛtti*; pp. 98-101.
4. Dharmakīrti; *P.V.*; IV. 116-119. *Svārthānumāna-pariccheda*; pp. 17-18. M.N. *Vṛtti*, p. 400.
5. Arcaṭa; *H.B.T.*; pp. 3-5, 20.
6. Dharmakīrti; *P.V.*; II. 5-7. M.N. *Vṛtti*; pp. 102-103.
7. Dharmakīrti; *P.V.*; I.287, III.1. M.N. *Vṛtti*; pp. 97, 257-258. also Durveka Miśra; *Dharmottara-pradīpa*; II.3, pp. 86-87.
8. Dharmakīrti; *P.V.*; II. 60-61. M.N. *Vṛtti*; pp. 119-120. also Arcaṭa; *H.B.T.*; pp. 177-185.
9. Arcaṭa; *H.B.T.*; Section 29, p. 41.
10. Dharmakīrti; *H.B.*; pp. 54, 64-66.
11. *Ibid*; p. 52.
12. Arcaṭa; *H.B.T.*; pp. 37-40.
13. Dharmakīrti; *Vādanyāya*; (with *Vipañcitārthā* of Śāntarakṣita), pp. 6-7; also Dharmakīrti; *H.B.* pp. 70-71. Arcaṭa; *H.B.T.*; pp. 4-5. Dharmakīrti; *P.V.*; II.81-122; III. 16-22. M.N. *Vṛtti*, pp. 126-137; 264-266. Prajñākara Gupta; *P.V.A.*; pp. 228-232.
14. Arcaṭa; *H.B.T.*; p. 5, pp. 23-24.
15. *Ibid*; pp. 4-5.
16. *Ibid*; pp. 28-30.
17. Prajñākara Gupta; *P.V.A.*; III.1, pp. 467-470.
18. *Ibid*; II. 537-541, pp. 461-463.

19. Dharmakīrti; *P.V*,; II.1. M.N. *Vṛtti*, pp. 257-258.
20. Dharmakīrti; *P.V.*; IV.1, M.N. *Vṛtti*, p. 363.
21. Prajñākara Gupta; *P.V.A.*; III.1, pp. 467-469. also Durveka Miśra; *Dharmottara-pradīpa*; pp. 87-90.
22. Durveka Miśra, *Dharmottara-pradīpa*; pp. 87-89, 150-151.
23. Prajñākara Gupta; *P.V.A.*; pp. 468-474.
24. Dharmakīrti; *P.V.*; II. 123-133; M.N. *Vṛtti*; pp. 138-140.
25. Dharmakīrti; *H.B.*; p. 52, *P.V.*; III.1, *Svārthānumāna-pariccheda*, pp. 1-12. M.N. *Vṛtti*, pp. 257-258, also Karṇakagomin; *P.V.T.*; pp. 1-12.
26. Dharmakīrti; *P.V.*; II. 174-186. M.N. *Vṛtti*, pp. 153-157.
27. Dharmakīrti; *P.V.*; II.123. M.N. *Vṛtti*, pp. 138-139.
28. Prajñākara Gupta; *P.V.A.*; III.1, pp. 467-470.
29. Dharmakīrti; *P.V.*· I.1-7, M.N. *Vṛtti*, pp. 3-8.
30. Arcaṭa, *H.B.T.*; pp. 6-8.
31. Vātsyāyana, *Nyāya-Bhāṣya*; I.i.3, pp. 182-183.
32. Uddyotakara; *Nyāya-Vārtika*; I.i.1, pp. 23, 31-33.
33. Gautama; *Nyāya-Sūtras*; I.i.5. also *Nyāya-Bhāṣya* and *Nyāya-Vārtika* on it. pp. 291-293.
34. Udayana; *Pariśuddhi*; I.i.5, pp. 338-339.
35. Gautama; *Nyāya-Sūtras* (also Vāstyāyana's *Nyāya-Bhāṣya* and Uddyotakara's *Nyāya-Vārtika*); I.i.5; pp. 291-293.
36. Uddyotakara; *Nyāya-Vārtika*; I.i.5, pp. 293-303.
37. Jayanta Bhaṭṭa; *Nyāya-Mañjarī*; part II, pp. 130-131. also Bhāsarvajña; *Nyāya-Bhūṣaṇa*; pp. 272-273.
38. Arcaṭa; *H.B.T.*; sections 17-18, pp. 28-29.
39. *Ibid*; section 18, pp. 28-29, also p. 152.
40. Dharmakīrti; *P.V.*; II-61-64, M.N. *Vṛtti*; p. 120.
41. Arcaṭa; *H.B.T.*; p. 46.
42. Vātsyāyana; *Nyāya-Bhāṣya*; I.i.5, p. 291.
43. Uddyotakara; *Nyāya-Vārtika*; I.i.5, p. 296.
44. Bhāsarvajña; *Nyāya-Bhūṣaṇa*; p. 272.
45. Translation from Tibetan version of *Pramāṇa-samuccaya-kārikās*, Mdo-ce-volume, Peking edition. Translated into Sanskrit by myself.

CHAPTER III

STRUCTURAL CONDITIONS OF ANUMĀNA

In the last chapter, we analysed the nature of *Anumāna* and argued that *Svārthānumāna* constitutes its epistemic condition. While analysing the nature of *Anumāna*, we said that *Parārthānumāna* is not a different kind of *Anumāna* at all in the strict sense of the term, since it is nothing else but a linguistic expression of what has been already cognised inferentially. In the previous chapter, it was argued that epistemologically *Svārthānumāna* is of primary importance. In this and the succeeding chapters we intend to argue that it is structurally and regulatively prior as well. That is, the structural and regulative conditions of *Svārthānumāna* are the necessary and sufficient conditions of *Parārthānumāna* as well.

Further, it was argued, at the end of the last chapter, that the structure or constitution of inferential cognition needs to be discussed and considered at the level of *Svārthānumāna* itself. Any piece of information that gives rise to indirect cognition (*Parokṣa-jñāna*) is not and cannot be called an inferential cognition simply because it has certain form and content of its own. Indirect cognition must be capable of being presented in an argumentative form. Otherwise, even plain narration or description etc. would enjoy the status of inferential cognition, just because they make us cognise indirectly and have certain form and content. Hence, any form and content giving rise to indirect cognition is not to be reckoned as an inferential cognition. Then, the necessary and/or sufficient structural conditions, which need to be satisfied, so that an indirect cognition could be counted as an inferential cognition, is a question to which close attention needs to be paid. In response to this methodologically important question, it seems, Dharmakīrti argues that *Pakṣa*, *Sādhya* and *Hetu* are necessary and sufficient for entertaining an indirect knowledge-claim. This does not, however, mean that conditions sufficient for inferential cognition, viz. *Pakṣa, Sādhya* and *Hetu,* are also sufficient for certifying the said kind of cognition. There, as will be argued later, we require additional conditions to be fulfilled, although they cannot be at variance with the structural conditions already mentioned. In other words, the structural conditions given by him for both cognition (*Svārthānumāna*) as well as its certification or vindication (*Parārthānumāna*) are just the same.[1]

Moreover, it seems, the question of viability or tenability of such an inferential cognition arises on the level of *Svārthānumāna* itself. Still further, whether such an inferential or discursive cognition is valid and/or sound and reliable is a question that is pertinent on the level of *Svārthānumāna* itself. That is why we started our methodological inquiry into the analysis of *Anumāna* right from *Svārthānumāna.*

After knowing the reasons why our inquiry opened with *Svārthānumāna,* it needs to be argued that all the important questions regarding *Anumāna,* viz. structure or constitution, the content and form, validity and/or soundness, etc., are connected with *Svārthānumāna,* since it is *Svārthānumāna* which opens the very possibility of their being discussed in the framework of *Anumāna.* Now, in this chapter, we wish to discuss and critically consider the questions or issues concerning the structural conditions of *Anumāna.* For, unless we fulfil structural or constitutive conditions along with the regulative conditions, viz. *Vyāpti* and *Pakṣadharmatā,* the questions of inferential cognition being valid or invalid, sound or unsound, acceptable or unacceptable do not arise.[2] Even though *Svārthānumāna* opens the very possibility of inferential cognition, it in itself is not sufficient for giving rise to valid inferential cognition. It must have certain form and content, and that too must be regulated by certain conditions. Then alone can it be cognitively significant. And further, validity or invalidity, soundness or unsoundness of an argument will require certain additional conditions to be fulfilled.[3] So, the discussion of the constitutive or structural conditions of *Anumāna* seems appropriate to be undertaken with reference to *Svārthānumāna,* and this would be our task in this chapter.

Before we begin discussing structural conditions of *Anumāna* according to Dharmakīrti, meaning of the expression 'structural conditions of *Anumāna*' and the way these conditions are related to fashioning and formulating an argument and to giving rise to inferential cognition needs to be explained. This will engage our attention in the first section. For understanding their proper function and role we would have to investigate into their nature and significance. That would be our task in the second section, while in the third section we shall investigate into Dharmakīrti's distinctive contribution with regard to explication of their nature and significance, in contrast to his inter- or intra-school predecessors or contemporaries.

I. The Function and Role of Structural Conditions of Anumāna:

Structural or constitutive conditions of *Anumāna* are determinative of its very structure, constitution or, what comes to the same, its very format.[4] They structure or constitute its form. In the preceding chapter, we saw that *Svārthānumāna* amounts to fashioning or formulating an argument, entertaining an indirect knowledge-claim concerning *Sāmānya-lakṣaṇa.* If structural or constitutive conditions are not fulfilled then it would no longer be possible for us to fashion or formulate an argument, or it would not be possible for us to entertain an indirect knowledge-claim concerning *Sāmānya-lakṣaṇa.*[5] That is why they are held to be structural or constitutive conditions of *Anumāna,* in the sense that unless they are fulfilled there will be no formulation of *Anumāna*, and, consequently, no indirect knowledge-claim concerning *Sāmānya-lakṣaṇa*, or its cognition.[6]

Given then that structural or constitutive conditions of *Anumāna* are decisively important, the question is: On what basis are they decided? And further, on what basis is their methodological appropriateness or otherwise envisaged? For, if their choice and selection are made at random, there will be no end to differences of opinion, and, consequently, there would also be no way to get out of them. Fortunately their choice is not a random choice. In order to choose them properly the principle of economy can be exploited as a decisive principle. The question that may be asked is: minimally how many and which constituents should an *Anumāna* have in order to get fashioned or formulated? In answer to this it is said that if the three pillars of *Anumāna* are given, along with their interconnections, it should be possible to formulate an argument or entertain any knowledge-claim inferentially.[7] Here it may be asked: Why should the consideration of the principle of economy weigh so heavily with us? The answer is that it is intuitively obvious, methodologically appropriate and philosophically rewarding to hold that we should not bring in any additional consideration if it is needless to do so, and if as a result of such a move we are not forced to suffer a heavy loss in terms of explanation. Dispensable considerations should always be said good-bye to, for otherwise our explanation of anything is likely to be unnecessarily complex and complicated, giving rise to further needless confusion and error.[8]

Secondly, the nature and structure of inferential cognition play an important role in determining the structural conditions of *Anumāna*. For, it is not merely enough to fashion and formulate an argument, or entertain an indirect knowledge-claim (*Parokṣa-jñāna*) concerning *Sāmānya-lakṣaṇa*, the object of inferential cognition. It must, in principle, be objective, sharable, capable of being articulated or communicated.[9] If this condition fails to be satisfied then there would not be any difference between perceptually and inferentially entertained knowledge-claims except that the former would be concerning *Svalakṣaṇa* and the latter concerning *Sāmānya-lakṣaṇa*, since both of them would be incommunicable. Hence, while deciding structural or constitutive conditions of *Anumāna* we must not ignore communicability, although mere communicability about anything does not automatically guarantee its being factual, since communicability concerning something that is merely coherently possible or conceivable is, methodologically speaking, perfectly legitimate.

Thirdly, while considering constitutive or structural conditions of *Anumāna*, one has to keep in mind that, according to Buddhists, *Parokṣa-jñāna* is made available to us only through *Anumāna*.[10] Likewise, one will have to think of the nature of *Sāmānya-lakṣaṇa*, for the whole structure of *Anumāna* itself is geared to the cognition of the characteristic features of the *Prameya* called *Sāmānya-lakṣaṇa*. That is, through *Anumāna* we should only be able to gain an indirect cognition of *Sāmānya-lakṣaṇa*, failing which *Anumāna* would lapse into *Aparokṣa-jñāna*, with the difference that whereas the object of *Pratyakṣa* is *Svalakṣaṇa*, that of *Anumāna* is *Sāmānya-lakṣaṇa*. To pave the way for something of this kind would do an irreparable damage and violence to Dharmakīrti's analysis of *Anumāna* and explication of its nature and structure.

Accordingly, while discussing structural constituents of *Anumāna* according to Dharmakīrti, we would have to bear carefully the following points in mind:

(1) *Sāmānya-lakṣaṇa* is an object of inferential cognition. But perceptual cognition is not a pre-condition of it.[11]

(2) Whatever is cognised inferentially need not exist actually and factually. By the same token, it need not be non-existent too.[12] Likewise, it need not be necessarily absurd (*Vikalpa*) or purely ficticious (*Bhrānta*).[13] Without being anything of these sorts it could be coherently conceivable, possible, and its being instantiated need not be ruled out in advance.

(3) For inferential cognition its verbalization is not a pre-condition, although it must be communicable in principle. Thus, we can and must be able to entertain an indirect knowledge-claim without its being verbalised or communicated. That is, even in solitude we should be able to entertain an inferential knowledge-claim all by ourselves, and hence conversational, debating or dialogical situation is not a pre-condition of inferential cognition as *Nyāya* philosophers are prone to hold, although an already fashioned and formulated argument could always be used in such a situation.[14]

All these points, mentioned above, perhaps, function as methodological and/or intuitive constraints while determining the structural conditions of *Anumāna* at the hands of Dharmakīrti. Here the sole question that is sought to be investigated into is: What sort of structure should *Anumāna* have in order that inferential cognition may arise (*Utpatti*) or be certified (*Jñapti*). However, this does not mean that the sort of cognition under consideration originates from the particular format or structure, or that it itself certifies it. Rather, inferential cognition originates or we are enabled to certify it via a particular structure, although inferential cognition and the structure of inference are inalienably (*Avinābhāva*) connected with each other.

With this, we return to the seminal question raised earlier: What is it that is necessary for entertaining inferential knowledge-claim as an indirect knowledge-claim? As an answer to this Dharmakīrti replies that given *Pakṣa*, *Sādhya* and *Hetu* one can always fashion and formulate an argument and entertain an inferential knowledge-claim.[15] Granted that they are enough or sufficient to fashion, formulate and entertain an inferential knowledge-claim are they merely the necessary structural conditions of *Anumāna* but not the sufficient? And if so, what are the additional sufficient conditions? How are the necessary and/or sufficient conditions to be decided? Such questions need to be considered carefully.

It appears that Dharmakīrti is methodologically right in determining the structural conditions of *Anumāna*. The structural conditions that he has stipulated are necessary and are context-freely determined. It will be pointed out later that they are context-freely sufficient as well. Naturally, it becomes clear that he is making a distinction between necessary and sufficient conditions. One can consider necessary and sufficient conditions of something contextually or context-freely. Contextually considered, one may come to stipulate some additional necessary and/or sufficient conditions of something, which context-freely may be redundant and dispensable. Further, while deciding necessary conditions of something, considerations other than methodological may weigh heavily with somebody. As a result, at his hands such necessary conditions may additionally come to be stipulated as, methodologically considered are dispensable. Dharmakīrti is not responding to a question as to what conditions, on whatever ground it may be, could be held necessary structural conditions of *Anumāna*. In other words, he is not interested in the inventory of all the possible necessary or sufficient structural conditions of *Anumāna*. He is rather responding to the seminal question as to what minimum structural necessary and sufficient conditions should an *Anumāna* satisfy in order that it may context-freely be fashioned or formulated at all.

The structure or constitution of *Anumāna* on Dharmakīrti's reckoning, is not merely a heap or pile of its structural constituents, viz. *Pakṣa*, *Sādhya* and *Hetu*. Nor are these constituents designed to be interconnected with one another in whatever fashion one may deem it fit to do so. Their organisation or interrelationship has very close connection principally with two fundamental aspects of *Anumāna*, viz. its regulative conditions[16] and its validity and/or soundness.[17] We briefly outline these points below without anticipating too much of our argument in later chapters.

Though *Pakṣa, Sādhya* and *Hetu* are given as the necessary constituents of *Anumāna*, it is necessary to link them with one another. Without their being connected one cannot hope to have inferential cognition at all. That is, *Pakṣa*, *Sādhya* and *Hetu* need to be connected with one another with the help of regulative conditions. For making inferential cognition possible both structural and regulative conditions need to be fulfilled. Then and then alone can one hope to have inferential cognition, and not otherwise. Of the two regulative conditions of *Anumāna*, viz. *Vyāpti* and *Pakṣadharmatā*, while the former establishes connection between *Hetu* and *Sādhya*, the latter establishes it between *Pakṣa* and *Hetu*. A detailed investigation into the connection between structural and regulative conditions of *Anumāna* and its implications would be the theme of our inquiry in the next chapter.

Further, fulfilment of structural and regulative conditions make it possible to have inferential cognition, or to fashion and formulate an argument. But merely because an argument has been fashioned it does not automatically guarantee that it should be valid and/or sound. Likewise, just because one has come to entertain an indirect knowledge-claim this in itself does not warrant that it is tenable. Constitutive conditions of *Anumāna* like *Hetu* have an important bearing upon validity and/or soundness of an argument via its peculiar characteristics like *Pakṣa-sattva*, etc. So also, constitutive conditions of *Anumāna* have an important bearing on the warrantability of an inferentially entertained indirect knowledge-claim. We shall have an occasion to look into this aspect of them at greater length in the fifth ehapter.

Having considered the function and role of the structural conditions of *Anumāna* according to Dharmkīrti, we proceed in the next section to analyse the nature of each of them and argue as to why each of them needs to be considered to be so.

II The Nature of Structural Conditions

As observed earlier, it is not merely enough to stipulate the structural conditions of *Anumāna*. They need to be shown to be its necessary and sufficient constitutive conditions. Further, Dharmakīrti is interested in establishing that *Pakṣa*, *Sādhya* and *Hetu* are context-freely necessary and sufficient constitutive conditions of *Anumāna*.[18] Accordingly, on the basis of a fairly detailed exposition of the nature of each of them it needs to be shown why and how all of them are held to be so. Further, it needs also to be argued that no more condition is required to be added to them, nor is any of them dispensable. It is to an exercise of this kind that we turn in this section.

With a view to making an inquiry outlined above and vindicating the claims mentioned earlier, five important points need to be borne in mind:

(i) Dharmakīrti makes a distinction between contextual and context-free considerations.
(ii) He, likewise, makes an important distinction between necessary and sufficient conditions of *Anumāna*.
(iii) In this, his orientation is basically methodological and so extra-methodological considerations, if any, need to be relegated to the background.
(iv) He refuses to stick dogmatically to common-sense, not because he is its sworn enemy, but rather because, in his view, a philosopher must have freedom to uphold even a counter-intuitive consideration if it is methodologically warranted, and
(v) He is not prepared to sacrifice the principle of economy on the altar of convenience.

With this brief background, we turn to a detailed consideration of the nature of each of the structural conditions of *Anumāna* accepted by Dharmakīrti and also why they are held as indispensable. First, coming to *Pakṣa* or what Dharmakīrti calls *Anumeya*.[19] Dharmakīrti explains the nature of *Pakṣa* as *Anumeyaḥ dharmī, sādhya* (*viśiṣṭa*) *dharmatvāt*.[20] *Pakṣa* is (called) a *Dharmī* due to its being characterized (*Dharmatvāt*) by a *Sādhya* (as capable of being) particularized (*viśiṣṭa*). Thus understood, *Pakṣa* is a reference-point such that if a *Hetu* related to *Sādhya* is related to it (*Pakṣa*), then, on that basis, *Sādhya* could be related to it (*Pakṣa*). Such a reference-point may be available in a given situation either as a variable or as a constant.[21] In the former case, it (the reference point) does not cease to be conceivable, although it is not instantiated being merely general or coherently conceivable, while, in the latter case, it is both coherently conceivable as well as instantiated or particularized, however accidentally it might be, although it does not cease to be general.[22] Coherent conceivability is a minimum condition *Pakṣa* is required to satisfy and hence it need not necessarily be factual, and although it may not in this way be factual, it does not cease to be a reference-point on that count. Due to this sort of consideration concerning *Pakṣa* at the hands of Dharmakīrti, it remains context-free and he has no compunction to hold that inferentially entertained knowledge-claims could be entertained in a merely coherently conceivable world as well.[23] From this it is obvious that such knowledge-claims as could be entertained in a non-empty, actual world are not and need not be ruled out. That *Pakṣa* is, in this way, sought to be understood as a reference-point in Dharmakīrti's treatment of *Auumāna* could be further reinforced with the help of two points: (i) With reference to *Puruṣārthasiddhi*[24] it operates as a reference-point effecting or rather enabling us to effect *Heyopādeyatā* which is instrumental to it.[25] (ii) Object of inferential cognition is always *Sāmānya-lakṣaṇa*, which although perfectly conceivable coherently is not necessarily instantiated, though it is instantiable in principle.[26] But just because an instantiable *Sāmānya-lakṣaṇa* is not as a matter of fact instantiated, this in itself does not forbid it to become object of inferential cognition.[27]

Secondly, *Pakṣa* determines the range within which the *Sādhya* could be discovered provided it is discoverable, or at least considered as coherently conceivable. To speak metaphorically, *Pakṣa* is like a pond or lake in which fishes of *Sādhya* could be angled with the help of the angle of *Hetu*. The range that *Pakṣa* in principle could be said to be making available could be contextually delimited or circumscribed with reference to an epistemic constraint of curiosity (*jijñāsā*)[28] and, accordingly, Dharmakīrti also describes *Pakṣa* to be *Jijñāsitaviśeṣo dharmī*.[29] Thus, here the methodological and epistemic considerations concerning *Pakṣa* seem to reinforce and strengthen each other to decide its nature as a structural determinant of *Anumāna*. Peripherally, however, this aspect of the nature of *Pakṣa* originates from, and remains characterizable with reference to, *Hetu*-centricity of *Anumāna*.

Coming to *Sādhya*. Prior to an inferential cognition, *Sādhya* is never given to us, directly or indirectly.[30] That *Sādhya* is not given cognitively prior to inferential cognition is not a matter of description but rather of the stipulation of the precondition of an inferential situation.[31] It is not given not because it cannot be given, but rather because with its being given the very need and propriety of inferential cognition terminates; and the whole inferential exercise itself becomes redundant.[32] Although it is not given, it must, at the same time, not be simply incapable of being given.[33] For, if it is incapable of being given even as a possible object of coherent cognition, it will be impossible to infer it as a result of inferential cognition. Thus, the possibility of *Sādhya* being inferred must never be dismissed in advance, for that will mark an impossibility of inferential cognition. Further, the *Sādhya* that we cognise or are enabled to cognise need not necessarily be actual and existent. Even if it is merely coherently conceivable, this in itself does not pose a barrier to its being inferred. However, whether the *Sādhya* is actual or coherently possible our cognition of it, as a result of inference, must always be indirect, since by its very nature and design *Anumāna* can furnish us only with indirect cognition (*Parokṣajñāna*).[34] With these preliminaries we turn to consider *Sādhya* as a structural condition of *Anumāna*.

As is well known, *Sādhya* is that which is inferred. It is related to *Hetu* on the one hand through *Avinābhāva Niyama* or *Vyāptī* and could be or possibly is connected to *Pakṣa* as a *Dharma* of it on the other.[35] *Hetu* is the indicator of *Sādhya* and *Sādhya* is that which is indicated by it.[36]

From an epistemological point of view, since *Sādhya* is to be inferred, its nature cannot be depicted and determined prior to its being inferred. Since it happens to be cognised through an indirect knowledge that we wish to have, we can at the most say that such an inferred *Sādhya* is connected with *Hetu* consistently; otherwise if there is a *Sādhyābhāva* then there will automatically be *Hetvabhāva*.[37]

On this background, it should be clear why Dharmakīrti does not define *Sādhya*. However, he says that *Sādhya* is *Jijñāsita Dharma*, i.e., a coherently conceivable *Dharma* of *Pakṣa* made available. That is why *Pakṣa* is sought to be understood as *Jijñāsitaviśeṣo dharmī*. Further, since *Sādhya* is inferred on the basis of *Sādhana* (*Hetu*), or since it is *Gamya* which happens to be indicated by *Gamaka* (*Hetu*),[38] *Hetu*-centrality of *Anumāna* makes its headway here as well. One thing, however, is clear. The *Sādhya* to be inferred could minimally be said to be coherently conceivable, factuality not being its pre-condition, although its factuality is not precluded or ruled out in advance. Thus, as *Hetu* is related to *Pakṣa* on the one hand and to *Sādhya* on the other, so too *Sādhya* is related to *Hetu* on the one hand through *Gamya-Gamaka-bhāva*, and to *Pakṣa* as its *Dharma* on the other. It is this sort of alignment and organisation of them that spells out the structure or constitution of *Anumāna*, the very framework of indirect cognition (*Parokṣajñāna*).[39]

The reason why *Sādhya* needs to be considered as a structural condition of *Anumāna* is that if it were not so, the process of inferring would lack an appropriate terminus and it would remain a matter of endlessly connecting one thing with another. In the absence of *Sādhya* resorting to *Anumāna* would be a redundant and futile exercise. Likewise, in its absence *Gamya-Gamaka-bhāva* would collapse, *Vyāpti* as a regulative condition of *Anumāna* would not be available, and *Pakṣa* would cease to be *Jijñāsitaviśeṣaḥ*. Thus understood, in its absence the very possibility of the framework of *Anumāna* would be annihilated and everything would be a matter of direct cognition. Hence, it is essential to acknowledge *Sādhya* as a necessary structural condition and component of *Anumāna*.

To Turn to *Hetu*. *Hetu* is a *Gamaka* in the sense that indirect knowledge (*Parokṣa-jñāna*) is made possible only through *Hetu*.[40] Without *Hetu* one cannot have cognition of *Sāmānya-lakṣaṇa*,[41] and thus understood inferentially, *Hetu* is a precondition of indirect cognition, and since, according to Dharmakīrti, indirect cognition becomes possible only through *Anumāna, Hetu* is its precondition as well.[42]

Hetu being essential for getting indirect cognition, it is accepted as a structural condition of *Anumāna. Hetu* is a characteristic feature (*Asādhāraṇa-dharma*) of *Pakṣa*[43] and hence related to *Pakṣa* through *Pakṣadharmatā*.[44] On the other hand, it is related to *Sādhya* through *Vyāpti*, a *Niyama* called *Avinābhāva*.[45] Thus *Hetu* is related to both *Pakṣa* and *Sādhya*. Obviously, it plays an important role in the format of *Anumāna*. But its cognitive role, too, is important. For, it is the *Gamya-Gamaka-bhāva* around which the whole framework of inferential cognition and/or its certification revolves. As a consequence, *Hetu* is an essential and important constituent of *Anumāna*.

Inference is a mode of inferring *Sādhya* on the basis of *Hetu*. Hence, it is also called *Sādhana* or *Liṅga*. *Hetu* is the indicator of *Sādhya* but from whatever *Hetu* that is available, the legitimate and requisite *Sādhya* cannot be inferred.[46] *Hetu* remains a proper indicator of the legitimate *Sādhya*, provided there is a certain relation .between *Hetu* and *Sādhya* (i.e. *Avinābhāva*). If *Hetu* obtains, *Sādhya* cannot fail to obtain and conversely, if *Sādhya* fails to obtain then *Hetu* must also fail to obtain.[47]

Hetu is also called as *Vyāpya* and obviously *Sādhya* as *Vyāpaka*. *Vyāpya* depends upon *Vyāpaka* in the sense that the latter is ontologically prior, while the former is epistemologically prior. Sometimes there is an extensional equinumerosity of *Hetu* and *Sādhya*. But *Hetu* is never more *Vyāpaka* than *Sādhya*. Hence, *Hetu* is either less than or equal to *Sādhya* in extension but never more.[48]

Likewise, *Hetu* is called *Gamaka* too. With the help of *Gamaka* one can get the knowledge of *Gamya* (*Sādhya*). But converse of it will not hold good, i.e. from *Sādhya* one cannot know *Hetu* Thus, *Gamya* or *Sādhya* cannot be epistemically prior. The relation between *Hetu* and *Sādhya* is thus known as *Gamya-Gamaka-bhāva*.[49] In between these two, *Gamaka* (*Hetu*) is always given to us. And on the basis of *Gamaka*, we attempt to get an indirect knowledge about *Gamya* (*Sādhya*). This knowledge of *Sādhya* needs to be certified. In this kind of certification, too, *Hetu* plays an important role. For, *Hetu* being already given, at least as coherently conceivable, its knowledge is reliable and certain.[50] It is the starting point of indirect cognition concerning *Sāmānya-lakṣaṇa*, and since *Anumāna* is the gate-way of indirect-cognition, *Hetu* occupies a decisive place and plays a central role in its format.

That is why when one deals with *Anumāna* one deals primarily with *Hetu*. We have to start with *Hetu* in order to formulate an argument. Secondly, the consideration of the tenability or otherwise of an argument also depends upon *Hetu*. Thirdly, with reference to constitutive conditions of *Anumāna* like *Pakṣa*, *Sādhya* etc. or with reference to the regulative conditions of it, viz. *Vyāpti* and *Pakṣadharmatā*, too, *Hetu* has an important role to play and, in its absence, neither of them would be available. We shall have an occasion to consider regulative conditions of *Anumāna* in the next chapter.

Having considered individually the constitutive or structural conditions of *Anumāna* according to Dharmakīrti, close attention needs to be paid to two further questions arising in the context under consideration:

(a) examination of the role of each of them on the count of *Hetu*-centrality of *Anumāna*, and
(b) critical consideration whether *Pakṣa*, *Sādhya* and *Hetu* are also sufficient constitutive conditions of *Anumāna*.

It is to the consideration of them in the same sequence that we now turn.

When one considers something as a centre, it could be considered so either structurally or functionally. With reference to considering the centre of *Anumāna*, it is the structural centrality of it that is at stake. There, again, the principal concern is that of methodology, and hence any sort of extra-methodological consideration could at the most be allowed to play only a reinforcing and strengthening role here. Accordingly, the question is: Which structural component of *Anumāna* could, and needs to be, held methodologically central to its format, such that the whole structure of *Anumāna* could be said to be revolving around it? In answer to this question, Dharmakīrti seems to uphold the *Hetu*-centrality of *Anumāna*, and his treatment of *Anumāna* in his various treatises could be held as significantly directed at establishment of this point of seminal significance. Further, since

Svārthānumāna is the very heart-core of *Anumāna*, and since *Parārthānumāna* is nothing else but verbalised *Svārthānumāna*, it is enough to show that *Hetu*-centrality of *Anumāna* structurally holds with regard to *Svārthānumāna*. We have observed already that *Gamya-Gamaka-bhāva*, *Vyāpti* and *Pakṣadharmatā*, each of which plays a decisive role in the framework of *Anumāna*, revolve around *Hetu* as its structural component. It would be argued later, that in the consideration of validity and/or soundness of an argument, or that of *Hetvābhāsas*, too, it is *Hetu* which again occupies a central place. Hence *Hetu*-centrality of *Anumāna* comes out on various counts. Consequently, among the structural conditions of *Anumāna*, *Hetu* gets precedence and priority over others.

From among the structural conditions of *Anumāna*, the sort of position and importance that is decisively enjoyed by *Hetu* cannot be said to be enjoyed either by *Pakṣa* or *Sādhya*. For, even though *Pakṣa* is structurally important and essential, some of the important aspects of the format of *Anumāna* like *Vyāpti*, *Pakṣadharmatā*, *Gamya-Gamaka-bhāva* cannot in any way be said either to be decisively determined by or to revolve around *Pakṣa*. Likewise, although *Sādhya* is an important structural component of *Anumāna*, it cannot be its centre, principally for the following reasons: (a) *Pakṣadharmatā*, one of the regulative conditions of *Anumāna* is totally independent of *Sādhya* and another, viz. *Vyāpti* cannot be said to be revolving around it; (b) *Gamya-Gamaka-bhāva*, too, cannot be said to be revolving around it; and (c) assigning any decisive place to it in precedence over the one assigned to *Hetu*, would totally reverse the *Vyāpya-Vyāpaka-bhāva* between them and consequently would destroy the very framework of *Anumāna*. Accordingly, neither *Pakṣa* nor *Sādhya* can be held to be central to the framework of *Anumāna*, methodologically or otherwise.

The problem of *Hetu*-centrality is, further, peculiar and unique only with reference to *Anumāna* or *Parokṣa jñāna*. For, it is only in the domain of indirect knowledge that we are required to resort to discursive reasoning, it being its gate-way, and it is with reference to employment of arguments as a means of indirect cognition that an inquiry into the framework of *Anumāna* becomes in order and in turn opens the door of its *Hetu*-

centrality, especially when methodological and context-free considerations remain uppermost.

The contention that *Hetu* is methodologically at the centre of the format of *Anumāna* is not to be mistaken for the contention that *Hetu* is merely essential and indispensable structural component of *Anumāna*. For, this kind of status is enjoyed by *Pakṣa* and *Sādhya* as well. *What it means is that every methodologically important aspect of the framework and format of Anumāna could be satisfactorily made sense of only insofar as, and to the extent to which, its consideration revolves around that of some aspect or the other of the nature and significance of Hetu as a structural component of it.* Since we shall have later on an occasion to look into the details of various aspects of this contention and its implications we refrain from anticipating our argument there.

With this we turn to the second important question raised above, viz. whether the structural conditions of *Anumāna* accepted by Dharmakīrti—*Pakṣa*, *Sādhya* and *Hetu*—could also be held sufficient over and above their being accepted as necessary. If they are held to be insufficient two requirements would have to be fulfilled: (a) some additional condition would be required to be shown as essential for being incorporated in the context-free consideration of *Anumāna* as its sufficient condition, and (b) such a move would have to be shown as methodologically defensible. For, it is these two considerations, viz. consideration of the format of *Anumāna* context-freely and giving methodological consideration precedence over every other sort of consideration, which seem to weigh heavily, if not altogether exclusively, with Dharmakīrti. Hence, substitution of contextuality consideration for context-free consideration of the format of *Anumāna* would mark a decisive shift from Dharmakīrti's procedure. But, likewise, giving precedence to an extra-methodological consideration over methodological consideration would bring in such a reversal of it that it would be inconsistent with Dharmakīrti's procedure. Accordingly, the proper question to answer would not be whether someone other than Dharmakīrti has brought in any factor other than *Pakṣa*, *Sādhya* and *Hetu* in his consideration of the format of *Anumāna* and whether it could be incorporated into Dharmakīrti's analysis of it, but rather whether it was essential for Dharmakīrti to incorporate any other constituent into the structure of *Anumāna*, at least as a sufficient condition of it, over and above those which he has already incorporated. Thus put, the answer to it is not far to seek and not very difficult to get either. His contention would be: Methodologically and context-freely considered, *Pakṣa*, *Sādhya* and *Hetu* are not only constitutively necessary conditions of *Anumāna*, but its sufficient conditions as well. This would mean that only in the presence of each one of them would we be able to fashion and formulate an argument context-freely and not in the absence of any one of them. If any additional condition is attempted to be smuggled in, no matter whether necessary or sufficient, it could only be at the cost of confusing context-loadedness with freedom from contextuality or else at the cost of giving some sort of extra-methodological consideration precedence over the methodological. That is why, he repudiates any of such suggestions uncompromisingly, no matter whether it comes from a Buddhist philosopher of the eminence of Diṅnāga or from a *Naiyāyika* like Uddyotakara. We shall have an occasion, later on, to take a passing note of such responses on the part of Dharmakīrti in the proper context.

So far we have given an account of the constitutive conditions of *Anumāna* as Dharmakīrti understood them and outlined the rationale behind it. To complete this discussion, it is necessary to look briefly into Dharmakīrti's distinctive contribution to the acceptance and justification of the methodologically context-free consideration of *Hetu*-centric structural framework of *Anumāna*, in the light of his responses to the suggestions coming from the adherents of Buddhism and *Nyāya*. It is to this that we turn in the next section.

III. *Dharmakīrti's Uniqueness*

In this section we hope to point out Dharmakīrti's peculiarity in formulating the characteristic sort of the structural framework of *Anumāna*. The structural conditions, it was argued above, which he has laid down are minimally necessary for both cognition as well as certification of indirect knowledge-claims. Accepting the methodological constraint of *Hetu*-centricity and yet not losing the track of intuitive constraint, viz. communicability, one can formulate, a framework of *Anumāna* in which *Pakṣa*, *Sādhya* and

Hetu are its necessary and sufficient structural conditions and in which context-freely *Hetu*-centricity is not lost sight of. Given this framework, it could be shown that some of the structural conditions of *Anumāna*, whether necessary or sufficient, that others talk of are either methodologically ill-founded and hence unacceptable, or else contextually loaded and are, on that account, (context-freely considered) redundant and dispensable. This way Dharmakīrti's uniqueness, not only in formulating structural conditions of *Anumāna* but also in establishing *Hetu*-centrality of it, at least structurally, could be brought out. We propose to do this exercise on two levels: on the one hand looking to Dharmakīrti's responses to the contention put forth by his Buddhist predecessors to see whether and to what extent, if at all, he was influenced by them, and, on the other hand, by paying attention to his responses to some of the contentions put forth by his *Nyāya*-predecessors.

Turning first to the *Nyāya* school. For, the grounds of his criticism of some contentions put forth by *Nyāya* philosophers would automatically take care of some of the points raised by the pre-Dharmakīrti Buddhist philosophers. Hence, to avoid duplication, we turn to the *Nyāya* position first.

As is well known, *Naiyāyikas* accept five (structural) constituents (*Pañcāvayava*) of *Anumāna*.[51] Apart from differences on this count between *Nyāya* and Dharmakīrti, let us take a quick look at some other points of difference between them on the background of which his responses to some of the contentions of *Nyāya* could be better understood, and their implications appreciated.

(i) Though both accept communicability as a necessary condition of *Anumāna*, whereas for the *Nyāya* it is pre-determined by experience,[52] for Dharmakīrti it is anchored minimally in coherent conceivability.[53] As will be evident later, this difference makes a profound impact on the structural conditions of *Anumāna* they respectively accept.

(ii) For *Naiyāyikas*, *Anumāna* is an *Avayavī* (an organic-whole) and five constituents (*Pañcāvayavas*) are its parts.[54] And though the whole is constructed out of parts, it is not just a bundle of them;[55] it has its own status apart from them. That is why each *Avayava* is presented as a sentence or a proposition. Further, for them communicability is the primary characteristic of *Anumāna*, and cognition is determined by it. Consequently, the structure and format of *Anumāna* gets, in their thought, automatically moulded accordingly. Whereas in the case of Dharmakīrti, cognition being primary, *Avayavas* need not be expressed in a sentential or a propositional form. The structural conditions of *Anumāna* he speaks of, viz. *Pakṣa*, *Sādhya* and *Hetu*, appear more like terms in sentences rather than sentences themselves.

(iii) The number of constituents, we are told by Vātsyāyana, is determined by two factors: (a) the number of *Pramāṇas* accepted,[56] and (b) the view that conclusion of every argument should be yielded jointly by all the *Pramāṇas* accepted.[57] This seems to have been influened by *Pramāṇa-saṁplava* accepted by *Naiyāyikas*.[58] Since they accept four *Pramāṇas*, five constituents of *Anumāna* are accepted on these two considerations. Further, each of the four accepted *Pramāṇas* is held to determine its respective *Avayava*.

Though Dharmakīrti accepts two *Pramāṇas* and three *Avayavas* of *Anumāna*, he does not believe that the *Avayavas* have any bearing on the *Pramāṇas* accepted or that the conclusion of an argument is yielded jointly by all the accepted *Pramāṇas*. This is in accordance with *Pramāṇa-viplava* that he accepts.[59]

Further, Dharmakīrti does not accept *Avayava-Avayavī* model of *Anumāna*; for him *Anumāna* is not an *Avayavī* made up of parts. He speaks of structural conditions of *Anumāna*, but they can hardly be confused with its *Avayavas*.[60]

(iv) In the case of the *Nyāya*, stipulation of the *Avayavas* of *Anumāna* not, as will be seen later, being governed by primacy of methodological considerations, extra-methodological considerations play an important role.[61] Whereas in Dharmakīrti's framework of *Anumāna*, extra-methodological considerations have no important role to play in determining the structure and format of *Anumāna*. It is strictly and primarily governed methodologically.[62]

On this general background, let us turn to consider the nature of each *Avayava* accepted by the *Nyāya*. This is not done in order to understand this aspect of the *Nyāya*-Buddhist controversy regarding the nature of *Anumāna* in details but just to know the methodological grounds on which Dharmakīrti rejects them and to bring out the uniqueness of his position.

The following are the necessary and sufficient constitutive conditions of fashioning and formulating an argument (*Anumāna*) according to the *Nyāya*:

(1) *Pratijñā*[63]—Concerning it we are told that it is accepted because of *Śabda-pramāṇa* (*Āgama*).[64] It is supposed to enunciate the point sought to be established (*Sādhya*) through *Anumāna*.

Dharmakīrti rejects *Pratijñā* as a necessary or sufficient constituent of *Anumāna* on the following grounds: (a) Statement or enunciation of *Sādhya* cannot methodologically be held to be constitutive of *Anumāna*. (b) There is no need to accept *Śabda* (*Āgama*) as an independent *Pramāṇa*, and the structural constituents methodologically need to have no bearing on the *Pramāṇas* that are accepted. (c) *Pratijñā* cannot be a structural condition of *Anumāna*, for without *Pratijñā* it is perfectly legitimate and warrantable to have inferential cognition. (d) Likewise, *Pratijñā* is also not essential for communication of *Anumāna*. In fact cognitive and communicative aspects of *Anumāna* do not make any difference to the number of constitutive conditions of *Anumāna*. Likewise, *Pratijñā* has nothing to do with cognitive aspect of *Anumāna*, and for communication of the latter it is dispensable. (e) Lastly, debating context cannot peculiarly be said to be connected with *Anumāna* as *Naiyāyikas* hold, both for cognition and/or communication.[65]

(2) Coming to *Hetu*, the second *Avayava*. Though *prima facie* it appears that Dharmakīrti and *Naiyāyikas* agree on acceptance of *Hetu*, yet its role and nature in their respective theories of *Anumāna* is different. For, *Naiyāyikas* accept *Hetu* as a representative correspondent of *Anumāna Pramāṇa*.[66] On the other hand, Buddhists, and especially Dharmakīrti, accept *Hetu* not as a representative of *Anumāna* but as the centrally important structural condition of *Anumāna*.[67] In *Nyāya*, *Hetu*[68] plays a different role in cognition and communication, while according to Dharmakīrti, it plays the same role. Accordingly, it is highly doubtful whether adherents of *Nyāya* can strictly uphold and defend the thesis of *Hetu*-centrality of *Anumāna* context-freely.

(3) Thirdly, *Udāharaṇa*[69] is another *Avayava* of *Anumāna* accepted by the *Nyāya*. It is an illustrative example and its

acceptance is held to be essential on two grounds: (a) it is a representative of *Pratyakṣa* as a *Pramāṇa*, and (b) perceptibility is accepted as a pre-condition of *Anumāna*. Appeal to actual experience is a commitment with *Nyāya*.[70]

On the contrary, Dharmakīrti rejects *Udāharaṇa* as a constitutive condition of *Anumāna*[71] on the following grounds:

(i) For the possibility of inferential cognition or communication, mere coherent possibility or conceivability is enough and insistence on actuality is too stringent a methodological demand.

(ii) Secondly, it is methodologically too stringent to hold that perceptibility is a pre-condition of *Anumāna*. Although inferential cognition need not be ruled out by convergence on facts, to insist upon it as a pre-condition of it is unwarrantable, for it elevates contextuality to universality.

(4) Fourthly, *Upanaya*[72] is an *Avayava* accepted by *Naiyāyikas*. *Upanaya* is reaffirmation of the subject to be proved, on the basis of *Udāharaṇa*. We are further told that *Upanaya* is a representative of the *Upamāna Pramāṇa* accepted by *Nyāya*.[73]

Dharmakīrti rejects *Upanaya* as a constitutive condition of *Anumāna* for *Upanaya* has no role to play in *Anumāna*—cognitively or communicatively.[74] Further, *Upamāna* as an independent *Pramāṇa* is rejected by him, subsuming it under *Anumāna*. Moreover, since through this *Avayava Udāharaṇa* is brought in by back-door, it amounts to reinforcing elevation of contextuality to the level of universality which is indefensible.

(5) Lastly, *Nigamana*[75] is accepted as an indispensable *Avayava* of *Anumāna* by *Naiyāyikas*. They argue[76] that *Nigamana* (final conclusion) is a re-statement of *Pratijñā* (enunciation), on the basis of the statement of *Hetu*. It is essential as a connecting thread of all the four, above-mentioned, constituents. It also is a consequence of their subscription to the view that conclusion of every argument must be entailed by all the accepted *Pramāṇas* jointly.

On the contrary, Dharmakīrti rejects *Nigamana* as a constitutive condition of *Anumāna*.[77] For, according to him, what one has (already) proved need not be re-stated. Further, *Nigamana* is neither cognitively nor communicatively necessary.[78] Various accepted *Pramāṇas* have nothing to do with *Anumāna* and its subject-matter, viz. *Sāmānya-lakṣaṇa*, and to hold that conclusion of every argument is jointly yielded by the totality of accepted *Pramāṇas* is to bring in an extravagant and dispensable doctrine of *Pramāṇa-saṁplava*, for it goes against the principle of economy.

There are only two determinative or regulative conditions of *Anumāna* according to Dharmakīrti, viz. *Vyāpti* and *Pakṣadharmatā*.[79] So far as their account at the hands of *Nyāya* predecessors of Dharmakīrti is concerned, it is enough to state, at this juncture, that whereas their account of *Vyāpti* is confused, cognisance of *Pakṣadharmatā* is not taken at all. We shall have an occasion to look at the salient features of this aspect of the debate between them in the next chapter, where we propose to consider in detail regulative conditions of *Anumāna*.

From the above discussion it should be clear that Dharmakīrti criticises and rejects contentions of others, whereby extra-methodological considerations are brought into the framework of *Anumāna*. He also gives the appropriate grounds on which he shows their futility and hence unacceptability. Further, he also succeeds in proving their contestability and non-acceptability not only within the Buddhist framework but also in such a framework of *Anumāna*, as is formulated in a methodological perspective context-freely. This implies that by contrast the structural or constitutive conditions of *Anumāna* laid down by Dharmakīrti are backed by proper methodological and context-free considerations. They are supported by the principle of economy, wherever it is necessary to do so.

Now, we turn to the Buddhist camp, especially pre-Dharmakīrti philosophers. Starting from Nāgārjuna, it is not clear whether he was ready to accept *Anumāna* as a *Pramāṇa*—much less what structure and format of it he was ready to uphold and defend. Hence the question of appropriateness or inappropriateness of it just does not arise.

Coming to Maitreyanātha, Asaṅga, Vasubandhu and Diṅnāga. Though they, perhaps, accept *Avayavas* more or less on the same grounds as those of *Naiyāyikas*, they differ in their explication of their nature. But since arguing for *Hetu*-centrality of *Anumāna* is our primary concern and, given that the impact of pre-Dharmakīrti (Buddhist) philosophers on him in this context is of secondary importance, it is enough to remark that Dharmakīrti seems to be much more methodologically accurate and precise in stipulating the structural conditions of *Anumāna*. For, none of them, it seems, has argued for *Hetu*-centrality or made such philosophically rewarding distinctions, viz. empty and non-empty domain, coherently possible and actual world, necessary and sufficient conditions, fashioning and formulating an argument and communicating it, debate and non-debate context in which *Anumāna* is used, etc. To present this point in clearer perspective and as a random-sample we take some issues or points for brief consideration.

First, though Vasubandhu defines *Pratijñā* in a way that is much closer to the way Dharmakīrti understands *Pakṣa*,[80] yet he allows himself to commit certain mistakes. That is why *Pratijñā* is rejected by Dharmakīrti in any form, whether suggested by *Naiyāyikas* or Buddhists like Vasubandhu. Instead, he accepts *Pakṣa* on methodological grounds. Secondly, Diṅnāga accepts *Dṛṣṭānta* as a necessary condition of *Anumāna*, but Dharmakīrti, off and on, vehemently criticises the grounds on which he does it.[81] For, even though *Dṛṣṭānta* takes care of applicability principle and hence avoids mere imagination, yet to insist on the fulfilment of the demand made by the principle of applicability is found to be methodologically too stringent. Hence, on methodological ground and on the ground of freedom from context, he prefers to remain satisfied with possibility of instantiability and does not convert it into a pre-condition of inferential cognition.[82]

Thus, after knowing the rationale behind Dharmakīrti's rejection of *Pañcāvayavas* of *Naiyāyikas*[83] and his grounds for refuting the contentions of his Buddhist predecessors concerning constitutive conditions of *Anumāna*, it is necessary to deal with his treatment of regulative conditions of *Anumāna*, viz. *Vyāpti* and *Pakṣadharmatā*, and show that even with reference to them *Hetu*-centrality of *Anumāna* is the principal issue before Dharmakīrti. There, we are going to discuss and critically evaluate his reasons for accepting the regulative conditions of *Anumāna*, and explore their connections with cognitive and certificatory aspects of *Anumāna*, its structural conditions and also its reference to validity and/or soundness. Thus, merely arguing for *Hetu*-centricity of *Anumāna* on the structural level is not enough; we need also to argue for it on the level of regulative conditions of *Anumāna* as well. That is our task in the next chapter.

Notes and References

1. Arcaṭa; *H.B.T.*; pp. 4, 61-65, 71-72.
2. Durveka Miśra; *Dharmottara-pradipa*; pp. 89-90.
3. Dharmakirti; *P.V.*; III. 1-2, M.N. *Vṛtti*; pp. 257-259.
4. It needs to be noted that Dharmakīrti distinguishes between *Sādhanas* (instruments of indication) [*Vādanyāya* pp. 5-6] and *Samudāyins* [*Svārthānumānapariccheda* p. 1] . Although, in his view, *Hetu-vacana* or *Pakṣa-vacana* are relevant in *Parārthānumāna*, they can neither be held *Sādhana* of *Gamya-Gamaka-bhāva* between *Hetu* and *Sadhya*, nor *Samudāyins* (structural components) of *Anumāna*. While on the *Nyāya*-view, *Anumāna* is an *Avayavī*, in Dharmakīrti's view it is a mode of cognition—indirect cognition—and cognition in itself cannot be understood as an *Avayavī*, although complex it could be. Accordingly, though it has structure, it does not have parts. Here we need not enter further into the details of this aspect of the *Nyāya*-Buddhist controversy.
5. Arcaṭa; *H.B.T.*; pp. 3-7.
6. Dharmakirti; *H.B.*; pp. 52-53.
7. *Ibid*; pp. 68-72.
8. Karṇakagomin; *P.V.T.*; pp. 4-12.
9. Prajñākara Gupta; *P.V.A.*; pp. 169-175, 483-488.
10. Arcaṭa; *H.B.T.*; pp. 3, 4, 39.
11. Dharmakirti; *H.B.*; pp. 52-54, 70-71, also Arcaṭa; *H.B.T.*; pp. 3-5, 37-40.
12. Arcaṭa; *H.B.T.*; pp. 4-5, 14, 23, 46-49, 152-153, 220-225.
13. *Ibid*; pp. 28-32, 36, 41, 104, 145-146.
14. Prajñākara Gupta; *P.V.A.*; pp. 484-494. also Arcaṭa; *H.B.T.*; pp. 39-40, 61-70, 87-88, 214-228.
15. Dharmakirti; *H.B.*; pp. 52-53. *Svārthānumāna-pariccheda*; pp. 1-5. Karṇakagomin; *P.V.T.*; pp. 4-20. M.N. *Vṛtti*; pp. 257-258.
16. Arcaṭa; *H.B.T.*; pp. 6-10.
17. *Ibid*; pp. 10-11, 54-55, 204-206.
18. Dharmakirti; *H.B.*; pp. 52-54, 69-72. Arcaṭa; *H.B.T.*; pp. 6-10, 204-206. Durveka Miśra; *H.B.T.A.*; pp. 257-266.
19. Dharmakīrti; *Svārthānumāna-pariccheda*; pp. 1-5, 70-73, *P.V.*; III.1, IV. 189-194. M.N. *Vṛtti*; pp. 257, 426-428.
20. Dharmakīrti; *H.B.*; pp. 52-53. *N.B.*; p. 24. Durveka Miśra; *Dharmottara-pradīpa*; pp. 24-26, 90-97. Arcaṭa; *H.B.T.*; pp. 16-17, 68-69, 220-225.
21. Dharmakīrti; *H.B.*; pp. 52-53. M.N. *Vṛtti*; pp. 367-370, 403-410,

421-422. Karṇakagomin; *P.V.T.*; pp. 4-15. Durveka Miśra; *Dharmottara-pradīpa*; pp. 96-99.
22. Dharmakīrti; *Svārthānumāna-pariccheda*; pp. 1-5. Durveka Miśra; *Dharmottara-pradīpa*; pp. 96-99.
23. Arcaṭa; *H. B.T.*; pp. 10-11, 14-17, 220-225.
24. *Ibid*; pp. 4-5, 39-40, 220-228.
25. Prajñākara Gupta; *P.V.A.*; pp. 467-475.
26. *Ibid*; pp. 235-247. Arcaṭa; *H.B.T.*; 23-28, 35-41, 45-50.
27. Arcaṭa; *H.B.T.*; pp. 33-41.
28. Dharmakīrti; *Vādanyāya*; p. 60.
29. Dharmakīrti; *N.B.*; p. 24, 60. also Durveka Miśra; *Dharmottara-pradīpa*; pp. 89-100, 175-179.
30. Dharmakīrti; *P.V.*; III. 202-219, 288-293, *Svārthānumāna-pariccheda*; pp. 1-7. M.N. *Vṛtti*; pp. 320-326, 348-349. Karṇakagomin; *P.V.T.*; pp. 4-25.
31. Arcaṭa; *H.B.T.*; pp. 6, 61-75.
32. *Ibid*; pp. 40-50, 56-58.
33. *Ibid*; pp. 61-75.
34. Dharmakīrti; *P.V.*; III. 183-193, *Svārthānumāna-pariccheda*; pp. 62-64. M.N. *Vṛtti*; pp. 315-317.
35. Dharmakīrti; *H.B.*; pp. 52-54. *Svārthānumāna-pariccheda*; pp. 1-5, 12-14. *P.V.*; I. 287, III. 1 M.N. *Vṛtti*; pp. 97, 257.
36. Dharmakīrti; *P.V.*; II. 57-84, III. 187-192. *Svārthānumāna-pariccheda*; pp. 62-64. M.N. *Vṛtti*; pp. 314-316.
37. Arcaṭa; *H.B.T.*; pp. 6-20, 73-74. Durveka Miśra; *Dharmottara-pradīpa*; pp. 90-99, 176-180.
38. Durveka Miśra; *Dharmottara-pradīpa*; pp. 91-100. Dharmakīrti; *P.V.*; III. 1-3, 15-32, M.N. *Vṛtti*; pp. 257-259, 264-270. Prajñākara Gupta; *P.V.A.*; pp. 488, 490-494, 644-646.
39. Arcaṭa; *H.B.T.*; pp. 9-20, 41-43.
40. *Ibid*; p. 4, 10-11, 15-16, 18-19. Dharmakīrti; *P.V.*; I. 286-287. II. 58-64, 78-82, 90-100, III. 47-49.
41. Dharmakīrti; *P.V.*; I. 286-287, III. 47-49.
42. Dharmakīrti; *H.B.*; pp. 52-54, 68-72. Arcaṭa; *H.B.T.*; pp. 2-7. Durveka Miśra; *H.B.T.A.*; pp. 257-260.
43. Dharmakīrti; *H.B.*;pp. 52-54. *Svārthānumāna-pariccheda*; pp. 1-7.
44. Arcaṭa; *H.B.T.*; pp. 14-19.
45. *Ibid*; pp. 6-20.
46. Dharmakīrti; *N.B.*; pp. 21-26. *P.V.*; III. 27-32. M.N. *Vṛtti*; pp. 268-269.
47. Arcaṭa; *H.B.T.*; pp. 9-11, 44-50.
48. *Ibid*; pp. 17-30, 220-228.
49. Dharmakīrti; *H.B.*; pp. 70-72. *Svārthānumāna-pariccheda*; pp. 1-7.
50. Dharmakīrti; *N.B.*; pp. 21-31.
51. Gautama; *Nyāya-Sūtras*; I.i. 32.
52. Uddyotakara; *Nyāya-Vārtika*; I.i.1, I.i.5.

53. Dharmakīrti; *H.B.*; pp. 70-72. *P.V.*; IV. 151-163.
54. Dharmakīrti; *Vādanyāya*; (also Śāntarakṣita's *Vipañcitārthā*); pp. 59-60.
55. Arcaṭa; *H.B.T.*; pp. 182-197, 204-215, 220-228.
56. Vātsyāyana; *Nyāya-Bhāṣya*; I.i.1.
57. *Ibid*; I.i.1, I.i.3, I.i.5, I.i. 32-39.
58. Vātsyāyana; *Nyāya Bhāṣya*; I.i.1, *also* Uddyotakara; *Nyāya-Vārtika*; I.i.1.
59. Arcaṭa; *H.B.T.*; pp. 63-73.
60. *Ibid*; pp. 57-58.
61. Dharmakīrti; *H.B.*; pp. 52-54, 65-72.
62. Arcaṭa; *H.B.T.*; pp. 7-12, 54-57, 204-231.
63. Gautama; *Nyāya-Sūtras*; I.i.33.
64. Vātsyāyana; *Nyāya-Bhāṣya*; I.i.1.
65. Dharmakīrti; *H.B.*; pp. 66-70. *P.V.*; IV. 164-175. *Vādanyāya*; pp. 58-65. *N.B.*; p. 53.
66. Vātsyāyana; *Nyāya-Bhāṣya*; I.i.1.
67. Arcaṭa; *H.B.T.*; pp. 6-11.
68. Gautama; *Nyāya-Sūtras*; I.i. 34-35.
69. *Ibid*; I.i.36.
70. Uddyotakara; *Nyāya-Vārtika*; I.i.1, I.i.32, I.i.36-37.
71. Dharmakīrti; *P.V.*; III.27, IV. 165-188. *H.B.*; pp. 52-54, 66-70. *N.B.*; pp. 91, 93-94, 102-104. *Vādanyāya*; pp. 59-64.
72. Gautama; *Nyāya-Sūtras*; I.i.38.
73. Uddyotakara; *Nyāya-Vārtika*; I.i.38.
74. Śāntarakṣita; *Vipañcitārthā* on *Vādanyāya*; pp. 60-61. Arcaṭa; *H.B.T.*; pp. 71-72.
75. Gautama; *Nyāya-Sūtras*; I.i.39.
76. Uddyotakara; *Nyāya-Vārtika*; I.i.39.
77. Dharmakīrtī; *P.V.*; IV. 150-170. Arcaṭa; *H.B.T.*; pp. 70-72.
78. Arcaṭa; *H.B.T.*; pp. 70-75.
79. Dharmakīrti; *H.B.*; p. 52, *P.V.*; III.1. *Svārthānumāna-pariccheda*; pp. 1-2.
80. Uddyotakara; *Nyāya-Vārtika*; I.i.33. also see (Vācaspati Miśra; *Nyāya-vārtika-tātparya-ṭikā* and Udayana's *Pariśuddhi* on it).
81. Dharmakīrti; *P.V.*; IV 120-170. M.N. *Vṛtti*; pp. 401-409.
82. Arcaṭa; *H.B.T.*; pp. 62-75, 200-208.
83. Dharmakīrti; *H.B.*; 70-72, *Vādanyāya*; pp. 60-65.

CHAPTER IV

REGULATIVE CONDITIONS OF ANUMĀNA

In the second and the third chapters we saw, with the help of appropriate illustrations, that the frameworks of *Anumāna* accepted by *Naiyāyikas* and Buddhists, especially by Dharmakīrti, are fundamentally different, at least with regard to the epistemic and constitutive conditions of *Anumāna*. We also brought out *Hetu*-centricity of *Anumāna* as envisioned by Dharmakīrti with reference to the two above-mentioned aspects of the framework of *Anumāna*, which is our main concern here. However, to further elaborate the argument and to show the *Hetu*-centricity of *Anumāna* as sought to be established by Dharmakīrti, it is necessary to argue that this feature is also shared by regulative conditions of *Anumāna*, *Trairūpya* and *Tridhātva* of it, the conditions of its validity and/or soundness as also by *Hetvābhāsas* etc. Otherwise, our exercise will remain partial, incomplete and, hence, unjustifiable. This residual task will occupy our attention from this chapter onward. Of this, we first take up the consideration of regulative conditions of *Anumāna*.

In the preceding chapter it was argued that the kind of knowledge we have with the help of *Anumāna* is basically *Hetu*-centric and becomes available to us through *Hetu*-centric structural feature of it. With the help of *Anumāna* alone, we can have *Parokṣa-jñāna* (of *Sādhya*). Since it is impossible without *Hetu*, it is obviously the *Hetu* which determines it. However, such a knowledge becomes possible not through random or mechanical connection of *Hetu* and *Sādhya*, but rather only through a particular relation between them—the relation regulated by a rule of *Vyāpti*.[1] Otherwise, knowledge by description gained without *Anumāna* would also have to be counted as species of *Parokṣa-jñāna*. What needs, however, to be clearly comprehended is that an indirect knowledge gained through *Anumāna* cannot fail to be *Hetu*-centric. Such a rule i.e. *Vyāpti* is one regulative condition of *Anumāna*. Likewise, the relation between *Pakṣa* and *Hetu* cannot be of any random kind; it needs to be regulated by a characteristic feature called *Pakṣadharmatā*,[2] which is another regulative condition of *Anumāna*.[3] Just as for the emergence of indirect knowledge on the basis of *Anumāna*, certain constitutive conditions need to be fulfilled, so too certain regulative conditions. Both these kinds of conditions are required to be fulfilled simultaneously and neither disjunctively nor successively, although there is a certain priority about them such that if the regulative conditions are not fulfilled then the constitutive conditions cannot be fulfilled, i.e. the constitutive conditions cannot be fulfilled independently of the regulative conditions.[4] We proceed to a detailed consideration of them.

In this chapter, we will argue that even the regulative conditions of *Anumāna* are *Hetu*-centric. Our full argument would be presented in five sections: The first deals with the nature and role of *Vyāpti* and *Pakṣadharmatā*. The second takes up the consideration of *Pakṣadharmatā* as a regulative condition. The third section deals with the nature of *Vyāpti* (*Niyama*) while the fourth discusses applicability of *Vyāpti*. In the last section we shall argue for *Hetu*-centrality of the regulative conditions of *Anumāna*. We hope that this will facilitate the establishment of the whole framework of *Anumāna*, at least at the level on which an argument can be entertained as *Hetu*-centric.

Before we take up the task of the first section in hand, a word about 'regulative conditions' is in order. They are comparable to rules of a game, if constitutive conditions could be comparable to rules in the game. Regulative conditions are normative in character and supply directional guidelines. Such conditions, further, may be regulative, contextually or context-freely. However, in either case, their nature and status, with respect to structural conditions remains the same insofar as they regulate or govern interrelationship among structural conditions. Nevertheless, the jurisdiction of their governance as also the flexibility or rigidity they bring in remain different. Implications of these general remarks would be clear as we proceed.

I. Necessity of the Regulative Conditions

It is essential to connect the structural constituents of *Anumāna*, viz. *Pakṣa*, *Sādhya* and *Hetu* with one another for the simple reason that inferential cognition is neither cognition of these discrete constituents, nor will it arise if they are not connected. For, in the absence of such a connection, the very essence of knowledge viz. *Avisaṁvādakatva* (non-inconsistency) will get compromised. Obviously, in that case, it will not give us any cognition, leave alone its being certified and/or communicated. But mere connection of every sort will not ensure this. To connect *Hetu* with *Pakṣa* appropriately we have to accept *Pakṣadharmatā* and to connect *Hetu* with *Sādhya* the rule of *Vyāpti* has to be followed, so that appropriate *Sādhya* may become available to us, which is of the nature of *Sāmānya-lakṣaṇa*.

Generally speaking, *Vyāpti* should be acceptable to everybody who accepts inferential cognition. The only question is: how to interpret *Vyāpti*? And secondly, prior to Dharmakīrti, in the *Nyāya*-tradition and also perhaps in the Buddhist tradition, nobody, it seems, had thought of *Pakṣadharmatā*, much less articulate and explicate it. And though *Naiyāyikas* posterior to Dharmakīrti are inclined to accept it, they have not understood its meaning and implications properly and seem to have failed to realise its appropriate role and function. Hence, no wonder, their engagement with *Pakṣatā* fails to be a substitute for *Pakṣadharmatā*.[5]

It is sometimes asserted that *Pakṣadharmatā* is not a contribution of Dharmakīrti but of Diṅnāga[6] or, perhaps, even of Vasubandhu.[7] There are, however, reasons to believe that the credit with regard to both the regulative conditions viz. *Vyāpti* and *Pakṣadharmatā* goes to Dharmakīrti. This is, however, not our principal engagement; we shall, therefore, draw upon this aspect of the intra-Buddhist and *Nyāya*-Buddhist controversy only insofar as it is essential for our argument.

Since, the very concept of *Pakṣadharmatā* is uniquely and pioneeringly interpreted by Dharmakīrti and since, given *Pakṣadharmatā* alone, one can coherently conceive of relating *Pakṣa* to *Hetu* appropriately, it is first essential to analyse and explain the very concept of *Pakṣadharmatā*.

Like *Vyāpti*, *Pakṣadharmatā* has an important role to play as a regulative condition of *Anumāna*, although neither of the two on its own is either necessary or sufficient as a regulative condition of *Anumāna*. Given *Pakṣadharmatā* but not *Vyāpti* what at the most could be claimed is the possibility of legitimately connecting *Hetu* with the given *Pakṣa* and nothing else. To open the possibility of *Sādhya* being legitimately connected with *Pakṣa*, *Avinābhāva* (of *Sādhya* and *Hetu*) along with *Pakṣadharmatā* is required. And further, if *Avinābhāva* alone is given, without *Pakṣadharmatā*, *Hetu-Sādhya* relation will be regulated but not *Hetu*'s legitimate relation with *Pakṣa*; and if merely *Pakṣadharmatā* is given without *Vyāpti*, relation between *Hetu* and *Pakṣa* would be channelised, but that between *Hetu* and *Sādhya* would remain unregulated. Hence, in order that *Sādhya* as related to *Pakṣa* may legitimately be inferred at all both *Vyāpti* and *Pakṣadharmatā* are required. They both jointly as well as severally operate as regulative conditions of *Anumāna*.

Earlier, in the last chapter, we saw the nature of *Pakṣa*. While discussing it, we pointed out that *Pakṣa* is called *Dharmī*, because, and insofar as, *Sādhya* as *Dharma* is predicable of it. Now, here we will point out that *Pakṣadharmatā* guarantees certain relation between *Pakṣa* and *Hetu*, as *Hetu* is an *Asādhāraṇa Dharma* of *Pakṣa*. Thus, *Pakṣa* is *Dharmī*, not only with reference to *Sādhya* alone but also with reference to *Hetu*, and the relation between these two *Dharmas*, viz. *Hetu* and *Sādhya*, is regulated by *Vyāpti*.[8]

II. *Consideration of Pakṣadharmatā*

Now, the *Dharma-Dharmī* relation between *Hetu* and *Pakṣa* is monodirectional such that it is *Hetu* which is related to *Pakṣa* as a *Dharma* of it, and it is this which is given to us through *Pakṣadharmatā*.[9] Likewise, *Pakṣadharmatā* relation also is monodirectional such that it is never given in the direction from *Pakṣa* to *Hetu*.[10] For, *Hetu* being *Asādhāraṇa Dharma* (unique or uncommon feature) of *Pakṣa*, it is always predicable of it, whereby *Hetu* automatically stands related to *Pakṣa* or it cannot fail to be related to *Pakṣa*, insofar as it is an *Asādhāraṇa Dharma* of it.[11] While *Hetu* is an *Asādhāraṇa Dharma* of *Pakṣa* it must neither be capable of being given as a natural consequence of *Pakṣa* nor should it be derivative from it,[12] and yet it should mark *Pakṣa* off from other possible objects in such a way that it is predicable only of *Pakṣa*.[13] If *Hetu* is either generative from or subsumable under *Pakṣa* then such a relation between them would be regulated by *Vyāpti*, as we shall see later, and in that case we would not need *Pakṣadharmatā*.[14] In order that the relation between *Hetu* and *Pakṣa* does not lapse into that between *Hetu* and *Sādhya*, *Hetu* needs to be such an *Asādhāraṇa Dharma* of *Pakṣa* that it could be regulated by *Pakṣadharmatā* only. By way of an example one may cite a daughter's relation with her mother. If, on the contrary, *Pakṣadharmatā* is sought to be understood from the side of the *Pakṣa* to that of the *Hetu*, then we would miss *Asādhāraṇatā* feature of it, for more than one *Dharma* could be predicable of it. For instance, a mother's relation to her children.[15]

Thus, *Pakṣadharmatā* ensures a relation of *Hetu* to *Pakṣa*, such that *Hetu* is *Asādhāraṇa Dharma* of it. This relationship can never be accidental, contextual, exception-tolerant, and uncertain.[16] However, it is not a rule-governed feature of *Hetu*, though it is such that it marks off its relationship with *Pakṣa* from its relationship with *Sādhya*.[17] In other words, it is regulative of *Hetu*'s relation with *Pakṣa*.

Peripherally, it needs here to be pointed out that there is a difference between *Pakṣatā* and *Pakṣadharmatā*. From the point of view of *Hetu*, *Pakṣadharmatā* is a feature of *Hetu*, since, *Hetu* is an *Asādhāraṇa Dharma* (uncommon feature) of *Pakṣa*. And any *Dharma* (feature) cannot be talked of without *Dharmī* (of which it is a feature). Hence, *Hetu* is said to be *Pakṣadharma* and its feature that it is *Asādhāraṇa Dharma* of *Pakṣa* is indicated by *Pakṣadharmatā*. On the contrary, *Pakṣatā* is indicative of a general or unique feature of *Pakṣa* such that contextually the *Sādhya* could only be related to it, provided its relation with *Hetu* is regulated by *Vyāpti* and *Hetu*'s relation with *Pakṣa* is regulated by *Pakṣadharmatā*. Thus, while *Pakṣatā* marks off *Pakṣa*'s relation with *Sādhya*, *Pakṣadharmatā* marks off *Hetu*'s relation with *Pakṣa*.

Moreover, *Pakṣadharmatā* also needs to be distinguished from *Pakṣa-sattva* and *Sapakṣa-sattva*, i.e. the first two conditions of the validity of an argument. *Pakṣadharmatā* is a relation between *Hetu* and *Pakṣa* and is a regulative condition for the formulation of an argument, while *Pakṣa-sattva* and *Sapakṣa-sattva*, as will be argued in the next chapter, are the necessary conditions which a valid argument needs to satisfy. *Pakṣadharmatā* opens the very possibility of entertaining of an argument,[18] whereas *Pakṣa-sattva* and *Sapakṣa-sattva* tell us whether such an entertained argument is viable or not, insofar as it is or it is not valid. Accordingly, *Pakṣa-sattva*, *Sapakṣa-sattva* etc. cannot be held to be conditions regulative of entertaining of an argument as *Pakṣadharmatā* is.

Secondly, whereas *Pakṣadharmatā* is regulative of the relation between *Hetu* and *Pakṣa*, *Pakṣa-sattva* and *Sapakṣa-sattva*, etc., are characteristic features of the *Hetu* of a valid argument alone,[19] such that if the concerned *Hetu* does not fulfil such conditions the argument in which it figures must turn out to be invalid giving rise to a *Hetvābhāsa*. On the contrary, *Pakṣadharmatā*, as pointed out above, is a regulative condition of the formulation of an argument. Consideration of validity is consequential upon the formulation of an argument and cannot be held determinative of it.

Thirdly, *Pakṣa-sattva* determines, as it were, the range of *Pakṣadharmatā* in the case of valid arguments, while *Pakṣadharmatā* always falls within the jurisdiction of it.[20] For, while *Pakṣadharmatā* gives rise to the cognition of such *Hetu* as is a unique feature of *Pakṣa* alone, *Pakṣa-sattva* alone may give us such a *Hetu* as is not a unique feature of *Pakṣa.*[21]

Lastly, whereas neither *Vyāpti* nor *Pakṣadharmatā* is a classificatory feature of *Anumāna*, *Pakṣa-sattva*, *Sapakṣa-sattva* etc. are classificatory features of *Anumāna* insofar as they are the features or marks of only a valid argument.

Granted that *Pakṣadharmatā* is necessary for governing the relation between *Hetu* aud *Pakṣa*, why should *Vyāpti* be considered a regulative co-condition of *Anumāna* along with *Pakṣadharmatā*? And, further, what is the relationship between these two regulative conditions themselves? It is to these questions that we now turn.

In the above discussion, the nature and role of *Pakṣadharmatā* was made clear and, later on we are going to do a similar exercise with reference to *Vyāpti*. However, before we move to the consideration of the nature and role of *Vyāpti*, it is necessary to pay attention to the need of accepting *Vyāpti* as an additional regulative condition and note the contours of their relationship, so that it will enable us to comprehend the nature and function of *Vyāpti*.

One cannot think of *Pakṣadharmatā* alone as a regulative condition of *Anumāna*. For, *Pakṣadharmatā* governs the relationship of *Hetu* to *Pakṣa*, whereas *Vyāpti* regulates the relation between *Hetu* and *Sādhya*. Mere regulation of *Hetu-Pakṣa* relation is not enough, nor does regulation of *Hetu-Sādhya* relation automatically take care of the former. Indirect cognition which *Anumāna* makes available to us is that of *Sādhya*, and it cannot be had if we just have cognition of the relationship between *Hetu* and *Pakṣa*, or, for that matter, of a relation between *Hetu* and *Sādhya* unmediated by *Vyāpti*. The *Hetu* which is connected with *Pakṣa* through *Pakṣadharmatā* is required to be shown to be related to *Sādhya* through *Vyāpti*. It is not merely *Hetu-Pakṣa* relation that is required to be regulated. Likewise, *Hetu-Sādhya* relation, too, is necessary to be regulated, for, as we shall argue later, any sort of relation between *Hetu* and *Sādhya* is not conducive to the emergence of cognition through *Anumāna*. Hence, *Vyāpti* and *Pakṣadharmatā* go together as regulative conditions of *Anumāna*. Further, they function and operate on equal level, viz. if any one of the two is absent, inferential cognition will just not arise. Both function and operate as regulative conditions in giving rise to *Parokṣa-jñāna* through *Anumāna*. *Vyāpti* and *Pakṣadharmatā*, thus, are the conditions of the very possibility of *Anumāna*, such that if any one of them is absent, *Anumāna* would just be impossible. Hence, they are jointly and individually regulative conditions of *Anumāna*.

Thus, while the pillars of *Anumāna*, viz. *Pakṣa*, *Sādhya* and *Hetu*, bring out principal supports on which it stands, *Vyāpti* and *Pakṣadharmatā* exercise and exhibit their control over them in such a way that they turn out to be the very foundations of *Anumāna*, it is within their regulative jurisdiction alone (other things remaining the same) that the intended *Sādhya* can be inferred. However, this does not mean that *Vyāpti* and *Pakṣa-dharmatā* are determinative of every feature of *Anumāna*. But they are the conditions of the very possibility of *Anumāna*, and consideration of validity and other features of *Anumāna* is consequent upon the formulation of *Anumāna*.

III. General Nature of Vyāpti

Now, to turn to the nature and function of *Vyāpti*, as one of the regulative conditions of *Anumāna*. In order to understand the nature and role of *Vyāpti*, two questions need to be asked: (i) How does *Vyāpti* relate *Hetu* to *Sādhya*? and, (ii) What is meant by *Vyāpti*?

There is no doubt that *Sādhya* is made available to us on the basis of *Hetu*, and the relation between *Hetu* and *Sādhya* is governed by *Vyāpti*. *Hetu* is *Liṅga* (indicator) of *Sādhya* which is *Liṅgi* (the indicated). Though it is accepted that *Vyāpti* regulates the relation between *Hetu* and *Sādhya*, there is a difference of opinion regarding the nature of *Vyāpti* between two camps—Buddhism and *Nyāya*. We propose to look into some points of this sort below.

First of all, there arises a question whether *Vyāpti* is a *Niyama* or a relation. While answering to it, Dharmakīrti, it seems, claims that it is not a relation (*Saṁbandha*); rather, it is a rule (*Niyama*) governing the relation (between *Hetu* and *Sādhya*). Between *Hetu* and *Sādhya*, it is the former which is epistemically prior, and that is why it is held to be *Gamaka* (indicator) of *Sādhya* (*Gamya*—the indicated). However, in order of being, it is *Sādhya* which is prior, and *Hetu* is posterior.[22] But since our present engagement with them is in the domain of epistemology and methodology, we need not pay attention to the second kind of priority. It is this epistemic relation between *Hetu* and *Sādhya* which is envisaged to be regulated by a rule called *Vyāpti*.

If *Vyāpti* is a *Niyama*, a question arises: What kind of *Niyama* is it? According to Dharmakīrti, it is *Avinābhāva-Niyama*. Thus, it becomes essential to explain and analyse the nature of *Vyāpti* in terms of *Avinābhāva-Niyama*.[23]

Vyāpti is a *Niyama* (rule) regarding *Saṁbandha* (relation) between *Hetu* and *Sādhya*.[24] But *Saṁbandha* itself is not a rule, nor is rule itself a *Saṁbandha*, although there can be a rule governing *Saṁbandha* whether the *Saṁbandha* under consideration is between separable relata or between distinguishable relata.[25] Further, the rule may be of two principal kinds: contextual and universal. Likewise, it is incorrect to equate a rule with technique, although there may be a rule governing a technique. With these preliminaries we turn to *Vyāpti* as a *Niyama*.

We shall have, later on, an occasion to investigate into peculiar features of *Vyāpti* as a *Niyama*. For the present, let us look to it generally as a regulative condition of *Anumāna*. First of all, it is regulative in a two-fold way: cognitively and methodologically. In its cognitively regulative aspect, it ensures indirect cognition of *Sādhya*, while in its methodologically regulative aspect, it ensures that only certain kind of knowledge-claim becomes available to us argumentatively. That is, on the one hand, it regulates certain aspect of our cognition, viz. indirect cognition, and, on the other hand, it also regulates structural format of *Anumāna*, within the framework of which indirect knowledge-claims could be formulated or advanced.

Secondly, we said *Vyāpti* as a *Niyama* regulates a relation. But it does not regulate any and every kind of relation. Rather, it regulates only *Vyāpya-Vyāpaka* kind of relation.[26] However, this does not mean, in any sense, that *Vyāpti* is generative of *Vyāpya-Vyāpaka* relation. This amounts to saying that given *Vyāpya-Vyāpaka* kind of relation, *Vyāpti* regulates it, although it does not generate it.[27]

Thirdly, if *Vyāpti* is a *Niyama* the question arises: How is it required to be interpreted and why? We turn briefly to the consideration of this issue. While dealing with *Vyāpti*, one finds that many ways of interpreting it are resorted to and a variety of *Niyamas* like *Sāhacarya* (co-existence), *Anyathānupapatti* (impossibility of being given otherwise), *Avyabhicāra* (necessity of non-transgression) and *Avinābhāva-Niyama* (invariable/exceptionless rule) is invoked in the process.[28] It needs to be considered as to which alternative of them is acceptable to Dharmakīrti and what is the rationale of it. Dharmakīrti seeks to understand it in terms of *Avinābhāva-Niyama*. Let us explain its rationale.

According to him, mere accidentality (*kādācitkatva*) of their being found together (*Sāhacarya*)[29] through repeated observation of such instances (*Bhūyodarśana*)[30] cannot bring forth necessity, which *Vyāpti* as a regulative condition has to have. *Sāhacarya* implies that the two things (*Hetu-Sādhya*) are found together. This could, however, be true contextually. But just by finding two things together contextually one cannot guarantee their being together context-freely and invariably. An attempt to interpret *Vyāpti* in this way also seems to bring in three further questionable claims: (a) all our knowledge-claims need to be empirically backed, (b) definitional and criterial considerations boil down to the same, and (c) any principle can be adopted solely on the ground that it does not depart from common-sense. Dharmakīrti obviously, on methodological grounds, would not be prepared to subscribe to these views. However, going into greater details of these views here would be a digression and we, therefore, refrain from it.

Similar observations also remain in order in face of the interpretation of *Vyāpti* in terms of *Sahopalaṁbha-Niyama* (simultaneity) at the hands of some Buddhist and as *Sāmānādhikaraṇya* at the hands of *Nyāya* philosophers.[31] For example, to say that there is a relation of *Vyāpti* between *Pṛthivī* and *Gandha* or between *Pṛthivītva* and *Gandhavattva* is to give this kind of interpretations of *Vyāpti*, where the *Vyāpti* under consideration can at most be said to obtain contextually, and not because *Gandhavattva* is *Svabhāva* of *Pṛthivī*. Further, the relation under consideration may be accidental and may lack inevitability, necessity, exceptionlessness, universality, freedom from context, etc., in terms of which *Vyāpti* could legitimately be held to be a regulative condition of *Anumāna*.

In case of *Sāmānādhikaraṇya-saṁbandha*, advocated by *Naiyāyikas*, it needs to be understood that it is a relation and as a relation it can neither be elevated to the status of a rule, nor can it be substituted for it. They further classify *Vyāpti* into three kinds: *Anvayī*, *Vyatirekī* and *Anvaya-vyatirekī* which are said to give us, correspondingly, three kinds of *Anumāna*. In the opinion of Dharmakīrti, *Vyāpti* as a regulative condition of *Anumāna* is a rule, and is uniformly applicable, no matter what kind of argument comes to be framed under its purview. And if *Vyāpti* is really to be understood as a regulative condition of *Anumāna*, then this is how it should be. Classification of *Vyāpti* would not be available unless it is confused with something else and methodological considerations are relegated to the background. Next, the *Nyāya* philosophers further contend that our cognition of *Vyāpti* is derived from repeated observation of similar instances.[32] This makes it a generalization from experience and, consequently, its universality remains contextual and not context-free, as demanded by Dharmakīrti. It amounts to confusing between regulative and applicative aspects of *Vyāpti*.

Similarly, *Avyabhicāra-Niyama* interpretation of *Vyāpti* advocated by Vaiśeṣikas and Sāṁkhyas, too, remains questionable. *Avyabhicāra-Niyama* (non-obtainability of one without the other) is certainly one of the important considerations.[33] However, *Vyāpti* cannot be equated with it. For, according to Dharmakīrti, on this interpretation of *Vyāpti*, *Asādhāraṇa Dharma* of something comes to be confused with it. A *Dharma* may be connected with a particular thing inalienably and even naturally, and yet it cannot be a regulative rule—using which one can prove necessary, exception-intolerant relation between *Hetu* and *Sādhya*. So *Avaśyaṁbhāvitva* not being conjoined with it, it cannot be equated with *Vyāpti* at all.

Lastly, coming to *Anyathānupapatti* of Jainas.[34] This interpretation of *Vyāpti*, too, does not give the true connotation of the term. That we have not noticed an instance going contrary to our experience makes *Vyāpti* anchored in experience and this cannot be mistaken for inevitability, exception-intolerance built into it as a context-free regulative principle.

Thus, till now, we have considered different notions of *Vyāpti* accepted by different schools of Indian Philosophy to mark them off from the Buddhist conception of *Vyāpti* and found that they seem to fail to be methodologically acceptable. To understand the methodological importance of Dharmakīrti's conception of *Vyāpti* as a rule it is essential to see what are the salient features of *Vyāpti* as a *Niyama*. To consider it we turn to the next section.

IV. *Salient features of Vyāpti as a rule*

In the last section, we saw that *Vyāpti* means *Avinābhāva-Niyama*. It is a regulative rule, which spells out the condition that needs to be fulfilled for the emergence of *Anumāna*. It regulates the relationship between *Hetu* and *Sādhya* in *Anumāna*. Any relation between them not conducive to and determinative of *Anumāna*, *Sāhacarya*, *Anyathānupapatti*, *Sahopalaṁbha-Niyama etc.*, is rejected on the ground of their being methodologically unsatisfactory. According to Dharmakīrti, there are certain salient features of *Vyāpti* as a regulative rule, viz. *Avinābhāva*, *Avyabhicāra*, *Avaśyaṁbhāva* etc. to which we propose to turn in this section.

Here it needs to be pointed out that the salient features of *Vyāpti* are not, as a rule, regulative of *Anumāna* on their own; rather, it is *Avinābhāva-Niyama* which is regulative of it. These features are not determinants of the *Niyama* but indicative of some important aspects of it. As indicators, they are not determinants themselves. And further, the *Niyama*, being determined by itself, cannot be determined by anything else. On the contrary, the moment we say that it is determined by something else, it will lose its status as a basic regulative principle of *Anumāna*. Secondly, *Vyāpti* as a *Niyama* exhibits all these features simultaneously and yet one cannot mistake one for the other. For, each feature is indicative of a different aspect of the rule. The meaning and significance of each feature is independent and different from that of another and yet these features could be spelt out significantly and relevantly with reference to one common rule, viz. *Vyāpti*. It is through these features of it that we are able to comprehend the unique nature of *Vyāpti* as a regulative condition of *Anumāna* as given by Dharmakīrti.

Turning first to *Avinābhāva*.[35] If there is *Avinābhāva* between *Hetu* and *Sādhya* then it implies that if *Hetu* is given, *Sādhya* cannot fail to be given and if *Sādhyābhāva* is there, *Hetvabhāva* too must be there. Thus, the relationship between *Hetu* and *Sādhya* is reciprocal. This kind of *Avinābhāva* ensures that *Vyāpti* needs to be understood consistently, and context-freely. If this does not happen, then *Vyāpti* as a regulative principle and condition of *Anumāna* cannot give direction to the fashioning of any argument. Given that there is *Vyāpya-Vyāpaka* relation between *Hetu* and *Sādhya* through *Avinābhāva*, it so happens to be regulated that, it cannot, even contingently, be the case that *Hetu* is there but not the *Sādhya*. This kind of relation between them is given to us at least on the level of coherent conceivability. Its actually being instantiated need not be ruled out, though it cannot be made its precondition. Thus, context-free never-failingness of *Vyāpti* is brought out by *Avinābhāva*.

Now coming to *Avyabhicāra*.[36] We saw that *Avinābhāva* brings out context-free never-failingness of *Vyāpti* as a regulative condition of *Anumāna*. But why should *Vyāpti* be so conceived? Because of its *Avyabhicāritva*, i.e. exceptionlessness. Cognitively considered comprehension of *Avinābhāva* as a feature of *Vyāpti* is prior. But comprehension of this in itself does not provide the rationale as to why *Vyāpti* needs to be so understood. Such a rationale is sought to be provided through another feature of it, viz. *Avyabhicāra*. However, concerning exceptionlessness it may be asked: Is this assumed or is there any rationale for saying so? It is sometimes sought to be made sense of in terms of *Aprayatnāntarīyakatā*.[37] What it means is that *Vyāpti* is held to be inevitable or exceptionless because, one cannot, with all one's efforts, repudiate it or, what comes to the same thing, find an exception to it. This rationale of the inevitability seems to smack of at least two troubles about it: (a) this rationale is basically anthropocentric in character in the sense that if our best efforts cannot disprove a certain thesis, this in itself does not, and cannot, establish the impossibility of its disproof. Similarly, even after very hard effort we might have failed to discover *Vyāpti* to be ridden with exception and from this failure might have concluded that therefore it is exceptionless or inevitable. If so, this is a weak rationale. (b) Such a rationale, further, makes *Vyāpti* as a regulative condition of *Anumāna* depend upon something else, and to the extent to which this is done, it is hard to accept it as a basic regulative condition. *Vyāpti* is certainly context-freely exceptionless due to its being inevitable, but its inevitability does not spring from or happen to be determined by our failure to show it to be avoidable or exception-ridden. Accordingly, the rationale and the basis of holding *Vyāpti* to be exceptionless or inevitable must be sought elsewhere. This kind of rationale of exceptionlessness is sought to be provided through the third feature of *Vyāpti*, viz. *Avaśyaṁbhāva*.

Avaśyaṁbhāva as a feature of *Vyāpti*[38] tells us that it is necessary. Thus understood, *Vyāpti* is exceptionless because necessity is built into it and this built-in necessity makes it exception-intolerant context-freely. Since *Vyāpti* is a necessary rule, or since necessity is built into *Vyāpti*, its exceptionlessness springs from itself and hence is required to be justified or made sense of in terms of nothing else. This makes exceptionlessness non-contextual and cosmocentrically tenable. It is this feature of it that makes it basic as well.

Lastly, *Vyāpti* has yet another feature called *Niyāmakatva*,[39] i.e. it is regulative in character. Since in this way it is regulative as well as basic that it is accepted to be fundamental regulative principle or condition of *Anumāna*. In this way various features of *Vyāpti* are inter-related and not isolated.

Thus, *Vyāpti* as a *Niyama* operates within the framework of context-free, necessary and coherently conceivable domain. It is exception-intolerant, necessary and holds never-failingly, and universally.

Vyāpti exhibits these features. They are indicators of its nature but not regulative of it. And, further, *Vyāpti*, being regulative in character, makes it possible to have context-free applicability, i.e. no argument which is valid and/or sound falls outside the purview of *Vyāpti*; but so too it guarantees context-free, universal, non-accidental, never-failing relation between *Hetu* and *Sādhya*. Thus, the two important pillars of *Anumāna*, viz. *Hetu* and *Sādhya*, are context-freely, never-failingly and necessarily connected to each other through *Vyāpti* which is a self-warranting regulative rule.

In this context, it is essential to analyse and explain some of the important implications of accepting the principle that *Vyāpti* is a *Niyama*. Some of the important points of it we will discuss in what follows:

(i) *Vyāpti*, being a *Niyama*, is exception-intolerant. It is context-freely regulative of *Anumāna*.

(ii) *Avinābhāva* cannot be mistaken for *Vyāpya-Vyāpaka* relation.

(iii) Any *Liṅga-Liṅgi-Saṁbandha*[40] in itself cannot be context-free, universal. But that which falls within the range of *Vyāpti* as a *Niyama* is never contingent or accidental. Contextually, one can understand *Avinābhāva* in terms of *Liṅga-Liṅgi-Saṁbandha* but not *vice-versa*.

(iv) Coming to *Gamya-Gamaka-bhāva*. *Vyāpti* seeks to regulate it and is not determined by it.

(v) *Avinābhāva* is regulative of *Ādhāra-Ādheya-Saṁbandha* but *Ādhāra-Ādheya-Saṁbandha* is not determinative of *Avinābhāva*, even contextually.[41]

(vi) Neither comprehension nor certification of our knowledge of *Vyāpti* has anything to do with induction and inductive-procedure, and hence *Bhūyodarśana* as a pre-condition of the cognition of *Vyāpti* is unjustified. *Vyāpti* as a regulative condition of *Anumāna* applies not only to our arguments concerning the actual but also to those concerning the coherently possible. Dharmakīrti is not interested in considering the nature of *Vyāpti* insofar as it is applicable only to our arguments relating to things in this world. His primary interest is to spell out the nature and significance of *Vyāpti* as a regulative condition of *Anumāna* in such a way that it is understood as the condition of the very possibility of *Anumāna*.

Dharmakīrti is not interested in giving a descriptive account of the way we reason when we think about anything at all. Nor is he interested in giving an account of the psychological factors involved in the process of reasoning and the role they play in it. His concern with *Anumāna* may be said to be of offering its critique—spelling out the conditions of the very possibility of *Anumāna* in such a way that if and when they are fulfilled *Anumāna* being fashioned and formulated would remain a permanent possibility. All the three kinds of conditions of *Anumāna* he considers—epistemic, constitutive and regulative—are signally taken into account from the point of view of this single consideration. As he does not bring in any extraneous factors into his consideration except the possibility of *Anumāna*, his critique is not designed to be tailored to spelling out the possibility of sound arguments only. As will be observed later, arguments which are, on methodological grounds, valid without being sound are as legitimate as those arguments which are both valid as well as sound. Likewise, although he considers both *Vyāpti* and *Pakṣadharmatā* to be regulative conditions of *Anumāna*, he does not consider their permutations and combinations like *Parāmarśa* (as *Naiyāyikas* are prone to hold) to be an additional epistemic or regulative factor though he does believe that these two regulative conditions need to be fulfilled jointly as well as severally. His criticism of his adversaries—both intra-school or inter-school—is not directed at their demolition but rather at pointing out that their concern with *Anumāna* does not and cannot amount to be its *critique*, spelling out the conditions of its possibility and considering various problems concerning it in the light of the fulfilment of the conditions of its possibility.

Having considered the nature and significance of each of the two regulative conditions of *Anumāna*, viz. *Pakṣadharmatā* and *Vyāpti* we proceed, in the next section, to show that they are *Hetu*-centric.

V. *Hetu-centricity of Regulative Conditions*

The regulative conditions of *Anumāna*, viz. *Vyāpti* and *Pakṣadharmatā* are taken into account context-freely and methodologically in the coherently conceivable world with reference to the possibility of formulation of arguments. Hence, Dharmakīrti conceives of their nature differently from other thinkers. However, their uniqueness in itself does not guarantee their *Hetu*-centricity, nor the *Hetu*-centricity of *Anumāna* is determinative of the nature of *Vyāpti* and *Pakṣadharmatā*. So far we saw that *Vyāpti* and *Pakṣadharmatā* are the two necessary and sufficient regulative conditions of *Anumāna* which enable us to establish interrelationship between the three structural conditions of *Anumāna*, viz. *Pakṣa*, *Sādhya*, and *Hetu*, and that over and above these two it is redundant and methodologically unwarrantable to accept any additional regulative condition.[42] In case of structural conditions we have shown their *Hetu*-centricity and the way this feature paves a way for *Hetu*-centricity of *Anumāna*. Now we intend to show that *Hetu*-centricity is built into regulative conditions as well and hence an *Anumāna* they make possible remains nothing but *Hetu*-centric.

In the case of *Vyāpti* we said that *Vyāpti* helps us in relating *Hetu* to *Sādhya*, insofar as *Hetu* is *Vyāpya* and *Sādhya* is *Vyāpaka*. This mode of relating amounts to mapping *Sādhya* with the help of *Hetu* and thus revolves around *Hetu*. In this what matters is that *Hetu* is logically and epistemologically prior to *Sādhya*. Hence it is *Hetu* which is important. In the case of *Pakṣadharmatā*, too, we have seen that it is *Hetu* which plays a central role and, accordingly, its consideration is of central importance. Out of the three structural conditions of *Anumāna*,

Hetu and *Pakṣa* are connected with each other on the basis of *Pakṣadharmatā* where consideration of *Hetu* remains important. Likewise, in the case of *Vyāpti*, which enables us to connect the structural conditions of *Hetu* and *Sādhya*, it is the role of *Hetu* which is primarily important. The *Hetu*, however, involved in *Pakṣadharmatā* and the one that figures in *Vyāpti* cannot be different in the case of a single argument, whatever kind of argument it may be. Given this, *Vyāpti* together with *Pakṣadharmatā* furnishes a regulation in accordance with which *Sādhya* could appropriately be inferred to be connected with *Pakṣa*. Thus the two regulative conditions of *Anumāna* enable us to establish interconnection between the structural conditions of *Anumāna* and with reference to them too primacy of *Hetu* remains uppermost. Rather, primacy of *Hetu* is built into each of them. Since regulative conditions of *Anumāna* are *Hetu*-centric, the way they enable us to interconnect structural conditions of *Anumāna* also remains *Hetu*-centric in character.

If one considers *Vyāpti* and *Pakṣadharmatā* to be non-*Hetu*-centric, then *Anumāna* will be poly-centric or at least dual-centric. But so considered, the very possibility of *Anumāna* would be methodologically annihilated in its very conception. In order not to allow something of this kind to happen both *Vyāpti* and *Pakṣadharmatā* must have bearing on the same centre and this is ensured by the same *Hetu* figuring in both of them. They are shown to be *Hetu*-centric.[43] Rather, it is methodologically, as well as intuitively, necessary that for the very possibility of *Anumāna* they need to be *Hetu*-centric. And since structural conditions are *Hetu*-centric, intuitively as well as methodologically, regulative conditions, too, cannot fail to be *Hetu*-centric.

So far we considered epistemic, structural and regulative conditions of *Anumāna* and argued that they are basically *Hetu*-centric in character. We also argued that given these three types of conditions, *Anumāna* can always be fashioned and formulated, and that for its being so fashioned and formulated, no additional condition of any sort is required to be fulfilled. Now after arguments come to be formulated a number of important problems crop up and demand consideration. Such problems are: What are the kinds of arguments and on what basis are arguments methodologically appropriate to be classified?

What sort of considerations would matter for our being able to decide the validity and/or soundness of a given argument? What sort of fallacies are arguments prone to give rise to and what is their consideration determined by? We propose to take up such issues for consideration from the next chapter. Of them, we take up the issue of classification and validity of arguments with priority for consideration. Accordingly it becomes the theme of the next chapter.

Notes and References

1. Arcaṭa; *H.B.T.*; pp. 9-11, 17-19, 55-57.
2. *Ibid*; pp. 11-17.
3. Dharmakīrti; *P.V.*; III.1, *Svārthānumāna-pariccheda*; pp. 1-2.
4. Dharmakīrti; *N.B.*; pp. 21-25. Arcaṭa; *H.B.T.*; pp. 4, 6, 9, 10, 19.
5. Jagadīśa Tarkālaṅkāra; *Jāgadīśī-pakṣatā-prakaraṇe;* (see also Gaṅgeśa's *Tattva-cintāmaṇi*) *Anumāna-khaṇḍa*, *Pakṣatā-prakaraṇa*, pp. 5-10.
6. Diṅnāga: *Hetu-cakra-hamaru*; kārikās 1-5, and *Nyāya-mukha*; pp. 10-35.
7. Iyengar, H.R.R.; "The *Vādavidhi* and the *Vādavidhāna* of Vasubandhu"; pp. 10-19.
8. Arcaṭa; *H.B.T.*; pp. 11-24.
9. Dharmakīrti; *P.V.*; III.1, *Svārthānumāna-pariccheda*; pp. 1-2, M.N. *Vṛtti*; pp. 257-258.
10. Arcaṭa; *H.B.T.*; pp. 11-17.
11. *Ibid*; pp. 12-27; 41, 72.
12. Dharmakīrti; *N.B.*; pp. 51-53, 59-60.
13. Dharmakīrti; *P.V.*; III.1, *Svārthānumāna-pariccheda*; pp. 1-2. Durveka Miśra; *Dharmottara-pradīpa*; pp. 88-93.
14. Dharmakīrti; *H.B.*; pp. 52-54. *P.V.*; III.1-3, 16-26, 29-49. *H.B.T.*; pp. 6-19. Durveka Miśra; *Dharmottara-pradipa*; pp. 91-115.
15. Karṇakagomin; *P.V.T.*; pp. 4-20.
16. Arcaṭa; *H.B.T.*; pp. 6-17.
17. *Ibid*; pp. 6-7, 12-14.
18. Dharmakīrti; *P.V.*; IV. 180-198. M.N. *Vṛtti*; pp. 422-430.
19. Arcaṭa; *H.B.T.*; pp. 16-17.
20. Dharmakīrti; *N.B.*; (also Dharmottara's *N.B.T.*) ; p. 22. *Vādanyāya*; (also *Vipañcitārthā* by Śāntarakṣita); p. 59. Prajñākara Gupta; *P.V.A.*; pp. 484-485.
21. Arcaṭa; *H.B.T.*; pp. 9-21, 54-56, 204-228.
22. *Ibid*; pp. 222-228.
23. Dharmakīrti; *P.V.*; III.31-32. *Svārthānumāna-pariccheda*; pp. 13-14. M.N. *Vṛtti*; p. 269. Arcaṭa; *H.B.T.*; pp. 6-11, 55-56.

24. Dharmakīrti; *H.B.*; pp. 62-72. Arcaṭa; *H.B.T.*; pp. 6-8, 54.
25. Dharmakīrti; *Saṁbandha-parīkṣā*; p. 140. Karṇakagomin; *P.V.T.*; 97-102, 166-172, 412-430, 437. Arcaṭa; *H.B.T.*; pp. 15-19, 180-195.
26. Dharmakīrti; *P.V.*; III. 31-32, 39, *Svārthānumāna-pariccheda*; pp. 1-2, 12-13, 15-16.
27. Arcaṭa; *H.B.T.*; pp. 55-56.
28. See introduction to *H.B.* by Sukhalaji Sanghavi; p. xxiii.
29. Dharmakīrti; *P.V.*; III. 31-35, IV. 64, 200-205. *Vādanyāya*; p. 41. Arcaṭa; *H.B.T.*; pp. 6-11, 53, 77, 124, 155, 164.
30. Dharmakīrti; *H.B.*; pp. 70-71. *P.V.*; III. 132-134. *Svārthanumāna-pariccheda*; p. 42. Arcaṭa; *H.B.T.*; pp. 99-112, 225.
31. Uddyotakara; *Nyāya-Vārtika*; I.i.5.
32. Udayana; *Pariśuddhi*; I.i.5.
33. Durveka Miśra; *H.B.T.A.*; pp. 308-323.
34. *Ibid*; p. 374.
35. Dharmakīrti; *P.V.*; III.1, 31. *Svārthānumāna-pariccheda*; pp. 1-2, 12-14. Arcaṭa; *H.B.T.*; pp. 222-223.
36. Dharmakīrti; *N.B.*; (also Dharmottara's *N.B.T.*); pp. 29-30.
37. Arcaṭa; *H.B.T.*; p. 18. Durveka Miśra; *H.B.T.A.*; pp. 317-318.
38. Dharmakīrti; *P.V.*; III.32, *Svārthānumāna-pariccheda*; p. 34. Arcaṭa; *H.B.T.*; p. 8.
39. Arcaṭa; *H.B.T.*; 6, 54, 77, 125, 141.
40. Arcaṭa; *H.B.T.*; pp. 8, 20-22, 180-185, 192-193.
41. *Ibid*; pp. 8, 19, 22, 180-182.
42. Dharmakīrti; *H.B.*; pp. 55-56, 72. Arcaṭa; *H.B.T.*; pp. 55-56, 204-222.
43. Dharmakīrti; *H.B.*; p. 52. Arcaṭa; *H.B.T.*; 6-12.

CHAPTER V

VALIDITY AND/OR SOUNDNESS OF ANUMĀNA

In the preceding chapter, we considered that *Vyāpti* and *Pakṣadharmatā* are accepted as necessary and sufficient regulative conditions of *Anumāna* by Dharmakīrti on methodological count. Before that we also considered epistemic and constitutive conditions of *Anumāna*. These various kinds of conditions of *Anumāna* individually and collectively make it possible to formulate an argument. Consequent upon arguments being formulated, two questions of seminal significance arise: What are the principal kinds of arguments, and whether such arguments are valid and/or sound. We propose to discuss them in this chapter and argue that these considerations also are *Hetu*-centric in character.

This chapter has three main sections. In the first, we concentrate on the validity aspect of *Anumāna* and on a number of questions related with it. The second section deals with soundness aspect of an argument, in which various issues connected with empirical implications of *Anumāna* are discussed. The last section concentrates upon classifications of *Anumāna* and their methodological defensibility. We shall show that each of these sets of problems need to be dealt with in the light of *Hetu*-centricity of *Anumāna*.

It has been already observed earlier that *Svārthānumāna* and *Parārthānumāna* distinction itself is not a classification of *Anumāna*. Any basic consideration regarding *Anumāna*, except its communication, is basically connected with *Svārthānumāna*. Since *Svārthānumāna* is the cognitive aspect of *Anumāna*, it cannot be posterior to *Parārthānumāna* in order of knowing, for in the case of *Anumāna*, *Parokṣa jñāna* enjoys primacy over its communication. However, even epistemically considered, *Parokṣa jñāna* too requires a condition to be fulfilled viz. viability.

Likewise, given regulative and structural conditions of *Anumāna*, it may come to be formulated, although this in itself would not decide its acceptability. In order that it comes to be accepted it has to be valid, sound and also of a particular kind. Again, an *Anumāna* becomes valid, or sound on the one hand, and of particular kind on the other because and insofar as it fulfils certain conditions. Accordingly, fulfilment of epistemic, structural and regulative conditions on the one hand and (a) validity; (b) soundness; or (c) classification of *Anumāna* on the other would have to be shown to be connected with one another, and this needs further to be shown to have an important bearing on *Hetu*-centricity of *Anumāna*. This is the major task of this chapter. With these preliminary remarks, we turn to the consideration of validity.

I. Conditions of Validity

Before we start consideration of the conditions of validity of *Anumāna*, one point needs to be noted carefully, viz. *Anumāna* gives us *Parokṣa-jñāna* and hence it is intuitively clear that the conditions of its validity cannot be contrary to the requirements of *Parokṣa-jñāna*. On the other hand, methodologically considered they need to be formulated context-freely, to ensure their maximal universality.[1] Implications of this would be clear as we proceed.

We have already seen that there are two regulative conditions of *Anumāna*: *Vyāpti* and *Pakṣadharmatā*, and that each of them needs to be understood in the light of *Hetu*-centricity of *Anumāna*. Likewise, we also saw that there are three structural conditions of *Anumāna* and that with regard to each of them it is the consideration of *Hetu* that remains uppermost. With regard to the consideration of validity as well, the starting clue/s would have to be gathered from the consideration of the nature of *Hetu* itself. For, validity is a formal notion and, accordingly, consideration of validity of an argument amounts to discussing a question as to what form an *Anumāna* should have in order that it is formally held to be viable. Here viability needs to be understood not only cognitively but also with regard to formulation as well as justification of an argument.

Accordingly, it amounts to asking a question: On what ground are we—or rather Dharmakīrti—prepared to consider any indirect knowledge-claim minimally viable? Or else: What form should a minimally viable argument exhibit? The answer according to Dharmakīrti is: Any indirect knowledge-claim is viable provided it is capable of being formulated with the help of a viable argument and that any argument is held to be formally viable provided it is at least valid. Thus considered, being valid is the minimum condition determinative of the viability of an argument as an instrument of indirect knowledge-claim. This is the reason why we began with the consideration of validity of an argument. We will argue later on that in the view of Dharmakīrti a *Svārthānumāna* has an epistemic priority over *Parārthānumāna*, so too the consideration of the validity of *Anumāna* has a methodological priority over the consideration of its soundness. Further, since in order that an argument is held to be viable, it need not necessarily be both valid and sound, and since soundness of an argument is meaningless without its validity, the reason of which would be clear later on, it is necessary first to pay closer attention to the validity aspect of an argument.

We observed earlier that in Dharmakīrti's treatment of *Anumāna*, *Hetu* plays an important role. What then is validity of an argument determined by? Dharmakīrti holds that it is determined by *Trirūpatva* of *Hetu*, i.e. three important features of *Hetu*, viz. *Pakṣa-sattva*, *Sapakṣa-sattva* and *Asapakṣa asattva*. However, it is not merely a matter of enumeration of the conditions of validity which is at stake. Likewise, it is also not enough to consider whether they are necessary and sufficient. It is necessary to inquire into the logic and rationale involved in their being accepted as conditions determinative of validity. It is to the consideration of this that we give priority, for this aspect of theirs is logically and methodologically prior to the mode of the way their nature is explicated.

If this important aspect of theirs is lost sight of, then our treatment of them is likely to lapse into their mere enumeration and their explication merely into the order in which they are enumerated. Instead of this, the very logic and rationale of the order in which conditions of validity are enumerated needs to be probed into to bring out the depth of Dharmakīrti's vision concerning them. This is what we propose to do.

It has been brought out earlier that methodologically it is essential that regulative and constitutive conditions of the very possibility of an *Anumāna* formulated context-freely have to be satisfied. Given this, both the regulative conditions, viz. *Vyāpti* as well as *Pakṣadharmatā* bear directly upon *Hetu*, in the sense that whereas the first opens out the possibility of legitimately relating *Hetu* with *Sādhya*, the latter that of relating *Hetu* with *Pakṣa*. On the other hand, out of the three structural conditions of *Anumāna*, viz. *Pakṣa*, *Sādhya* and *Hetu*, it is *Hetu* which is most important. Further, out of the two regulative conditions, it is *Pakṣadharmatā* which regulates relation between *Hetu* and *Pakṣa*. Given this, we shall argue that one aspect of the relation between *Hetu* and *Sādhya* (i.e. coherently conceivable domain) together with *Pakṣadharmatā* is the starting point of spelling out the conditions of the validity of an argument, while another aspect of the relation between *Hetu* and *Sādhya* (i.e. empiricality aspect) together with *Pakṣadharmatā* is the starting point of spelling out the conditions of the soundness of an argument, and that the former of them is prior and methodologically sufficient to make an argument minimally viable. Accordingly, we first turn to the consideration of validity.

Given this, let us combine two considerations: *Pakṣadharmatā* and the centrality of *Hetu* out of the structural conditions of *Anumāna*. As a consequence, it follows that if this is to be minimally satisfied for the viability of *Anumāna*, then *Hetu* must be, in principle, capable of being related, in a methodologically appropriate way, to *Pakṣa*.[2] This is not only required by *Pakṣadharmatā* but a certificate to that effect has to be issued, as it were, by *Pakṣa-sattva* of *Hetu*. That is why, perhaps, Dharmakīrti considers it a primary condition of the validity of an argument. For, if this condition of validity is not satisfied, then it is pointless to consider whether any other condition of it is satisfied. We shall return to this point later.

Pakṣadharmatā, however, should not be confused with *Pakṣa-sattva* although they are often confused with each other. The former is a regulative condition of *Anumāna*, whereas *Pakṣa-sattva* is a condition of validity of *Anumāna*. Secondly, in case of non-fulfilment of regulative condition one cannot formulate an *Anumāna*, while in the case of non-fulfilment of a validity condition we have *Hetvābhāsa* i.e. in the former inferential cognition itself is just not available, whereas in the case of the latter the available inferential cognition would not be reliable and acceptable i.e. valid. Thirdly, fulfilment of regulative condition of *Pakṣadharmatā* is logically prior, while that of *Pakṣa-sattva* is logically posterior. Lastly, *Pakṣadharmatā* opens out the possibility of *Hetu* being related to *Pakṣa*, while *Pakṣa-sattva* issues an assurance that it is so related in a certain way. Given this, the regulative condition called *Pakṣadharmatā* should not be confused with the condition of validity called *Pakṣa-sattva*. For, in that case all formulated arguments will be automatically characterised as valid, and in such a situation distinction between validity and invalidity itself will vanish. Unfortunately, this sort of mistake seems to be committed, at least partly, by Diṅnāga,[3] as in his view *Pakṣadharmatā* guarantees validity of an *Anumāna*. Moreover, he also seems to accept reducibility of *Vyāpti*, another important regulative condition, to *Pakṣadharmatā*. This means that *Pakṣa-sattva* as a condition of validity needs to be distinguished from *Pakṣadharmatā*.

While formulating the conditions of validity appropriately, certain points, according to Dharmakīrti, need to be borne carefully in mind:

(i) They need to be formulated with a view to making the largest number of arguments logically viable.

(ii) They need to be formulated in accordance with the principle of economy, i.e. they need to satisfy the minimum conditions of validity. We shall note below that both these principles are unfortunately disregarded by *Naiyāyikas*.

(iii) They need to be formulated both context-freely as well as situation-freely. We shall argue below that both these considerations have been ignored by adherents of *Nyāya*, since they hold that non-empty world and debating-situation are essential for the consideration of validity of an argument.

(iv) Validity of an argument should not be mixed up with soundness of it. For whereas, as would be discussed later, validity could be considered without commitment to certain kind of non-empty world, soundness cannot be.

(v) Since validity is a formal notion, its consideration should revolve only around the form of an argument and deducibility of the conclusion of an argument from its premises.

every other sort of consideration being extraneous to it. It needs, however, to be understood as a built-in feature of valid arguments alone, and that it cannot be engineered into them at will at all, whatever kind of their nature may be.

(vi) Lastly, the consideration of validity of an argument primarily and basically revolves around characteristic features of *Hetu*.

With this we return to *Pakṣa-sattva*. It is a primary condition of validity and its fulfilment is directly related to *Pakṣadharmatā*. '*Pakṣa-sattva*' literally means that *Hetu* must be obtainable on *Pakṣa*.[4] And *Pakṣa* is that whose *Dharma*, i.e. *Sādhya* is going to be inferred. Thus *Pakṣa-sattva* could be interpreted as the groundwork of the inferability of *Sādhya* on the given *Pakṣa*. Let us, however, look to it a bit more closely. *Pakṣadharmatā* as a regulative condition opens out the possibility of *Hetu* being related to *Pakṣa* as an *Asādhāraṇa dharma*[5] of it. But for the emergence of indirect cognition of *Sādhya* this much is not enough, even though through *Vyāpti* we are given that *Hetu* is related to *Sādhya*. What sort of status should *Sādhya* enjoy which we cognise indirectly? We cannot say anything a priori. But the modes of its determination can be laid down as well as distinguished from each other. Now *Pakṣa* as a *Dharmī* may either just be coherently conceivable or else may be factual. Given this, what sort of status should *Hetu* enjoy as its *Asādhāraṇa dharma*? One answer is that it should enjoy at least parity of status with that of *Pakṣa*. But for the emergence of an indirect cognition of *Sādhya* and for our being able to decide the status of *Sādhya* in relation to that of *Pakṣa* we need to be given an assurance about parity between the status of *Pakṣa* and that of *Hetu*. *Pakṣa-sattva* gives us that assurance, whereby we are given that *Hetu* enjoys parity of status with *Pakṣa*. If *Pakṣa* is merely coherently conceivable then it is enough that *Hetu* too should just be coherently conceivable, while if the former is actual then the latter too needs to be actual.[6] Thus, in order of being it is the status of *Pakṣa* which is primary but epistemologically, however, it is the status of *Hetu* which is primary, since cognitively we map the status of *Sādhya* through inference on the basis of that of *Hetu*. But we also get a clue to the status of *Pakṣa*, although that is not our concern in inference, since *Hetu* has parity of status with *Pakṣa*. *Pakṣa-sattva* is assurance of parity of status of *Hetu* with *Pakṣa*. This assurance in itself does not lay down that *Pakṣa* must be factual or actual as its precondition; nor does it demand similar actuality of *Hetu*. What is enough for validity of an argument is an assurance of the parity of status between *Hetu* and *Pakṣa*. That is all. With this assurance, as one important condition of it, we can not only construct a valid argument but also show validity of an already given valid argument in such a way that such an exercise fulfils the general conditions of knowledge like *Avisaṁvādakatva*, *Avijñātārtha-prakāśakatva* and *Vyavahartavyatva*. Thus understood, mere coherent conceivability of *Pakṣa* and its parity with *Hetu* in order of being, or conversely, mere coherent conceivability of *Hetu* and its parity with *Pakṣa* is strong enough a starting point of the consideration of the validity of an argument, since parity of status is a reciprocal relation. Thus, *Pakṣa-sattva* as a condition of validity gives us an assurance of a parity of status between *Hetu* and *Pakṣa*. It need not be construed in the *Ādhāra-Ādheya* mould[7] and said that what it gives us is obtainability of *Hetu* on *Pakṣa*, especially since Dharmakīrti does not understand *Vyāpti* in terms of *Sāmānādhikaraṇya*[8] as adherents of *Nyāya* do. If we construe it in the *Ādhāra-Ādheya* mould, we will introduce a distortion into his analysis of *Anumāna*.

Dharmakīrti does not, however, discuss conditions of validity of an *Anumāna* merely by enumerating them. He also lays down a principle regarding them and brings out as to why they need to be considered to be so, i.e. he provides a rationale of them.[9] Let us briefly look into it so that in the light of it discussion of the other conditions of validity could be facilitated. Now, whatever be the status of *Pakṣa*, whether merely coherently conceivable or actual, it is intuitively clear that there would be other objects, remembering that in Dharmakīrti's conception the world is essentially pluralistic. Now these other objects could broadly be classified into those which are similar to *Pakṣa* and those which are dissimilar to it. No matter, further, whether they are similar or dissimilar, they would also enjoy a certain ontological status. In the case of similar objects it would further be held that they are similar to *Pakṣa* at least insofar as they enjoy a parity of status with it, while in the case dissimilar objects it could likewise at least be said that they do not enjoy the parity of status with *Pakṣa*, enjoying or not enjoying parity of status itself being the ground of their similarity or dissimilarity with *Pakṣa*. Given this, it may be asked: If *Hetu* enjoys a parity of status with *Pakṣa*, what sort of status *Hetu* could have in comparison with the objects which are either similar or dissimilar to *Pakṣa* and, accordingly, enjoy or do not enjoy parity of status with it? The answer is obvious: *Hetu* should enjoy a parity of status with the objects which enjoy parity of status with *Pakṣa*, since they are similar to it and also since the *Hetu* enjoys a parity of status with *Pakṣa*. Conversely, *Hetu* should not enjoy parity of status with the objects which do not enjoy parity of status with *Pakṣa*, since they are dissimilar to it and also because *Hetu* enjoys parity of status with *Pakṣa*. While the former ensures consistency, the latter scrupulously avoids inconsistency. And this is precisely what is sought to be assured through the other two conditions of validity, viz. *Sapakṣa-sattva* and *Asapakṣa-asattva*. We proceed to give an outline of them.

'*Sapakṣa-sattva*' literally means obtainability of *Hetu* on *Sapakṣa*, and *Sapakṣa* is that which is similar to *Pakṣa*.[10] This is a very prosaic way of clarifying the meaning of *Sapakṣa-sattva* and fails to bring out as to why on earth it should be held to be a condition of the validity of an *Anumāna* at all. In the light of the rationale we explicated above, it becomes abundantly clear that *Hetu* must enjoy a parity of status with all those objects which enjoy a parity of status with *Pakṣa*, and to ensure the validity of an argument, we must have this sort of assurance at our disposal. It is this which *Sapakṣa-sattva* provides, and failing that we would come to decide upon validity of an argument in an incoherent and indefensible way. Accordingly, if *Pakṣa* is merely coherently conceivable then *Hetu* too would be similarly coherently conceivable, and objects similar to *Pakṣa* would also likewise be coherently conceivable and the status enjoyed by *Hetu* would likewise have parity with that enjoyed by objects similar to *Pakṣa*, for they are similar to it precisely because they enjoy a parity of status with it.

Lastly, *Asapakṣa-asattva*. '*Asapakṣa-asattva*' literally means impossibility of the obtainability of *Hetu* on objects dissimilar to *Pakṣa*.[11] Instead of putting it in such a literal fashion let us try to make sense of it within the framework of the rationale we provided above. Objects dissimilar to *Pakṣa* must be so because they do not enjoy parity of status with it. Now, *Hetu* enjoys parity of status not only with *Pakṣa* but also with those objects which enjoy parity of status with *Pakṣa* (*Sapakṣa-sattva*). Further, the objects dissimilar with the latter i.e. *Sapakṣa* (*Asapakṣa-asattva*)[12] cannot enjoy a parity of status with it, and such an absence of parity of status in relation to *Sapakṣa* would also automatically be absence of parity of status with *Pakṣa*, since *Pakṣa* and *Sapakṣa* enjoy parity of status. Hence, the status enjoyed by the *Hetu* must also be dissimilar to that enjoyed by such dissimilar objects, since it has a parity of status with *Pakṣa*. Thus, *Asapakṣa-asattva* assures us that *Hetu* does not and cannot enjoy parity of status with the objects which are dissimilar to the objects which are similar to *Pakṣa*, since *Pakṣa*, *Sapakṣa* and *Hetu* enjoy parity of status. Satisfaction of this third condition of validity ensures avoidance of inconsistency. Thus, starting with *Pakṣa-sattva*, with two further assurances, viz. *Sapakṣa-sattva* and *Asapakṣāsattva*, consideration of consistency is allowed to be extended as far as it is required to be, and inconsistency is scrupulously avoided, minimum conditions for determination of validity are carefully laid down, such that each of them is essential and together they are sufficient.

There are certain fundamental points of difference between the ways in which conditions of validity of *Anumāna* are laid down by *Naiyāyikas* and Dharmakīrti. To highlight Dharmakīrti's insight with greater clarity, we propose to look briefly into them.

There is a difference between *Nyāya* and Dharmakīrti regarding considerations of *Anumāna* on a number of counts. Some of the important points of difference are as follows:

(i) *Naiyāyikas* believe, it seems, that every *Anumāna* that we put forward is always in a debate-context and hence in a social situation. So far as formulation as well as certification of an argument are concerned a debate-context itself is a pre-condition. On the contrary, Dharmakīrti very clearly holds, it appears, that a debate-context is not a methodological pre-condition of formulation and/or certification of *Anumāna*.

(ii) *Naiyāyikas* hold that perceptibility is a pre-condition of *Anumāna*, whereas Dharmakīrti considers this to be methodologically too strong a requirement.

(iii) Since, further, *Naiyāyikas* hold that conclusion of every argument concerns actually real objects, it is necessary that actual non-empty world is the only world on which it should have a bearing. Dharmakīrti, on the contrary, holds that methodologically this demand is too restrictive. In consequence, at the hands of *Nyāya*, requirements of validity and those of soundness of an argument are not distinguished, leave alone demarcated; at the hands of Dharmakīrti they are clearly demarcated.

(iv) As noted in the preceding chapter, for *Nyāya*, *Vyāpti* is a relation, for Dharmakīrti it is a rule.

Since *Naiyāyikas* believe that debating-situation and social-context are essential for formulation of an argument, it is but natural for them to hold, likewise, that they are also necessary for the consideration of validity and/or soundness of an argument. Hence, over and above the three seminal conditions of validity considered above, they raquire two more conditions to be satisfied, in order that argument may not turn out to be vulnerable in a debating-situation. They are: *Asatpratipakṣatva* and *Abādhitaviṣayatva*. The first of these is brought in to ensure that our arguments do not have that sort of vulnerability built into them as a result of which they could be exploited by our adversaries against us. The second, on the contrary, is brought in to ensure that we do not contradict ourselves while debating, otherwise we would come to defeat our claim by ourselves! None of these, however, could be considered to be a legitimate condition determining validity. Moreover, they cannot also be held to be bringing in such a feature of *Hetu* which is important for the determination of validity, since debating-context and social-situation are not inalienably connected with *Hetu*.

We may mention here in passing, without going into further details, that in pre-Dharmakīrti period none of the philosophers from *Nyāya* school has given any condition/s of validity and/or soundness. Likewise, although it is claimed that they considered *Vyāpti* crudely, there is no mention of *Pakṣadharmatā*. It is only after Dharmakīrti elaborately discussed them and brought out their implications, that *Nyāya* thinkers, too, started talking about them. Though in this they seem to be indebted to him, no one of them has acknowledged it. But even after they started talking about them, they did it in such a way that some of their prior commitments made independently were neither compromised nor were given up. Thus, they started defining *Pakṣa* as *Dharmī*, for it possesses both *Sādhya-dharma* as well as *Hetu-dharma*. Hence, it made it possible for them to interpret *Vyāpti* in terms of *Sāmānādhikaraṇya*, which, as mentioned earlier, is a relation and not a rule as Dharmakīrti understands it.

Though both *Naiyāyikas* and Dharmakīrti accept *Pakṣa-sattva*, *Sapakṣa-sattva* and *Asapakṣa-asattva* (*Nyāya* prefers to understand it as *Vipakṣe asattva*) to be determinative of validity, the crux of the difference between them concerning their nature and significance lies in how to interpret the term '*Sattva*'. Dharmakīrti prefers to accept coherent conceivability-framework to be methodologically sufficient with regard to validity and hence interprets '*Sattva*' as parity of status,[13] whereas *Naiyāyikas* advocate that '*Sattva*' needs to be interpreted in terms of actuality or factuality, as they stick to their commitment of considering empiricality as a pre-condition of *Anumāna*. Secondly, Dharmakīrti articulates a uniform rationale as to why they need to be considered as conditions determining validity. In the case of *Nyāya*, not only a uniform rationale interconnecting all the so-called five conditions of validity enumerated by them is not articulated but, methodologically considered, it also seems, in principle, to be incapable of being articulated. Although those five conditions enumerated by them were held to be characteristic marks of a *Sat-hetu*, they are not so, especially because, as observed earlier, at least *Asatpratipakṣatva* and *Abādhitaviṣayatva* seem to be springing from such considerations as have nothing to do with any bearing that regulative conditions of *Anumāna* have on *Hetu* as a structural condition of *Anumāna*. Thirdly, the context of debate and social situation are not necessary conditions of the advent of *Anumāna* as *Naiyāyikas* hold, since it is dictated and necessitated neither by the requirements of the satisfaction of regulative conditions nor by the constitutive conditions of *Anumāna*. In fact, as noted earlier, the account of the regulative conditions of *Anumāna* at the hands of Dharmakīrti's *Nyāya*-predecessors itself was incomplete insofar as they did not acknowledge *Pakṣadharmatā*. Fourthly, whereas methodological considerations like maximal universalizability combined with economy of detrminants of validity gets precedence at the hands of Dharmakīrti, in the *Nyāya* treatment of validity these considerations seem hardly to be taken serious note of. Lastly, Dharmakīrti endeavours to formulate conditions of validity context-freely, whereas in the *Nyāya* treatment of them contextuality and commitment to actual non-empty world seems to have gathered exclusive significance. Hence, on methodological grounds, *Asatpratipakṣatva* and *Abādhitaviṣayatva*, which are held by *Nyāya* to be conditions determining validity, need, according to Dharmakīrti, to be dispensed with without any further ado about them.

So far we have looked into the methodologically important conditions determining validity of *Anumāna* and explained their salient features. Let us proceed briefly to consider *Hetu*-centricity of *Anumāna* with regard to consideration of validity of it. Any argument could minimally be held to be viable because, and insofar as, it is valid. Validity of an argument is a formal notion and needs to be understood accordingly. When in accordance with methodological considerations we succeed in stipulating the minimum number of conditions determining validity, our stipulation also entails a corollary of keeping the maximum number of arguments valid and, hence, viable. Those which would fail to be valid in spite of such a methodological precaution could be safely ignored as this is least likely to threaten our cognitive enterprise. We also saw that conditions of validity revolve around two principal considerations: *Pakṣadharmatā* as a regulative condition of *Anumāna* and *Trairūpya* of *Hetu*. It has already been argued in the preceding chapter that each of the regulative conditions of *Anumāna* is *Hetu*-centric in character and that regulative conditions of *Anumāna* also need to exhibit this feature, since they have a bearing on every major aspect of *Anumāna*. In the case of *Trairūpya* of *Hetu*, viz. *Pakṣa-sattva*, *Sapakṣa-sattva* and *Asapakṣāsattva*, it was separately shown that the principal consideration in each of them is that of *Hetu*. Thus, in their case, too, *Hetu*-centrality is almost analytic in character in the sense that they are shown to be built-in features of a *Hetu* that figures in a valid argument.

Likewise, on the level of the underlying rationale which interconnects the three features of a *Hetu* that figure in a valid argument, too, it was shown that they are so interconnected because, and insofar as, *Hetu* figures centrally in them. Thus *Hetu*-centrality also plays a decisive role with regard to consideration of validity of an argument.

The conditions of validity, it was further argued, are not only decisively important with regard to formulation of a valid argument but also with reference to its certification. A fuller implication of this remark would be apparent when we come to *Hetvābhāsas*, which have mainly to do with violation of conditions determining validity of an argument.

It is needless to say that such conditions as determine validity can neither be held to be *Pakṣa*-centric nor *Sādhya*-centric, as both regulative as well as structural conditions of *Anumāna* can neither be held to be *Pakṣa*-centric nor *Sādhya*-centric.

Having looked into the validity aspect of *Anumāna* and considered conditions determining validity in details and having shown their *Hetu*-centricity, we need to pay attention to another important aspect of *Anumāna*, viz. its soundness. It is to the consideration of this problem that we turn in the next section.

II. Soundness of an Argument

In the last section, we saw that formulation of an argument itself does not guarantee its validity. It is determined by *Trairūpya*, viz. *Pakṣa-sattva*, *Sapakṣa-satta* and *Asapakṣāsattva*, of *Hetu*. So, the claim advanced by *Nyāya* philosophers that five characteristics of *Hetu* determine the validity of an argument is methodologically indefensible. We saw that consideration of validity and consideration of the soundness of arguments are not the same thing—in fact, they are altogether different considerations; their rationale, therefore, needs to be differentially spelt out. Of this, we clarified the rationale of validity in the last section, while to clarify the rationale of soundness of an argument remains the task of the present section. We shall also have to spell out the methodological basis of the connection between considerations of validity and those of soundness. This section, therefore, would be given to the consideration of various problems concerning soundness of an argument and, at the end, we shall also argue that consideration of soundness, too, is basically *Hetu*-centric in character. While presenting an outline of Dharmakīrti's treatment of the soundneses of an argument we shall also spell out its major differences from that of his *Nyāya* and Buddhist predecessors with a view to bringing out the salient features of Dharmakīrti's treatment.

To begin with, consideration of the soundness of an argument stands in some kind of marked contrast, methodologically considered, to that of validity. We want to note these points of contrast carefully so that they do not get lost sight of:

(i) We observed that validity is a formal notion and revolves around the consideration of form of an argument. In this context, it is necessary to note that the form of an argument and the kind of an argument are two different things, and we shall have an occasion to return to this point in the next section. Meanwhile, let us note that by contrast consideration of the soundness of an argument has something to do with the content of it and, through the content with the truth of it. And the truth of an argument has two aspects: truth of premisses and that of conclusion. Accordingly, it would have to be seen as to how the truth of premisses enables us to decide the truth of the conclusion.

(ii) Validity can be investigated into contextually or context-freely, although context-free inquiry into it is methodologically superior to contextual one, since the former guarantees greater universalisability. Consideration of soundness, by contrast, is essentially contextual in character. Through its adherence to content and truth it brings in commitment to factual world, i.e. to the actual non-empty world. Validity, on the contrary, does not or rather need not bring in such a commitment, for form of an argument can be considered with reference to coherently conceivable world as well, although consideration of validity does not necessitate commitment to actual non-empty world. This is lost sight of sometimes, as will be shown later on to be happening in the system of *Nyāya*, which holds that considerations both of validity and soundness necessarily bring in commitment to actual non-empty world. This they try to justify on the ground of the applicability of an argument. But applicability is indeed twofold: applicability in thought and applicability to facts. Hence, it is unreasonable to understand applicability only in the latter sense.

(iii) Since the considerations of validity and soundness or those of form and content of an argument are different, the conditions that determine them too are different. So too, their respective rationales are different. This being the case, to seek to explicate the conditions that respectively determine them or their respective rationales as the same is methodologically unwarranted.

In spite of such differences, however, in the explication of validity or soundness of an argument certain common points remain and we propose to take note of them, their fuller implications becoming clear as we proceed:

(1) In both the sorts of considerations, methodologically speaking, principle of economy should not be allowed to be sacrificed at the altar of extra-methodological considerations.

(2) Formal and material, i.e. validity and soundness issues should not be mixed-up, for this is methodologically unwarranted.

Furthermore, in the opinion of Dharmakīrti, the way we make sense of the issues concerning validity and soundness of an argument should neither force us to make non-sense of *Parokṣa-jñāna* nor of those aspects of Buddha's philosophy which are capable of being interpreted within its framework, Moreover, he would also demand that in the Buddhist account of validity and soundness of an argument such concessions should not come to be made unwittingly, whereby those methodologically untenable implications of *Nyāya* inquiry are admitted into such a framework by back door and thereby coherence and methodologically appropriate orientation of it is either distorted or endangered. Lastly, although one need not swear by absolute departure from commonsense in one's treatment of these issues, one need not also make an advance commitment to it.

We saw earlier that according to Dharmakīrti *Trairūpya* together with *Pakṣadharmatā* enables us to spell out the format and the rationale of the consideration of the validity of an argument. Now, as observed above, since consideration of soundness of an argument has basically to do with the content or truth of it, its rationale needs to be spelt out differentially. In the case of consideration of validity, it is enough to start with a coherently conceivable *Hetu*. In the case of consideration of soundness, on the contrary, one has to start with actual or factual *Hetu*.[14] Having started this way, one may ask a question: What considerations need to be satisfied in order that starting with an actual *Hetu* we would be led to infer or have an indirect cognition of an actual or factual *Sādhya*? The truth of such an argument will have, on the one hand, to do with, the truth of premisses and, on the other, with that of conclusion, and such a conclusion would obviously be about the obtainability of *Sādhya*. We shall take up this question for consideration later on. Before that, we need to spell out the rationale of soundness. Secondly, one may ask: Which regulative condition of an *Anumāna*, together with which other consideration, has a decisive role to play with regard to the determination of the soundness of an argument and on what basis? We first take up this question for consideration.

Now, the only regulative condition of *Anumāna* which, in a methodologically appropriate way, enables us to connect *Hetu* (*Gamaka*) with *Sādhya* (*Gamya*) is the rule of *Vyāpti*. This rule, as a rule, is preservative of validity or of soundness of an argument, in the sense that as it does not make validity or soundness of an argument emerge, so too, it in itself does not distort it, such a distortion of them being primarily determined by disregard or violation of conditions that determine validity or soundness. Further, *Vyāpti* enables us to relate *Hetu* with *Sādhya* through their *Vyāpya-Vyāpaka* relation with each other.[15] Starting with actual *Hetu*, this *Vyāpya-Vyāpaka* relation, together with the rule of *Vyāpti*, enables us to spell out the rationale of the soundness of an argument. In the case of valid arguments, it operates minimally on the level of coherent conceivability, and thereby has no role to play with regard to the truth of an argument. Now, if an actual *Sādhya* is to be inferred then it can be done only if it is sought to be mapped out with the help of an actual *Hetu*, since in the *Vyāpya-Vyāpaka* relation in which they stand related, it is *Hetu* which is *Vyāpya* and it is *Vyāpaka* which can be mapped out with its help. Thus considered, actuality of *Sādhya* demands its parity with similar kind of *Hetu*. And having started with actual *Hetu*, with the help of the rule called *Vyāpti* and within the framework of *Vyāpya-*

Vyāpaka relation, we are enabled to comprehend indirectly an actual *Sādhya,* which has a direct bearing upon the truth of the conclusion of an argument. With the truth of *Hetu* and *Vyāpti* as a rule, truth of premisses too is assured. Thus, whereas actual *Hetu* furnishes assurance of truth of premisses, the other requisite true premiss would automatically be furnished through *Pakṣa-dharmatā,* as the same *Hetu* would be figuring in it as an *Asādhāraṇa dharma* of *Pakṣa.* Further, since *Vyāpti* is a rule and a rule is never true or false, though it may be tenable or otherwise, requisite assurance of the truth of premisses would thus be furnished. Given this, the truth of conclusion could also be assured.

We, however, said above that in the consideration of soundness of an argument *Vyāpya-Vyāpaka* relation, too has an important role to play. Now, as the truth of *Hetu* is assured through actual *Hetu* being given, the truth of *Vyāpya-Vyāpaka* relation too needs to be assured, so that when that is assured we may be led in a methodologically legitimate way to infer true *Sādhya.* *Vyāpti* as a rule is preservative, no matter whether of truth or coherent conceivability, and it is no magic to convert coherent conceivability automatically into truth. Accordingly, those conditions need to be fulfilled on which assurance of the truth of *Vyāpya-Vyāpaka* relation may be furnished to us. Without anticipating too much our later argument, we can say at this juncture that the truth of *Vyāpya-Vyāpaka* relation can be furnished only if it comes to be operative in an actual non-empty world, whereas assurance about it comes to us through the fulfilment of conditions that determine soundness which ensure that *Vyāpya-Vyāpaka* relation is operative contextually in a non-empty world. It is important to note that *Vyāpya-Vyāpaka* relation in itself is no assurance that it is or must be operative in an actual non-empty world alone, as it could be operative in merely coherently conceivable world as well. Or to put it differently, such a relation can be operative with regard to a coherently possible world as well, in which case assurance of truth would not be forthcoming, though of coherent possibility would be, and mere coherent possibility is neither actuality nor detrminative of factual truth. Further, operativeness of *Vyāpya-Vyāpaka* relation in a coherent non-empty world may bring forth two possibilities[16]: (a) it may be operative from actual *Hetu* to actual

Sādhya, in which case alone it can furnish an assurance of factual truth of an argument, provided conditions derminative of soundness of an argument are fulfilled, and (b) it may be operative from non-obtainability (*Anupalabdhi*) of *Sādhya* indicative of non-obtainability of *Hetu*, which is not indicative of soundness of an argument, although by the same token it does not rule out its validity, for there is no rule whereby it has been or could be decided in advance that if an argument is not sound it also cannot be valid.

Thus operativeness of *Vyāpya-Vyāpaka* relation in a non-empty world is decisively significant with regard to consideration of soundness of an argument, provided that the conditions decisive of the fact that it is so operative are fulfilled. Thus understood, operativeness of the *Vyāpya-Vyāpaka* relation in a non-empty world furrnishes the context of the consideration of the soundness of an argument together with *Vyāpti* as a regulative rule. Fulfilment of the conditions which determine soundness assures us on the one hand that *Vyāpya-Vyāpaka* relation is operative in a non-empty world, and, on the other hand, funishes an assurance of the truth of it, the other aspect of the truth of an argument being funished by *Pakṣadharmatā*. For, the same *Hetu* would figure in it which figures in the *Vyāpya-Vyāpaka* relation operative in the non-empty or actual world under the jurisdiction of the rule of *Vyāpti*. It is, as observed above, neither generative of validity nor of soundness of an argument, though it is preservative of both of them.

But it may be asked, why can conditions that determine validity themselves not be taken to be determinative of soundness? The answer is: Because of the following reasons: (i) There are at least some kinds of arguments, viz. *Anupalabdhi-Anumāna*, which, though they are methodologically valid, are not sound. (ii) Conditions determining validity and soundness are respectively different. (iii) What plays a decisive role in the determination of validity and furnishes its appropriate rationale is *parkṣadharmatā* togehter with *Trairūpya* of *Hetu*. In the case of soundness of an argument, on the contrary, it is *Vyāpya-Vyāpaka* relation figuring in a non-empty world together with *Vyāpti* which has a decisive role to play. Given this, (iv) the rationale of soundness revolves around parity of status between *Hetu* and *Sādhya*, whereas that of validity revolves around parity of status between *Hetu* and *Pakṣa*. (v) Lastly, whereas in the case of validity coherent conceivability is a minimal condition, in the case of soundness, truth and hence obtainability is a minimal condition. Thus understood, determination of the consideration of validity and that of soundness need to be differently made sense of. It would a be methodologically untenable move to confuse the two. However, whether it is validity or soundness, its principal consideration and its determinative conditions are required to be satisfied on the level of *Svārthānumāna* itself.

We distinguished above the domain of the consideration of soundness from that of the validity saying that whereas, minimally it is the consideration of the actual which is uppermost in the former case, in the latter case it is that of the coherently possible or conceivable. However, the actual must be coherently possible, though whatever is coherently possible need not be actual. If we understand the domain of coherently possible—logical as well as rational—then it would be seen to be wider, and the domain of the actual will be subsumable under it. This indicates methodological simplicity and clarity in the concerned philosophical inquiry and assures us that a viable sound argument also needs to fulfil the condition of validity.

Given this, one can clearly understand Dharmakīrti's insistence on making the distinction between validity and soundness.

(1) The domains of validity and soundness being different, it is essential to distinguish between them. For, the domain of validity accommodates that of soundness, since fact cannot transgress the limits of coherent possibility. Factual and actual world is one of the sub-sets of the totality of coherently possible worlds.

(2) Every valid argument, in principle, is instantiable. But as a matter of fact, it is not instantiated, may be because of its being empirically impossible, e.g. *Svabhāvānupalabdhi* or *kāryānupalabdhi*, or because of non-actuality, which is a contingent phenomenon. If we start from fact, on the contrary, our obtaining or not obtaining the inferred object will always be contextual or accidental.

It amounts to saying that since *Naiyāyikas* start their philosophical inquirty from our day-to-day experience, and put experienciability as a pre-condition of it, it is no wonder that their exercise remains delimited to the actual world or the world we live in. In principle also, it becomes impossible for them to transgress the limits of common-sense. Hence, as a result of it, soundness becomes the pre-condition of validity. It is nothing else but indicative of mixing two different kinds of issues, viz. philosophical inquiry and common-sensical inquiry, validity and soundness, contextuality and freedom from context. As a result, they land in a methodological confusion, mixing-up of different kinds of issues without inquiring into minimal conditions which context-freely are required to be satisfied.

With this, we turn to the consideration of those conditions which determine the soundness of an argument. In the opinion of Dharmakīrti, that sort of *Vyāpya-Vyāpaka* relation is determinative of soundness which is marked by the tie of *Svabhāva-pratibandha*,[17] for on the fulfilment of this condition alone can one thing indicate another. We turn to a detailed account of it.

Svabhāva-pratibandha means a natural in-separable tie[18] of one thing with another, such that through *Vyāpya-Vyāpaka* relation, given one of them the other cannot fail to be located. It is this feature of it which gives us the range of soundness. It may, however, be asked: What sort of natural tie is it which remains inalienable and as a result of which if one of the two things which are so connected is given, the other does not fail to be given? We have seen earlier that through *Vyāpya-Vyāpaka* relation it is always possible to map out *Vyāpaka* with the help of *Vyāpya*, since the range of *Vyāpya* is a proper sub-set of the range of *Vyāpaka*.[19] It is not this kind of set-sub-set relation that is under consideration in *Svabhāva-pratibandha*. For, it could be available in a coherently possible world as well. Under such a condition, it cannot enable us to have the range of the soundness of an argument, which is operative in the world of facts, and not merely in the world of coherent possibility. What is, on the contrary, wanted for soundness of an argument is a device using which we cannot, if one thing is given to us, fail to obtain another thing provided they are related through *Vyāpya-Vyāpaka* relation. Thus, here, the *Vyāpya-Vyāpaka* relation gives us the domain, as it were, within which *Svabhāva-pratibandha* gives us the range of the soundness of an argument. Thus understood, mere *Vyāpya-Vyāpaka* relation does not guarantee soundness of an argument. It, along with *Svabhāva-pratibandha*, is necessary to be given.[20]

This kind of *Svabhāva-pratibandha*, according to Dharmakīrti is basically of two kinds: (a) the nature of one thing is subsumable under that of another in such a way that if the subsumed thing is given, through *Vyāpya-Vyāpaka* relation, the thing under which it is subsumable cannot fail to be given. In other words, there is a *Tādātmya* relation between the two.[21] Here what is meant by *Tādātmya* is not what is normally understood by identity but rather what is meant by subsumption. (b) one thing emerges from the other such that the thing that has emerged being given, the thing from which it emerged cannot fail to be given. This kind of relation he calls *Tadutpatti*.[22] What is meant by it is the relation of 'emerging from'.

These two relations of *Tādātmya* and *Tadutpatti* are such natural inalienable ties between two things that if they are so related and if their *Vyāpya* is already given, the *Vyāpaka* cannot fail to be given. Or given the actuality of one, the actuality of the other cannot fail to be given. It is this kind of assurance that is required for the truth of an argument being certified or cognised legitimately. For, as observed earlier, soundness of an argument is concerned with its truth, or content, not with its form. That is why in Dharmakīrti's view *Tādātmya* and *Tadutpatti* need to be understood as determinants or conditions of soundness of an argument.[23] For, on their being fulfilled, soundness of an argument cannot fail to be given, since the truth of an argument around which soundness of an argument revolves would not fail to be assured on fulfilment of these two conditions. Since, further, the ties under consideration are neither arbitrarily engineered nor deliberately imputed to them, they are natural in the sense that the things under consideration are given to us as tied with each other with these ties. And over and above these two sorts of ties, there is none with the help of which two things could be tied with each other in such a way that if one of them is given, the other cannot fail to be given. Hence they constitute necessary and sufficient conditions of soundness of an argument—according to Dharmakīrti.

The reason why such a natural tie is held to be decisive is

that truth of an argument needs to be decided on the basis of facts, and facts are given to us; we discover them, we do not create them at will. Likewise, obtainability of facts needs to be decided on the basis of relations operative between them. As in the case of validity form of an argument is decisively important, so in the case of soundness of an argument facts are decisively significant. In the case of an indirect cognition that *Anumāna* makes available it is not their discreteness that is significant, but rather their connectedness. But such a kind of connectedness alone needs to be held to be significantly important for soundness of an argument which is neither arbitrary nor engineered by us. For, methodologically speaking, truth of an argument would be forthcoming only on the assurance of the truth of its premisses and that of its conclusion. But since truth of conclusion is derivative from that of premisses, from the assurance of the truth of premisses, that concerning the truth of conclusion would be automatically available, provided the facts of which they are the truths, are themselves inalienably related with each other. It is this sort of assurance that they are so related that comes from *Tādātmya* or *Tadutpatti* kind of natural ties between them. That is why they are and need to be considered to be conditions of soundness of an argument. Their arbitrary stipulation would be indefensible and methodologically untenable.

In the case of *Tādātmya* kind of *Pratibandha* between things, *Svabhāva-Hetu* brings out such a nature of one thing of the two as are related to each other with such a tie that it is subsumable under another. In the case of *Tadutpatti* kind of *Pratibandha*, on the contrary, the *Kārya-Hetu* brings forth effect and through *Vyāpya-Vyāpaka* relation assures us of the cause from which it emerged. It is only these two sorts of relations together with *Vyāpya-Vyāpaka-bhāva* which are important with reference to soundness of an argument. Other sorts of relations between things are irrelevant for consideration in the context of soundness of arguments[24] because through them things do not come to be related to each other inalienably, nor do they remain operative along with *Vyāpya-Vyāpaka-bhāva.*

For considering an argument to be viable, its truth, according to Dharmakīrti, need not be held to be its pre-condition. *Naiyāyikas*, on the contrary, hold that it is, since perception according to them is a pre-condition of *Anumāna*, and truth, they hold, has very decisively something to do with perception. Dharmakīrti, on the other hand, holds, on a methodologically reasonable basis, that viability of an argument can be accepted merely on the proviso that it is at least valid. For, as observed earlier, *Vyāpya-Vyāpaka-bhāva* in a coherently possible world merely would give us a valid argument, though not a sound argument. Likewise, as will be noted later on, *Anupalabdhi-Anumāna* is certainly valid although it is not sound. Accordingly, the range of valid argument is larger than that of sound arguments. Hence, validity of an argument need not guarantee its soundness as well, although these two features of arguments need not be so discordant with each other that an argument is prohibited from being simultaneously both valid and sound. Even if, in this way, a valid argument may not be sound, is a sound argument, necessarily valid in order to be held to be viable? Although there is a logical possibility of an argument being sound without being valid, Dharmakīrti does not take it seriously, for according to him, validity of an argument is a minimum condition of its viability. Given this, in his view, arguments may be held to be viable either because they are merely valid or because they are both valid and sound. Thus, in his view, soundness of an argument presupposes its validity but validity does not presuppose soundness. The range of valid arguments is larger than that of sound arguments, and accordingly, the range of sound arguments, in his view, is a proper sub-set of that of valid arguments. *Nyāya* philosophers, on the contrary, consider both validity and soundness to be necessary conditions of viability of an argument and, accordingly, hold the range of valid arguments and that of sound arguments to be coextensive. In fact, they do not distinguish between the two, since their methodology and its important presuppositions, some of which were outlined earlier, forbid them to do so.

In this context, it needs to be considered whether such a so-called constituent of *Anumāna* as *Udāharaṇa*, held to be necessary not only by *Nyāya* but also by such predecessors of Dharmakīrti as Diṅnāga, needs to be considered to be significant with regard to soundness of an argument if not with regard to its validity as well. We argued earlier that such constituents as *Pratijñā*,

Udāharaṇa, *Upanaya* and *Nigamana* accepted by *Nyāya* philosophers cannot, on any methodologically tenable ground, be held to be structural conditions of *Anumāna* since the very possibility of the formulation of *Anumāna* does not hang on them. Here we intend to argue briefly that *Udāharaṇa* can also not be taken as a determinant of its validity or soundness[25] according to Dharmakīrti. To take validity first. *Udāharaṇa* makes an instance or example available of the fact that *Hetu* is related to a thing which is similar to *Pakṣa*. Now, form of an argument which matters with regard to the consideration of its validity is determined mainly by two conditions, viz. *Pakṣa-dharmatā* and *Trairūpya* of *Hetu*, neither of which is determined by *Udāharaṇa*. It cannot even be mistaken for or confused with *Sapakṣa-sattva*, for that, too, as we saw earlier, is determined by similarity of something with *Pakṣa* because both of them enjoy a parity of status, which is neither determined by nor is required to be exemplified by *Udāharaṇa*. It would suffice even if it (*Sapakṣa*) is entertained on the level of coherent conceivability to assure *Anumāna* of consistency. Accordingly, validity of an argument cannot be held to be determined by or dependent upon *Udāharaṇa*. So it is dispensable with reference to it. With regard to soundness of an argument, too, the same thing holds. We proceed to show how, in Dharmakīrti's view, *Udāharaṇa* is dispensable with regard to soundness of an argument as well. We saw that in the case of the consideration of soundness of an argument what matters is *Svabhāva-pratibandha* together with *Vyāpya-Vyāpaka* relation, and the former of them is not determined by citation of an example. Nor is *Vyāpya-Vyāpaka-bhāva* required to be instantiated in order that, within its framework, *Svabhāva-pratibandha* may assure us of the truth of premisses and that of the conclusion. In fact, it is not *Vyāpya-Vyāpaka-bhāva* regulated by the rule of *Vyāpti* which an *Udāharaṇa* is said to be illustrating but rather *Vyāpya-Vyāpaka-bhāva* understood in terms of *Vyāpti*, where *Vyāpti* is sought to be understood as a *Saṁbandha* called *Sāmānādhikaraṇya* and not as a rule as is done by Dharmakīrti. And *Vyāpti*, understood in the latter sense, is not at all required to be instantiated. Given this, *Udāharaṇa* can also not be said to be important, decisively or otherwise, in consideration of the soundness of an argument.[26]

We saw earlier that, on Dharmakīrti's view, soundness of an argument presupposes its validity, although the converse of this is not acceptable to him. Likewise, although an invalid argument could, in principle, be sound, yet since, on Dharmakīrti's view, validity is a minimum condition of the viability of an argument, such an argument should be held to be unviable, due to its invalidity, in spite of the fact that it is sound. Further, mere unsoundness of an argument is no basis to dismiss it as unviable, since, insofar as it is valid, it remains viable. Thus, it seems, in consideration of the relationship between validity and soundness of an argument, along with methodological considerations, *Vyavahartavyatva* as a criterion of knowledge appears to have carried weight with Dharmakīrti. This does not, of course, mean that he would ever countenance sacrifice of consistency. For, if methodological considerations alone were to be held to be decisive, then there is no reason why he should not have considered sound but invalid arguments. Their non-consideration seems also to be backed by yet another reason: the domain of *Anumāna* is primarily the domain of reason, thought; and if any consideration is not at least backed by thought, then it has no business to be an object of an inferential cognition. This means that *Vyavahartavyatva* may either mean (1) *Vyavahartavyatva* with reference to facts alone in which case it would be object of perceptual cognition, or (2) in the domain of thought alone, or else (3) in the domains of both facts and thoughts; in the latter two cases it would be an object of inferential cognition. As in the case of perceptual cognition *Vyavahartavyatva* with reference to fact/s is a minimal condition, so too with reference to inferential cognition, *Vyavahartavyatva* with reference to thought is a minimal condition. Naturally, where the consideration concerning *Vyavahartavyatva* with regard to both facts and thought is at stake it is *Vyavahartavyatva* with regard to thought which needs to be held as primary, not only because *Vyavahartavyatva* in thought is no guarantee of *Vyavahartavyatva* with regard to fact, but also because inferential cognition, in Dharmakīrti's view, does not and need not presuppose *Vyavahartavyatva* in fact. We shall have an occasion to see some important implications of this distinction between domains of facts and of thought in the context of *Hetu*-centricity of *Anumāna* in the last chapter.

As we showed earlier, consideration of validity is basically *Hetu*-centric in character in Dharmakīrti, so it needs to be shown that discussion of soundness of an argument also is *Hetu*-centric in character. It is now to this that we turn. It may *prima facie* be held that since, according to him, the domain of sound arguments is a sub-set of the domain of valid arguments, and since valid arguments are already shown to be *Hetu*-centric in character, it automatically follows that sound arguments should also be *Hetu*-centric according to him. This would be an indirect way of establishing *Hetu*-centricity of the consideration of soundness at his hands. In spite of this, however, determinants of validity and those of soundness are different. Hence, over and above showing that consideration of validity is *Hetu*-centric in character according to Dharmakīrti, it needs separately to be shown that consideration of soundness is also so, otherwise one important aspect of *Anumāna*, viz. soundness, would miss *Hetu*-centricity, and this would cast aspersion on our central thesis that according to Dharmakīrti *Anumāna* is *Hetu*-centric.

We argued earlier that validity of *Anumāna* according to Dharmakīrti is *Hetu*-centric because its determinative conditions are so. We also saw that *Svabhāva-pratibandha* in general or *Tādātmya* and *Tadutpatti* in particular are, according to Dharmakīrti, conditions of soundness of *Anumāna*. We argued that it is not *Svabhāva-pratibandha* of any kind but only that which fits into *Vyāpya-Vyāpaka-bhāva* that is significant with regard to soundness. For that sort of *Svabhāva-pratibandha* alone could be non-accidental in character.[27] Moreover, in *Vyāpya-Vyāpaka-bhāva* under consideration, it is the role of *Hetu* as *Vyāpya* that is significant, for in that framework we try to map out *Vyāpaka* with the help of *Vyāpya*.[28] In the case of *Tādātmya* and *Tadutpatti* too, it is *Hetu* whose consideration is central. In the case of the former, the *Hetu* plays such a role with regard to subsumption, giving us the subsumable, which could be subsumed under its corresponding wider set. In the case of the latter. too, *Hetu* gives us *Kārya* starting from which we could indirectly be led to its corresponding cause. Thus considered, both on the level of

Vyāpya-Vyāpaka-bhāva and *Svabhāva-pratibandha* on the one hand, and *Tādātmya* or *Tadutpatti* on the other, it is centrality of *Hetu* which is at stake, and hence, accordingly, consideration of soundness also remains *Hetu*-centric in character at the hand of Dharmakīrti.

Now having argued for validity and/or soundness of *Anumāna* to be *Hetu*-centric it is essential to establish that similar feature is exhibited by classification of arguments and that *Hetu*-centrality is similarly at stake here also. It is to this consideration that we now turn in the next section.

III. Kinds of Anumāna

In the preceding two sections we have seen that the conditions of validity and/or soundness need to be considered, according to Dharmakīrti, in such a way that methodological issues and perspectives would be distinguished from extra-methodological ones. If the conditions of validity are concentrated upon, they are only three: *Pakṣa-sattva*, *Sapakṣa-sattva* and *Asapakṣa-asattva*, while any suggestion to accept any additional condition of validity is rejected on methodological grounds. Similarly, soundness is also shown to be determined by *Svabhāva-pratibandha* in general and *Tādātmya* and *Tadutpatti* in particular. It was further shown that, according to Dharmakīrti, arguments could perfectly be valid, without being sound, and it was further argued that both validity and/or soundness of an argument, in his view, are basically *Hetu*-centric in character.

With this background, we hope, in this section, to argue another important point concerning *Anumāna*, viz. methodologically *Anumāna* is classifiable into only three kinds viz. *Svabhāvānumāna*, *kāryānumāna* and *Anupalabdhi-anumāna*.[29] The other classifications of *Anumāna* given by adherents of different schools are methodologically inappropriate. Hence, classification of *Anumāna* into *Pūrvavat*, *Śeṣavat* and *Sāmānyatodṛṣṭa*, or that into *Kevalānvayī*, *Kevalavyatirekī* and *Anvaya-vyatirekī* etc. remain unacceptable to Dharmakīrti. For, these classifications are not backed by appropriate methodological considerations. Likewise, we shall inquire into Dharmakīrti's rationale of the classification of *Anumāna* and finally argue that even with regard to classification of *Anumāna* it is *Hetu* which has a central role to play and hence this aspect of *Anumāna* also is *Hetu*-centric in character. We proceed to discuss these points.

Before we begin discussing important aspects connected with classification of *Anumāna* and appreciate its rationale, certain preliminary considerations are in order. First, certain *prima facie* distinctions like *Svārthānumāna* and *Parārthānumāna* are not classificatory in character, for every consideration concerning any significant aspect of *Anumāna*, except its communication, needs to be taken into account on the level of *Svārthānumāna* itself. Secondly, classification of *Anumāna* is not methodologically required to be isomorphic with the distinction between valid and sound arguments. In fact, classification of *Anumāna* cuts across this distinction in such a way that one and the same kind of argument could be valid and/or sound depending upon whether or not conditions of its validity and/or soundness are fulfilled. Thirdly, classification of *Anumāna* cannot originate from classification of regulative conditions of *Anumāna*. First of all, there are no classes of regulative conditions of *Anumāna*, even though there may be, and indeed are, more than one regulative conditions of *Anumāna*. Yet each of them is a regulative condition, and their plurality is required to be accepted because relation between *Hetu* and *Pakṣa* as well as that between *Hetu* and *Sādhya* cannot be said to be regulated in a methodologically defensible way by the same regulative condition. Further, any of these regulative conditions, say *Vyāpti*, could be variously formulated—say, either the *Anvayī* way or the *Vyatirekī* way. Yet these different formulations boil down to the same regulative principle or rule. Hence, its different formulations are neither classificatory of it, nor have they anything to do with classification of *Anumāna*. Fourthly, any classification, including that of *Anumāna*, should not be consequential in the sense that it is done by looking to the consequence it gives rise to. Rather it should be sought to be accomplished by looking to the application of an appropriate *fundamentum divisionis* or methodologically appropriate principle of classification. Later on, we shall have an occasion to return to these points when we shall briefly consider the reasons as to why Dharmakīrti is not prepared to accept classification of *Anumāna* advocated by others. With these preliminaries we turn to Dharmakīrti's classification of *Anumāna* and bring out its rationale.

Classification of Anumāna

Whenever we classify, we are required to have an appropriate basis of classification, so that relying on it we would be able to classify without giving rise to confusion and error. In the case of *Anumāna*, it is classifiable into three kinds (*Tridhātva*) on the basis of the kind of classificatory characteristics or features *Hetu* has. Such classificatory features of *Hetu*, according to Dharmakīrti, are: (a) that *Hetu* may be of the same nature as *Sādhya* in terms of the coherently conceivable or of actuality, (b) that it may be of the nature of *Kārya* of the *Kāraṇa* which is *Sādhya*, and this sort of feature *Hetu* may again have either in terms of the coherently conceivable or of actuality, and (c) that *Hetu* may just not be obtained actually. Given these classificatory features, we get three principal kinds of *Anumāna*: *Svabhāvānumāna, Kāryānumāna* and *Anupalabdhi-anumāna*. Cognitively considered, when we know anything indirectly we may know it to be of the nature of something already known, or as a *Kāraṇa* of it or else find it absent because something else is absent. As one can see, these features of *Hetu* are exclusive in the sense that if *Hetu* is of the same nature as *Sādhya* then it cannot be its *Kārya*, and if it is a *Kārya* of it then it cannot be of the same nature as *Sādhya*. For, the view that *Kāryas* are of the same nature as their causes seems to go against both discreteness and change accepted by Buddhism. Likewise, a *Hetu* which does not obtain can neither be considered under *Svabhāva* nor *Kārya*, though coherent conceivability cannot be withdrawn from it. Of these three kinds of *Hetu*, the first two give us valid and/or sound arguments, while the third gives us only valid arguments.

Coming to *Anupalabdhi* first. Starting with *Anupalabdha* kind of *Hetu*, we cognise absence of something else indirectly. Such an absence of something may be cognised contextually or context-freely, though either way, knowability of such a thing cannot be ruled out in advance. *Anupalabdhi* cannot be equated with *Abhāva*.[30] For *Abhāva* is held to be a kind of real, while absence is not a thing.

Further, *Anupalabdhi* (non-obtainability) of a thing is instrumental to the determination of absence of something else, provided, of course, that their absences are connected with each other either through *Vyāpya-Vyāpaka-bhāva* (understood coherent conceivability-wise) or through empiricality. Accordingly, we get a number of varieties of *Anupalabdhi-Anumāna*,[31] into the detailed discussion of which we need not enter here. One thing, however, needs to be noted carefully: each of them remains *Hetu*-centric.

It is essential to note in this context that negative propositions depict *Anupalabdhi*, although *Anupalabdhi* does not determine negative propositions nor do negative propositions automatically imply *Anupalabdhi* of something.[32]

Similarly, *Svabhāvānumāna* and *Kāryānumāna* too, in which *Svabhāva*- and *Kārya-Hetu* are used, are classifiable in accordance with certain kind of classificatory features of *Hetu*.

Methodologically speaking, thus, *Hetu* alone remains at the centre of this classification of *Anumāna*, and, accordingly, classification of *Anumāna* also remains *Hetu*-centric in character. *Pakṣa* or *Sādhya* or *Pakṣadharmatā* or *Vyāpti* or any of their features cannot be methodologically warrantable basis of the classification of *Anumāna*.

With this background, it is important and interesting to consider briefly the classifications of *Anumāna* suggested by others and Dharmakīrti's reaction to them.

In the *Nyāya-sūtras* Gautamācārya has classified *Anumāna* into three categories, viz. *Pūrvavat*, *Śeṣavat* and *Sāmānyatodṛṣṭa*.[33] Unless we understand the meaning and the basis of such a classification it will not be proper to evaluate it. Vātsyāyana explains *Pūrvavat*[34] as that kind of *Anumāna* where we have a prior knowledge of effect on the basis of perception of its cause. On the other hand, *Śeṣavat*[35] means a posterior knowledge of cause derived from the perception of its effect. Whereas *Sāmānyatodṛṣṭa* could be taken in two senses: one, *Sāmānyataḥ dṛṣṭaḥ*, commonly seen. It means cognition of one thing on the basis of another or what is commonly seen; or second, *Sāmānyataḥ-adṛṣṭaḥ*, commonly unseen. That is, the knowledge of a thing which is not commonly seen. For example, observing affection, aversion and other qualities one can infer that there is a substance called soul. Vātsyāyana prefers the latter sense of *Sāmānyatodṛṣṭa*, whereas

Uddyotakara advocates the former.[36] Taking into account both the senses of it, the following points could be raised:

(i) Basically, the presupposition that seems to be behind this classification is that inference is nothing else but knowing things in the world through cause-effect relationship.[37] This itself is questionable for it does not take into account merely valid arguments or subsumptive inferences.

(ii) Inference need not be from perceived to unperceived,[38] as valid inferences are perfectly legitimate without the backing of perception.

(iii) The classification of *Anumāna* is based on the illustrations of it, and such a base is inappropriate. The basic objection is, however, that this classification does not have any uniform methodological principle backing it and hence, being arbitrary, it is unacceptable.

Another classification of *Anumāna* is attempted by Uddyotakara in his *Nyāya-Vārtika*. According to him, inference is *Liṅga-parāmarśa* aided by memory.[39] He classifies *Anumāna* into three kinds, viz. *Kevalānvayī*, *Kevala-vyatirekī* and *Anvaya-vyatirekī*.[40] He seems to have acknowledged the fact that inference is not based on cause-effect relationship but on *Liṅga-parāmarśa*. In such a *Liṅga-parāmarśa*, inferential knowledge is based on similarity or dissimilarity of *Udāharaṇa* with *Sādhya*, or positive or negative kind of *Vyāpti*.[41]

Without going into needless details, it may be observed against this classification that (a) it seems to employ more than one *fundamentam divisionis*; (b) it brings in points of extra-methodological significance like *Udāharaṇa* and elevates them to the status of methodologically significant points; (c) it takes different formulations of *Vyāpti* as its various kinds, without realising that through different formulations *Vyāptis* do not become many, and (d) it confuses between regulative condition of *Anumāna* and classificatory basis of it. As a result of this, none of them would be acceptable to Dharmakīrti as a proper classification of *Anumāna*.[42] It is a pity that in spite of Dharmakīrti's methodologically warranted objection to it, it continued to be accepted as appropriate classification of *Anumāna* not only in post-Dharmakīrti tradition of *Prācīna-Nyāya*[43] but also percolated it into *Navya-Nyāya*[44] and has impressed upon people that it is the only legitimate classification of *Anumāna*, especially since other classifications of it, though they come from Gautamācārya, were subsequently given up.

As contrasted with such attempts of classifying *Anumāna*, Dharmakīrti's classification seems to be presented more thoughtfully, on the basis of tenable methodological principle. It does not violate any of the major counts on which he objects to those classifications of *Anumāna* at the hands of his *Nyāya* adversaries. It also does not employ more than one *fundamentum divisionis* at a time. As any other consideration concerning *Anumāna* is *Hetu*-centric in character not only on the level of cognition of indirect knowledge or formulation of an argument but also on the level of their certification and/or communication, classification of *Anumāna*, too, likewise remains, in his view, *Hetu*-centric in character. Given this, we have so far inquired into every major aspect of *Anumāna* except one, viz. *Hetvābhāsas*, and have shown that in Dharmakīrti's consideration it remains basically *Hetu*-centric in character. It is to the consideration of *Hetvābhāsas* that we turn in the next chapter.

Notes and References

1. Arcaṭa; *H.B.T.*; pp. 3-7.
2. Dharmakīrti; *H.B.*; pp. 52-54. *Svārthānumāna-pariccheda*; pp. 1-2.
3. Diṅnāga; *Nyāya-mukha*; pp. 25-26, 42-43. Karṇakagomin; *P.V.T.*; p. 57. M.N. *Vṛtti*; p. 264.
4. Dharmakīrti; *N.B.*; (with *N.B.T.* of Dharmottara); pp. 21-23.
5. Dharmakīrti; *H.B.*; pp. 52-53. *P.V.*; III.1, IV.189, *Svārthānumāna-pariccheda*; pp. 1-2.
6. Arcaṭa; *H.B.T.*; pp. 219-228. Durveka Miśra; *H.B.T.A.*; pp. 406-410.
7. Arcaṭa; *H.B.T.*; pp. 8, 19, 22, 180-182. Dharmakīrti; *Svārthānumāna-pariccheda*; pp. 45-47.
8. Dharmakīrti; *P.V.*; III.84-86, 132-134. *Svārthānumāna-pariccheda*; pp. 28-29, 42-43. M.N. *Vṛtti*; pp. 286-287, 298-299. Karṇakagomin; *P.V.T.*; pp. 191-192, 260-265.
9. Dharmakīrti; *N.B.*; (also *N.B.T.* of Dharmottara); pp. 22-25. Durveka Miśra; *Dharmottara-pradīpa*; pp. 91-100.

10. Dharmakīrti; *N.B.* (also *N.B.T.* of Dharmottara); pp. 22-24. Durveka Miśra; *Dharmottara-pradīpa*; pp. 91-98. Arcaṭa; *H.B.T.*; pp. 68-69.
11. Dharmakīrti; *N.B.*; (also *N.B.T.* of Dharmottara); pp. 24-25. Durveka Miśra; *Dharmottara-pradīpa*; pp. 91-98. Arcaṭa; *H.B.T.*; pp. 68-69.
12. Dharmakīrti; *N.B.*; (also Dharmottara's *N.B.T.*); p. 25. Durveka Miśra; *Dharmottara-pradīpa*; p. 98.
13. Dharmakīrti; *P.V.*; III. 35-38, 185-219. *Svārthānumāna-pariccheda*; pp. 14-17, 61-73. M.N. *Vṛtti*; pp. 270-271, 314-324.
14. Dharmakīrti; *N.B.*; (also *N.B.T.* of Dharmottara); pp. 29-31. *P.V.*; II.97-99, III.197. M.N. *Vṛtti*; pp. 130-131.
15. Dharmakīrti; *H.B.*; pp. 53, 68. *Svārthānumāna-pariccheda*; p. 2- Arcaṭa; *H.B.T.*; pp. 17-19, 53-55.
16. Dharmakīrti; *N.B.*; (also *N.B.T.* of Dharmottara); pp. 28-32. Durveka Miśra; *Dharmottara-pradīpa*; pp. 108-116. Arcaṭa; *H.B.T.*; pp. 18-19, 39, 283.
17. Dharmakīrti; *P.V.*; III.2, 39, 283. *Svārthānumāna-pariccheda*; pp. 2-3, 15-16, 100, 116.
18. Dharmakīrti; *H.B.*; pp. 54-55. *N.B.*; (also *N.B.T.* of Dharmottara); pp. 29-31.
19. Arcaṭa; *H.B.T.*; pp. 18-19, 62, 74, 210-211. Karṇakagomin; *P.V.T.*; pp. 8-20, 107-109.
20. Dharmakīrti; *H.B.*; pp. 53-68. Arcaṭa; *H.B.T.*; pp. 9, 17-20, 50-56, 214-216.
21. Dharmakīrti; *H.B.*; pp. 55-63, 67. Arcaṭa; *H.B.T.*; pp. 6-9, 55, 76-79, 83. Durveka Miśra; *Dharmottara-pradīpa*; pp. 111-117, 129, 169.
22. Dharmakīrti; *H.B.*; pp. 63-64, 66-68. Arcata; *H.B.T.*; pp. 55, 88, 150-153. Durveka Miśra; *Dharmottara-pradīpa*; pp. 111-116, 169.
23. Dharmakīrti; *N.B.*; (also *N.B.T.* of Dharmottara) ; pp. 29-31. *P.V.*; II.71, 84, 98. III.2, 23, 31-32. IV. 11, 195-198, 208. *Vādanyāya*; pp. 6-19. M.N. *Vṛtti*; pp. 122, 127, 130, 259, 269, 367, 429-432. Arcaṭa; *H.B.T.*; pp. 6-20.
24. Arcaṭa; *H.B.T.*; pp. 150-166.
25. Dharmakīrti; *H.B.*; pp. 52-54, 70-72. *P.V.*; III. 267-268. *N.B.*; pp. *H.B.T.A.*; 91-94. Arcaṭa; *H.B.T.*; pp. 62-63, 70-78, 200-202. Durveka Miśra; pp. 408-409.
26. Dharmakīrti; *P.V.*; III. 27-32. *Svārthānumāna-pariccheda*; pp. 11-13, 76-89. Arcaṭa; *H.B.T.*; pp. 54, 70-75, 220-225.
27. Dharmakīrti; *H.B.*; p. 72. Arcaṭa; *H.B.T.*; pp. 69-95, 220-227. Dharmottara; *N.B.T.*; pp. 90-96.
28. Dharmakīrti; *H.B.*; pp. 54-55. *N.B.*, pp. 29-31.
29. Dharmakīrti; *H.B.*; pp. 54-68. *N.B.*; p. 25. *P.V.*; III. 1-2. *Vādanyāya*; pp. 6-7.
30. Dharmakīrti; *H.B.*; pp. 54, 64-68. Arcaṭa; *H.B.T.*; pp. 6-7, 50-55, 73-82, 145-149, 167-204.

31. Durveka Miśra; *Dharmottara-pradīpa*; pp. 100-106, 116-147.
32. Dharmakīrti; *H.B.*; pp. 64-72.
33. Gautama; *Nyāya-Sūtras*; I.i.5.
34. Vātsyāyana; *Nyāya-Bhāṣya*; I.i.5.
35. *Ibid*; I.i.5.
36. Uddyotakara; *Nyāya-Vārtika*; I.i.5.
37. *Ibid*; I.i.5.
38. Dharmakīrti; *H.B.*; p. 72. Arcaṭa; *H.B.T.*; pp. 6-10. Durveka Miśra; *H.B.T.A.*; pp. 382-403.
39. Uddyotakara; *Nyāya-Vārtika*; I.i.5.
40. *Ibid*; I.i.5.
41. Udayana; *Pariśuddhi*; I.i.5.
42. Dharmakīrti; *H.B.*; pp. 52-72. *Svārthānumāna-pariccheda*; p. 103.
43. For eg. in *Nyāya-vārtika-tātparya-ṭīkā* of Vācaspati Miśra, Udayana's *Pariśuddhi*, *Nyāya-Mañjarī* of Jayanta, *Nyāya-bhūṣaṇa* of Bhāsarvajña etc. one can find that they defend the classification of *Anumāna*, i.e. *Anvayī*, *Vyatirekī*, *Anvaya-vyatirekī*, advocated by Uddyotakara.
44. The same trend is followed by *Navya-Naiyāyikas* like Gaṅgeśopādhyāya and his followers like Gadādhara Bhaṭṭa, etc.

CHATPER VI

HETVĀBHĀSAS

In the preceding four chapters, we argued the major aspects of *Hetu*-centricity of *Anumāna* with regard to two important considerations concerning it, viz. its formulation and certification. In this chapter we hope, in the same way, to argue and show that fallacies incidental to certification of *Anumāna*, too, are *Hetu*-centric. *Prima facie*, one may say that if all the important considerations regarding *Anumāna*, viz. epistemic condition, structural conditions, regulative conditions, validity and/or soundness, classification etc. are *Hetu*-centric then violation of validity conditions, i.e. *Hetvābhāsas*, also cannot fail to be *Hetu*-centric. Although *prima facie* this may be the case, yet instead of presuming it to be so, it needs to be shown that it is so, and that this feature of them is backed by an appropriate methodological consideration. Likewise, if some considerations are tried to be smuggled in as *Hetvābhāsas* by somebody, they need to be shown to be indefensible on methodological grounds. It is to the consideration of this that the present chapter is devoted.

In the last chapter, we have seen that consideration of validity of *Anumāna* is more important than consideration of its soundness. For, viability of an *Anumāna* depends primarily upon its validity, and not on its soundness. An unsound argument may or need not be rejected, since, in spite of its being unsound, it may be valid and hence viable, although defect in it on account of unsoundness would have to be rectified. Validity depends upon *Trairūpya*,[1] whereas soundness is determined by *Svabhāva-pratibandha*.[2] And the conditions of validity and soundness being different, issues respectively connected with them must also be distinguished and tackled separately. Since, however, *Hetvābhāsas* are a direct consequence of the disregard of the conditions of validity,[3] and since they are given to us by *Trairūpya* of *Hetu*, in the consideration of *Hetvābhāsas* we shall have once again to look to *Trairūpya* of *Hetu*.[4] One thing, however, is certain. Neither in the consideration of validity nor in that of *Hetvābhāsas* are we required to look to anything else except the conditions that determine validity.

Given this general background, it is now possible to understand the meaning of '*Hetvābhāsa*.' By *Hetvābhāsa* we mean, normally, defect/s in *Hetu*.[5] When a man attempts to infer certain *Sādhya* with the help of certain defective *Hetu*, he is said to have recourse to *Hetvābhāsa*. Due to such an inappropriate use of *Hetu*, one, instead of cognising/proving the intended *Sādhya*, proves/cognises something else and does not succeed in proving the intended one and may prove as valid the very opposite of what he intended to prove.[6] But how does one select a faulty *Hetu* instead of a proper one? It is of course a mistake of the person who infers.[7] But a faulty *Hetu*, which gives rise to misunderstanding in him, is not fundamentally different from a proper one, for a faulty *Hetu* resembles a proper one in certain respects. It appears like a proper one, though, as a matter of fact, it is not. It is the superficial similarity between the two which causes the confusion.[8]

What is meant by *Hetu's* partial correctness and partial defectiveness? What it means is that a defective and a proper *Hetu* may resemble each other in certain respects, though not in every respect. Yet this kind of partial similarity of a defective *Hetu* with proper *Hetu* may lead one to confuse the two and employ a defective *Hetu* instead of a proper one to infer an intended *Sādhya* on its basis. Such a defective *Hetu* fulfils some conditions of a proper *Hetu*, though not all, and this is how a *Hetvābhāsa* arises.

Such a failure in locating defective *Hetu* and consequently using it instead of a correct one is not dependent upon the man who infers. Any person placed in that situation is likely to commit the same mistake. That is, *Hetvābhāsas* arise irrespective of the person concerned. But so, too, the place and time are not determinative of *Hetvābhāsa*. That is, the discussion and determination of *Hetvābhāsas* must be done context-freely,[9] according to Dharmakīrti. Whenever a *Hetu* fails to satisfy any one or two of the three conditions that determine validity, a *Hetvābhāsa* arises context-freely. The possibility of a defective *Hetu* not fulfilling all the three conditions of validity is ruled out, because in such a situation the defective *Hetu* will not appear like the proper one even superficially and, hence, will not fail to be detected as such and would not be employed in place of a correct one. The difference between a proper and an improper *Hetu* in such a case would be already apparent, and, given this, one would not deliberately employ such a defective *Hetu*.

According to Dharmakīrti, it seems, *Hetvābhāsas* could arise in case of *Svabhāvānumāna*, *Kāryānumāna* or *Anupalabdhi-anumāna* in the same way. For example, *Asiddha hetvābhāsa* may be located in *Anupalabdhi-anumāna* just as in *Svabhāvānumāna* or *Kāryānumāna*.[10] It is irrelevant which kind of *Anumāna* it is, for the classificatory conditions of *Anumāna* will not play any important role in marking the fallacy. Further, the important point to note relates to the condition/s of validity violated, the way it has been violated, the kind of *Hetvābhāsa* that emerges and the nature of the resultant *Hatvābhāsa*. Accordingly, the consideration as to the kind of *Anumāna* it arises in is irrelevant for the discussion and analysis of the nature of the concerned *Hetvābhāsa*. Moreover, such a mode of their explication is in accordance with the principle of economy and other appropriate methodological considerations.

Secondly, validity gives us the range of coherent possibility or conceivability, and soundness that of actuality, such that the latter is subsumable under the former. It is obvious that discussion of *Hetvābhāsas*, too, must be connected with the range of coherent possibility rather than that of actuality.[11] For consideration of viability of *Anumāna* is basic and primary. But the converse of this does not hold good. Hence, discussion of *Hetvābhāsas* on the level of actuality will not fetch greater dividends, as compared to that of coherent possibility. As in the case of every other aspect concerning *Anumāna*, Dharmakīrti shows deeper insight backed by appropriate methodological considerations, so too in the case of *Hetvābhāsas*. As a result, the discussion of *Hetvābhāsas* being connected with validity, its consideration marks the insightful understanding of the problem and yet it is simpler and clearer as compared with that at the hands of others.

Similarly, Dharmakīrti seems to be clear about the distinction between *Hetvābhāsas* and *Nigrahasthānas*.[12] *Hetvābhāsas*, he rightly points out, arise in the context of validity or invalidity of an argument,[13] whereas *Nigrahasthānas* arise in the context of *Vāda*, i.e. failure in justifying our own argument from *Vādī*'s side or failure in locating a defect in *Vādī*'s argument from *Prativādī*'s side.[14] In the case of the former, non-fulfilment of conditions of validity is responsible and in the latter the failure in persuading others is responsible. The former is the domain of logic, the latter is the domain of rhetorical epistemology. *Hetvābhāsas* could arise even if a single individual alone reasons, while the latter essentially requires and presupposes a social context.

In contrast to this, it is interesting and illuminating to see the *Nyāya* position. According to *Naiyāyikas*, *Hetvābhāsas*,[15] arise due to the failure in satisfying conditions of *Sat-hetu*, which are five, viz. *Pakṣa-sattva*, *Sapakṣa-sattva*, *Vipakṣāsattva*, *Abādhita-viṣayatva* and *Asat-pratipakṣatva*.[16] Since, unfortunately, they do not make any distinction between validity and soundness on the one hand and between logic and rhetoric on the other, naturally their treatment of *Hetvābhāsas* seems to be determined by extra-methodological considerations.[17]

Before we turn to Dharmakīrti's treatment of *Hetvābhāsas*, one point seems to be in order. From Dharmakīrti's point of view, one may argue that *Ātmāśraya*, *Anyonyāśraya*, *Anavasthā* etc. are not *Hetu-doṣas* and none of them in principle could be counted to be fallacious in the strict sense of the term. They are, however, sought to be avoided for considerations other than, and extraneous to, considerations of validity.

We have seen earlier that *Parokṣa jñāna* becomes possible principally because of *Hetu*. In the case of *Hetvābhāsa*, our inferential ambition is belied due to defects in *Hetu*. Hence, *Hetu* is the central consideration with regard to the resulting cognition—correct or faulty. Further, whenever we entertain *Anumāna*, it must be at least viable. And since validity is determinative of viability it becomes important. Any argument that fails to be valid must be formally defective and hence indicative of spoiling consideration of coherent conceivability itself, i.e. in such a case one fails to conceive coherently the inferred thing appropriately.[18] This does not mean actually locating the thing in the actual world. Rather, it means our inability to conceive coherently the sort of *Sādhya* that could be inferred from a defective *Hetu* or our inability to infer the intended one from a defective *Hetu*. For, in *Hetvābhāsa*-situation an appropriate *Hetu* comes to be unwittingly replaced by a defective one.

Any *Hetvābhāsa* arises due to violation or non-fulfilment of some or the other condition of validity that needs to be satisfied.[19] To point out the fallacy of such an argument in which *Hetvābhāsa* has arisen it is enough to point out what sort of inferentially disastrous consequence/s employment of a defective *Hetu* would lead to. Non-fulfilment of condition/s of validity itself turns out to be a mark of invalidity.[20] It needs, therefore, to be seen what consequences would arise if every condition of validity comes to be violated. This will also enable us to better appreciate the point that consideration of *Hetvābhāsa* also is *Hetu*-centric in character, as consideration of validity is.

According to Dharmakīrti, *Hetvābhāsa* arises when any of the conditions determining validity brought to our notice through *Trairūpya* of *Hetu* is violated singly or in combination.[21] We turn to a brief account of the three *Hetvābhāsas* accepted by him.

Coming first to *Asiddha*. When *Hetu* does not satisfy the condition of *Pakṣa-sattva*, *Asiddha Hetvābhāsa* arises.[22] The *Hetu* under consideration itself being doubtful, assurance of the very possibility of its being connected with the given *Pakṣa* itself does not seem to be forthcoming. In the absence of it, the possibility of *Sādhya* being connected with *Pakṣa* too becomes impossible to entertain. In other words, non-connectibility of the *Sādhya* with *Pakṣa*, due to non-connectibility of the *Hetu* with the given *Pakṣa*, is the cause of *Asiddha Hetvābhāsa*. In such a case *Avinābhāva* between such a *Hetu* and the intended *Sādhya* also is jeopardised and, in consequence, we are unable to infer the intended *Sādhya*.[23]

Since *Pakṣa-sattva* means an assurance concerning the possibility of connectibility of *Hetu* with *Pakṣa*, non-fulfilment of this condition implies that either this kind of assurance is impossible or else it is doubtful. In either case, however, inference of the intended *Sādhya* is jeopardised.

Dharmakīrti, it seems, classifies *Asiddha* into six varieties of it, viz. *Ubhayāsiddha*, *Prati-vādi-asiddha*, *Vādi-asiddha*, *Sandehāsiddha*, *Āśrayāsiddha* and lastly *Sarvagatāsiddha* in which he appears to be considerably under the influence of Diṅnāga. He explains and illustrates all of them very systematically. However, it is needless to go into their details, as he has not drawn any of their methodologically significant implications. Hence we leave them aside. What is important to notice, however, is that they jointly exhaust all the possible cases of *Asiddha Hetvābhāsa*—both contextual and context-free. Further, it needs to be emphasised that we are considering connectibility of *Hetu* in the coherently conceivable framework, and hence *Asiddha* is also dealt with on the plane of coherent conceivability.[24] It need not necessarily mean not getting actually the thing inferred, for it may be contingently present. To avoid confusion of contingent presence or absence with doubtful connectibility on the one hand and impossibility of connectibility on the other, he talks about coherent inconceivability of context-free connectibility of the *Hetu* with *Pakṣa*.[25]

In the pre-Dharmakīrti works, one finds some crude modes of considering *Asiddha Hetvābhāsa*. We propose to take a brief note of it. Diṅnāga, before Dharmakīrti, appears to talk about *Asiddha* in terms of *Adṛṣṭa*.[26] It may be due to his failure, as remarked earlier, to distinguish between validity and soundness and his advocacy of the view that *Dṛṣṭānta* is a constitutive condition of *Anumāna*. Due to this, the domain of coherent conceivability and actuality merge into each other. Hence, *Asiddha*, unfortunately, comes to be equated with *Adṛṣṭa*. Methodologically, it is incorrect on the part of Diṅnāga to do so. For, it marks confusion on his part, between actuality and coherent conceivability, and subscription to its implications.

On the other hand, *Naiyāyikas* and *Vaiśeṣikas*, too, understand *Asiddha* as absence of the intended *Sādhya* on the given *Pakṣa*.[27] Their analysis of the reasons which lead them to this sort of consequence is also equally ambiguous. For, in their view the *Sādhya* remains *Asiddha* either because *Hetu* is *Asiddha* or *Pakṣa* is *Asiddha*.[28] Thus understood, in their account emergence of *Asiddhatva* of *Hetu* does not necessarily revolve around defectiveness of *Hetu*. On this count, their account of *Asiddha* remains methodologically unsatisfactory. Uddyotakara, for instance does not define and explain *Hetvābhāsa*; he merely stipulates, with illustrations, different varieties of *Hetvābhāsas*[29]. But one could, through critical examination of those varieties, show that many of them overlap and that at least some of them are fictitious. However, here we need not do that exercise.

One may ask, however, why *Asiddha Hetvābhāsa* should be avoided. Its emergence in our thinking is held to be a methodological constraint in order to ward off inferences concerning fictitious or purely imaginary objects. This means that whatever we consider coherently conceivable should be serviceable (*Vyavahartavya*) in fact or in thought or in both. Conversely, we should not infer anything that fails to satisfy this demand.

Avoidance of *Viruddha*, another *Hetvābhāsa*, in our inference, on the contrary, is aimed at keeping it free from being infected with contradication and inconsistency (*Avisaṁvādakatva*). This could also, perhaps, be extended to consistency in our thought, action and modes of fellowship. But it is not our present concern. Therefore, we refrain from this kind of exercise.

Viruddha, Dharmakīrti understands, to be a *Heṭvābhāsa* which arises due to non-fulfilment of the conditions determining validity as *Sapakṣa-sattva* and *Asapakṣa-asattva*,[30] i.e. instead of having such characteristics as are conducive to the fulfilment of the conditions of *Sapakṣa-sattva* and *Asapakṣa-asattva*, the *Hetu* has such characteristics as are either contrary to them or are just their opposites. In the former case, we get *Anyabhāva-Hetu*, while in the latter we get *Bhāvavat-Hetu*. In both the cases. however, the *Sādhya* is connectible to *Asapakṣa* which it should not be and is inconnectible with *Sapakṣa* which also it should not be. That is why, such an inference is held to be unacceptable. If the *Hetu-dharma*, which should be connected with the *Dharma* of the intended *Sādhya* alone, is not so connected, and instead is connected with a *Sādhya* which is contrary to the intended *Sādhya* or is a contradiction of it then *Viruddha Hetvābhāsa* arises.[31]

Diṅnāga argues for *Viruddhāvyabhicārī* as a kind of *Viruddha Hetvābhāsa*,[32] which is, it seems, concerned with soundness rather than with validity of an argument. However, as pointed out earlier, *Hetvābhāsas* arise not because of unsoundness but because of invalidity. Hence, Dharmakīrti rejects *Viruddhāvyabhicārī-Hetvābhāsa* as a kind of *Viruddha*.[33]

Likewise, Dharmakīrti shows that *Viparyaya* or *Iṣṭavighātakṛta* accepted by some to be varieties of *Viruddha* are subsumable under the two earlier mentioned varieties of *Viruddha* and hence are dispensable.[34] Moreover, *Viparyaya* and *Iṣṭavighāta-kṛta* are said to arise not due to non-fulfilment of *Trairūpya* of *Hetu* but on account of our inferring *Sādhya-viruddha*. What is, further, meant by *Sādhya* here is not free from confusion, as very often the *Sādhya* of the principal argument is sought to be understood in the sense of *Pakṣa*. Thus, there is a confusion between *Sādhya* and *Pakṣa*.

Thirdly, coming to *Anaikāntika*. When *Sādhya* is not only connectible with *Pakṣa* or *Sapakṣa* but also with something else, though not with *Asapakṣa*, then *Anaikāntika* or *Savyabhicāra Hetvābhasa* arises.[35] In other words, *Sādhya* is connectible not only with that with which *Hetu* is connected but also that with which *Hetu* is not connected. Naturally, *Anaikāntika* is only of two kinds: (i) *Sādhāraṇa—Hetu* is connectible not only with *Sapakṣa* but also with *Asapakṣa* and (ii) *Asādhāraṇa—Hetu* is connectible with *Sapakṣa* as well as *Pakṣa*, with doubtful non-connectibility with *Asapakṣa* contextually as well as context-freely. But in either case the condition of *Asapakṣa-asattva* is not fulfilled and hence *Anaikāntika Hetvābhāsa* arises. What *Anaikāntika* implies is that we should not resort to arbitrariness and shifting of our stands in our reasoning and, thus, give rise to inconsistency.

Like *Asiddha* and *Viruddha*, Uddyotakara cites various examples of *Anaikāntika* and seeks to give the impression that these are the kinds of it. But illustrations themselves connot be differentiating criteria. Further, the kinds he distinguishes are overlapping, and indeed some of them are fictitious, not to talk of those which are subsumable under others. We, however, need not go into this question here.[36]

In the *Nyāya* school, nonetheless, we find a different class of *Anaikāntika* known as *Anupasaṁhārī* being consistently acknowledged. This kind of *Anupasaṁhārī Hetvābhāsa* arises, we are told, when one fails to cite an appropriate example in support of one's argument.

According to Buddhist philosophers in general and Dharmakīrti in particular, however, *Anupasaṁhārī* is not a different kind of *Anaikāntika* and hence need not be acknowledged. For, since *Dṛṣṭānta* or *Udāharaṇa* itself is subsumable under *Sapakṣa-sattva*, *Anupasaṁhārī* cannot methodologically be considered separately. He, first of all, refuses to accept *Dṛṣṭānta* or *Udāharaṇa* as a necessary constituent of *Anumāna*. For it serves no purpose—structural, regulative, validitatory or even of soundness. Hence, *Dṛṣṭānta* having no significant role to play, its not being cited cannot be considered to be determinative of *Hetvābhāsa*. Moreover, as in many cases, citing an example, although possible, may be dispensable; so, too, in some other cases it might not have been cited, as it cannot be—e.g. *Yat sat tat kṣaṇikam*/. Additionally, since empiricality is, according to Dharmakīrti, not a pre-condition of *Anumāna*, it is enough that we are able to entertain and certify an argument, and, therefore, to cite an example is a needless exercise.

As observed in the preceding chapter, according to *Naiyāyikas* a *Sad-hetu* needs to fulfil five conditions. Correspondingly, they acknowledge five *Hetvābhāsas*. Accordingly, in addition to the earlier mentioned three *Hetvābhāsas*, they also accept *Sat-pratipakṣa* and *Bādha* to be *Hetvābhāsas*.[37]

Before we turn to discuss them, some points need to be clarified, which are as follows:

(i) *Naiyāyikas*, before Dharmakīrti, did not analyse and explain the criteria of *Hetvābhāsas*, for they did not, it seems, think of the criteria on the basis of which an invalid argument may come to be shown to have emerged out of violation of some validating condition. It may be because of the lack of distinction between cognitive and certificatory epistemology or due to the commitment to *Pramāṇa-saṁplava*. Leaving it aside, for the present, it suffices to note that the definitions and formal criteria of *Hetvābhāsas* were not clear to them.

(ii) Further, the *Nyāya-vārtika* has not even defined or analysed the term '*Hetvābhāsa*', though it is classified on the basis of illustrations. Uddyotakara illustrates different varieties of *Asiddha*, *Viruddha* and *Anaikāntika*, and very casually tells us that they arise due to non-fulfilment of the conditions of *Pakṣa-sattva*, *Sapakṣa-sattva*, etc. In this he seems to be indebted to Diṅnāga. However, it seems that at least up to that time five conditions of *Sad-hetu* themselves were not formulated, leave alone their being used as a criterion of articulation of *Hetvābhāsas*. Though one comes across, for the first time in the

Nyāyamañjarī, these conditions and their analysis, they are not used appropriately even within the *Nyāya*-framework.

(iii) Uddyotakara tells us that there are 'n-number' of kinds of *Hetvābhāsas*; and although mentioning each of them is immaterial, he mentions only some of them as a sample. It is needless for our present purpose to touch upon every treatise in the pre- or post-Dharmakīrti *Nyāya* tradition.

(iv) The fourth and the fifth kinds of *Hetvābhāsas* are sometimes known, respectively, as *Prakaraṇasama*[38] and *Kālātīta*,[39] and sometimes as *Satpratipakṣa* and *Bādhita* or as *Sādhyasama* and *Atītakāla*. However the headings may differ, what they mean by them is the same. This is what we are told by later *Naiyāyikas*.

(v) *Satpratipakṣa* and *Bādhita* arise primarily in the context of *Vāda* because in *Vāda* we use *Anumāna* to justify our own position and criticise that of others. It is no wonder that while justifying our own position we should be in a strong position. Truth could be established in *Vāda*-context. For, it is acceptability or non-acceptability that is the mark of truth. If in *Vāda* our position is acceptable, we have succeeded in establishing truth. Hence, for establishment of truth *Vāda*-context becomes essential, and for acceptability strengthening of our argument becomes necessary. That's why fortification of our claim with the help of *Dṛṣṭānta* was considered important.

Given this, what is meant by *Satpratipakṣa*, needs to be seen. Since, *Asatpratipakṣatva*, as a mark of *Sat-hetu*, means absence, on the other side, of counter-balancing reason that could negate the *Sādhya*, its converse *Sat-pratipakṣatva* means availability of counter-balancing reason to the other side of the debate using which it refutes an argument advanced by their rivals. In such a case the party advancing the argument would lose its claim in face of a powerful counter-argument advanced by the other side. *Naiyāyikas* hold that not only for communication but also for formulation and certification of an argument debating-context and social-situation are essential conditions required to be satisfied.

On the other hand, Dharmakīrti seems to be methodologically right in making a distinction between formulating an argument and its communication. When we formulate an argument we do want to formulate it in such a way that it may not be invalidated. But to expect that it should not come to be so formulated that it might turn advantageous to someone else, or to expect that it should not force us to leave our commitments, like that of *Pramāṇa-saṁplava,* are extra-methodological demands made on formulation of an argument. Therefore, they are indefensible.[40] Even when we acknowledge plurality of *Pramāṇas*, it need not be acknowledged for the disclosure of the same feature/s of things. For, principle of economy demands that one *Pramāṇa* is enough to do that job. Likewise, if one person is enough to formulate an argument, it is needless to hold that there must be at least two, just because its communication is transitively sought to be understood. So too, secondly, one should not confuse between *Pakṣa* as a *Dharmī* and *Pakṣa* as a party in debate. Given these two important points, it is easy to see why *Asat-pratipakṣatva* and *Abādhitaviṣayatva* are not accepted as conditions determining validity of *Anumāna*, and, correspondingly, *Sat-pratīpakṣa* and *Bādhita* as *Hetvābhāsas.* Moreover, as seen earlier, subscription to *Avisaṁvādakatva* and *Avijñātārtha-prakāśakatva* as two general criteria of knowledge applicable to inferential knowledge as well, is a powerful enough device to keep off inconsistencies likely to crop up in our knowledge. If, on the contrary, *Abādha* is sought to be understood as a general criterion of knowledge then it remains difficult to understand why it should have been formulated in the context of *Anumāna* alone. On such methodological grounds, Dharmakīrti refuses to accept them to be *Hetvābhāsas.*

With this background in mind, let us, however, briefly explain what *Abādhita-viṣayatva* means, due to the non-fulfilment of which *Bādhita Hetvābhāsa* arises.

As *Abādhita-viṣayatva* means non-contradiction of the claim under consideration by another stronger claim, its violation implies that there arises a contradiction in the claim attempted to be established if it may be disproved on the basis of a stronger contradictory claim advanced on the basis of knowledge derived from the same mode or any other *Parmāṇa.* It means, our earlier knowledge-claim should not be contradicted by the information newly made available.

In this context, some of the major differences between the *Nyāya* and the Buddhist approach to *Hetvābhāsas* could briefly be taken into account. First of all, it needs to be understood that *Nyāya* conception of *Hetvābhāsa* is different from that of a Buddhist like Dharmakīrti. For, their conceptions of *Anumāna* themselves are different. Secondly, whereas Dharmakīrti seeks to consider *Hetvābhāsas* methodologically with reference to the conditions that determine validity, *Naiyāyikas* seem to confuse between methodological and extra-methodological considerations about it. Thirdly, *Naiyāyikas* hold that communicative situation is a necessary condition for the formulation of an argument, while for Dharmakīrti, those conditions which need to be necessarily satisfied for the formulation of arguments are the minimal conditions and a set of them does not and need not include social situation and debating-context. Fourthly, the *Nyāya* analysis of *Hetvābhāsas* is backed by their subscription to the doctrine of *Pramāṇa-saṁplava*, while in his treatment of them Dharmakīrti does not bring in his subscription to the doctrine of *Pramāṇa-viplava*. Fifthly, for *Naiyāyikas* the domains of validity and soundness are co-extensive and this conviction springs from their view that *Anumāna* needs to be backed by perceptual cognition, while for Dharmakīrti these two domains need to be distinguished. For, whereas the domain of validity is that of viability in thought, that of soundness has something to do with truth and so with actuality. All these and such other points in the *Nyāya*-Buddhist controversy are important and an inquiry into them would be fascinating. But this not being our present concern we leave them without going into further details.

From the above discussion of *Hetvābhāsas* at the hands of Dharmakīrti, it should be clear that his treatment of them is *Hetu*-centric. The methodological rationale by which it is guided is that of *Trairūpya* of *Hetu*. Since non-fulfilment of *Trairūpya* conditions is determinative of *Hetvābhāsa* and since *Trairūpya* as a condition determining validity is *Hetu*-centric, *Hetvābhāsas*, too, cannot fail to be *Hetu*-centric. Further, since any *Hetvābhāsa* arises out of violation of some condition/s of validity, it amounts to be dichotomously and oppositionally related with the context-free consideration of validity. The oppositional relation between *Hetvābhāsa* and validity is so decisive that any argument that gives rise to any *Hetvābhāsa* cannot be valid and hence viable. In his discussion of *Hetvābhāsas*, Dharmakīrti has consistently kept consideration of the methological aspect of the problem to be uppermost and has not allowed it to be adulterated by bringing in any extra-methodological consideration. This shows the depth of his insight as also clarity in his ideas.

Right from the second chapter we have seen that for Dharmakīrti, consideration of *Hetu* is the crux of all important issues concerned with *Anumāna*. Whether it is an issue of inquiring into epistemic, structural or regulative conditions of *Anumāna*, or of the consideration of validity and/or soundness aspects of it—inclusive of the discussion of *Hetvābhāsas* incidental to the violation of the conditions of validity—*Hetu* has remained, in one form or the other, central in the treatment of *Anumāna* at the hands of Dharmakīrti. He could be said to have worked out elaborately a consistent theory of *Hetu*-centrality of *Anumāna* and inquired into various implications of it. In this kind of treatment of *Anumāna*, some kind of methodological aspect of of the treatment of the problem has always remained decisive and he does not seem to have compromised with it on any ground, whatever be the dividends of such a compromise. Further, compared to the treatment of various aspects of *Anumāna* at the hands of his predecessors from both the camps of Buddhism and *Nyāya*, the clarity and profundity of understanding he evinces remains by far unmatched. Given this, he could be said to have pioneered and worked out the theory of *Hetu*-centrality of *Anumāna*, the salient features of which we have had an occasion to look into.

With the background of this discussion in our mind, we propose to investigate into some of the major implications of Dharmakīrti's theory of *Hetu*-centrality of *Anumāna* and see what modes of interconnection have shaped it. It is to this inquiry that we turn in the next i.e. the last chapter.

Notes and References

1. Dharmakīrti; *N.B.*; (also *N.B.T.* of Dharmottara); pp. 29-32. *Svārthānumāna-pariccheda*; pp. 1-3, 12-13. Arcaṭa; *H.B.T.*; pp. 6-11, 14-20, 23, 41, 220-228.
2. Dharmakīrti; *N.B.*; (also *N.B.T.* of Dharmottara); pp. 29-31. *H.B.*; pp. 71-72. Arcaṭa; *H.B.T.*; pp. 204-228.

3. Dharmakīrti; *N.B.*; (also *N.B.T.* of Dharmottara); pp. 67-85. *P.V.*; III.1, *Svārthānumāna-pariccheda*; pp. 1-3.
4. Arcaṭa; *H.B.T.*; pp. 6-11, 54-56, 204-228.
5. Dharmakīrti; *N.B.*; p. 67, *Vādanyāya*; pp. 64-68. *H.B.*; pp. 68-72. Arcaṭa; *H.B.T.*; pp. 6-16, 54-56, 85, 204-207.
6. Dharmakīrti; *P.V.*; III. 16-18. *Svārthānumāna-pariccheda*; pp. 7-13. M.N. *Vṛtti*; pp. 264-265. Karṇakagomin; *P.V.T.*; pp. 8, 57-63.
7. Dharmakīrti; *P.V.*; II. 58-61, III. 289-292, IV. 21-25. M.N. *Vṛtti*; pp. 119-120, 348-349, 370-372.
8. Durveka Miśra; *Dharmottara-pradīpa*; pp. 86-100, 188-239.
9. Dharmakīrti; *H.B.*; pp. 68-72. Arcaṭa; *H.B.T.*; pp. 6-11.
10. Arcaṭa; *H.B.T.*; pp. 8-11, 204-205. Prajñākara Gupta; *P.V.A.*; pp. 484-489.
11. Prajñākara Gupta; *P.V.A.*; pp. 508-511, 567-569, 577-580.
12. Dharmakīrti; *Vādanyāya*; (also Śāntarakṣita's *Vipañcitārthā*); pp. 4-6, 59-71, 129-136. Arcaṭa, *H.B.T.*; pp. 6-11, 204-205. Durveka Miśra; *Dharmottara-pradīpa*; pp. 222-224.
13. Chinchore, Mangala R.; *Vādanyāya: A Glimpse of Nyāya-Buddhist Controversy*;
14. Dharmakīrti; *Vādanyāya*; (also Śāntarakṣita's *Vipañcitārthā*); pp. 4-6.
15. Uddyotakara; *Nyāya-vārtika*; I.i.1.
16. Vācaspati Miśra; *Nyāya-vārtika-tātparya-ṭīkā*; I.i.5;I.ii.4-9. Jayanta; *Nyāya-mañjarī*; pp. 153-168.
17. Arcaṭa; *H.B.T.*; pp. 204-228.
18. Dharmakīrti; *N.B.*; (also *N.B.T.* of Dharmottara); p. 67. *H.B.*; pp. 68-72. Arcaṭa; *H.B.T.*; pp. 6-16, 54-56, 204-207.
19. Arcaṭa; *H.B.T.*; pp. 6-11, 204-205.
20. *Ibid*; 4-11, 203-211.
21. *Ibid*; 6-11; Durveka Miśra; *Dharmottara-pradīpa*; pp. 188-189.
22. Dharmakīrti; *N.B.*; (also *N.B.T.* of Dharmottara); p. 22. Durveka Miśra; *Dharmottara-pradīpa*; pp. 188-189.
23. Arcaṭa; *H.B.T.*; pp. 8, 10-11.
24. *Ibid*; pp. 204-228.
25. Dharmakīrti; *N.B.*; (also *N.B.T.* of Dharmottara); pp. 67-71. Durveka Miśra; *Dharmottara-pradīpa*; pp. 188-195.
26. Diṅnāga *Nyāya-mukha*; pp. 14-15. *Hetu-cakra-hamaru*; pp. 270-272.
27. The entire *Prācina-Nyāya* tradition of the *Sūtras*, the *Bhāṣya*, the *Vārtika*, the *Ṭīkā* and the *Pariśuddh* (*N.S.* I.ii.7) considers *Sādhya-sama* to be a variety of *Hetvābhāsa* instead of *Asiddha*. It is Jayanta, who for the first time, explains *Sādhya-sama* in terms of *Asiddha*. Vide *Nyāya Mañjarī* part II, pp. 162-167. In the *Navya-Nyāya* tradition the name *Asiddha* got precedence over *Sādhya-sama*, the latter no longer being noticeable in it.
28. Bhāsarvajña; *Nyāya-bhūṣaṇa*; pp. 309-313.
29. If one goes through Uddyotakara's *Nyāya-vārtika*, one finds that he

gives 16 examples under four heads and states that due to permutation and combination of them one can have 2032 varieties of *Hetvābhāsas*, and 'n number' of them are likely to arise due to the variation of person, place and time. And still, he maintains, they could be tackled under five principal heads.

30. Dharmakīrti; *N.B.*; (also *N.B.T.* of Dharmottara); pp. 73-79. Durveka Miśra; *Dharmottara-pradīpa*; pp. 198-213.
31. Arcaṭa; *H.B.T.*; pp. 44, 68, 75, 147-148, 204-220.
32. Diṅnāga; *Nyāya-mukha*; pp. 60-61.
33. Dharmakīrti; *N.B.*; pp. 79-80, 85-87. Arcaṭa; *H.B.T.*; pp. 215-220.
34. Durveka Miśra; *Dharmottara-pradīpa*; pp. 187-188, 211-213. M.N. *Vṛtti* on *P.V.*; pp. 363-391.
35. Dharmakīrti; *N.B.*; pp. 71-73, 80-85. Durveka Miśra; *Dharmottara-pradīpa*; pp. 195-198, 213-224.
36. Uddyotakara; *Nyāya-vārtika*; I.i.5, I.i.35, I.ii.4.
37. In the *Nyāya-sūtras* and the *Nyāya-bhāṣya* (I.ii.5-9), five *Hetvābhāsas* are enumerated and in the *Nyāya-vārtika* four reasons are mentioned due to which these five kinds of *Hetvābhāsas* arise. But, it is only after Dharmakīrti that five conditions of *Sad-hetu* and, corresponding to them, five kinds of *Hetvābhāsas* which arise due to their non-fulfilment are mentioned. However, neither Vācaspati nor Udayana discusses them critically. And even though Jayanta, for the first time undertakes such an exercise, he, too, attempts to interpret them in such a way that *Asiddha* could be fitted into *Sādhyasama* of the *Nyāya-sūtras*. This seems a dogmatic the tradition one subscribes to.
38. Gautama; *Nyāya-sūtras*; I.ii.7.
39. *Ibid*; I.ii.9.
40. Dharmakīrti; *H.B.*; pp. 66-72. Arcaṭa; *H.B.T.*; 6-11, 204-228.

CHAPTER VII

IMPLICATIONS OF HETU-CENTRICITY OF ANUMĀNA

In the preceding chapters we argued and presented, in broad outline, the different aspects of the theory of *Hetu*-centricity of *Anumāna* upheld by Dharmakīrti. We also pointed out that precedence given in it to methodological considerations of *Anumāna* does not water-down or annihilate *Hetu*-centricity of *Anumāna*. Rather, it reinforces and strengthens it. With regard to epistemic aspect of *Anumāna*, we saw, in fairly great details, that *Svārthānumāna* is an epistemological basis and foundation such that every major consideration concerning *Anumāna* must be available and discussed primarily with reference to it. For, except communication of an already formulated argument and problems incidental to it, *Parārthānumāna* brings forth no consideration concerning *Anumāna* which is novel and arises on its level for the first time. One may say, perhaps, that *Svārthānumāna* constitutes, as it were, an epistemic womb of the discussion of all the major aspects of *Anumāna*. Hence, we argued that, according to Dharmakīrti, *Parārthānumāna* is basically linguistic in character, while *Svārthānumāna* is epistemic in nature. It is by taking this aspect of it into account that we endeavoured to understand its nature and role as epistemic condition of *Anumāna*. Starting with this, on the background of a fairly detailed outline of the major contours and curvatures of the landmarks of Dharmakīrti's philosophy and its conceptual framework, we considered, with reference to every major aspect of *Anumāna*, how *Hetu*-centricity of it is at stake. Likewise, we endeavoured to show that this feature of the treatment of various aspects of *Anumāna*, at the hands of Dharmakīrti, remains a decisively significant feature and a strong and powerful thread unifying them all. Dharmakīrti could perhaps be said to be a Buddhist philosopher and logician *par excellence* in the sense that in the works of anyone else of his predecessors from the camp of *Nyāya* and Buddhism, *Anumāna* has hardly received such a comprehensive, varied, consistent and detailed treatment. His profound insight into the problem concerning *Anumāna* is revealed in his consideration of the nature and significance of *Vyāpti* and *Pakṣadharmatā* as regulative conditions of it, and *Pakṣa*, *Sādhya* and *Hetu* as its structural or constitutive conditions. We argued that all these aspects of *Anumāna* remain, in his thought, basically *Hetu*-centric in character.

With this background in mind, in the next two succeeding chapters we argued that not only in the consideration of validity and/or soundness of *Anumāna* but also of the *Hetvābhāsas* incidental to violation or disregard of the validating conditions of it, the major thrust and focus remain to be *Hetu*-centrality of *Anumāna*. Dharmakīrti has presented and delineated this point without sacrificing or diluting major methodological and intuitive constraints.

Given this, it could be held, it was argued, that in Dharmakīrti's treatment, *Anumāna* remains basically *Hetu*-centric in character and structure, function and implication with regard to every major aspect of it, and to disregard or ignore it would do considerable violence to our understanding of his treatment of *Anumāna*.

It would be a mistake to hold that all these various aspects of the *Hetu*-centrality of *Anumāna* at his hands have been presented in a single treatise of his, comprehensive or otherwise. Some of the treatises he wrote are comprehensive, others are devoted to a specialised treatment of a particular theme. Whereas his *Pramāṇa-vārtika* is a treatise of the the first kind, his other works like *Hetu-bindu*, *Vādanyāya*, *Saṁbandhaparīkṣā* are of the second kind. It would further be a mistake to hold that it is the same aspect of *Anumāna* which has been treated in various treatises of his, for in that case they would lapse into pointless duplication and mechanical repetition.

In such works as *Hetu-bindu*, *Santānāntarasiddhi*, etc., he has selected a particular topic or theme of seminal interest for specialised treatment. For instance, a comparatively small work, *Hetu-bindu*, though favoured by two extensive commentaries respectively by Arcaṭa and Durveka Miśra, is given to the presentation of his own theory of *Anumāna*. Elsewhere, it forms a part of his exposition, often in outline, of his philosophical position in *Pramāṇa-vārtika*, or of his thought in *Vādanyāya*. In all these works, at least with reference to his treatment of *Anumāna*, he seems to be interested in one central theme concerning it, viz. *Hetu*-centrality of *Anumāna* in its various aspects—generically or distributively. We argued for, and presented in fairly detailed outline, the various aspects of this kind of treatment of *Anumāna* at his hands. We also considered the cognitive and certificatory aspects of them and explicated the rationale of his treatment of particular aspects of it.

The remarkable consistency with which he has presented and worked out the theory of *Hetu*-centrality has certain implications of seminal significance. It is the object of this chapter to study them in outline. Such implications, we feel, need to be considered on four main levels: (a) General, (b) Methodological, (c) Epistemological, and (d) those which are important from the point of view of Buddhist Philosophy. We proceed to consider them in the same order.

I. General Implications

(a) *Unifying Focus and Perspective*: Dharmakīrti's theory of *Anumāna* has a unifying focus and perspective. The *Hetu*-centricity of *Anumāna* is allowed to emerge right from its conception and, both in its generic and aspectival consideration of its nature, it is never allowed to be ignored or diluted. Such a unifying focus concerning its treatment is exhibited in his various treatises, full length or short, major or minor.

(b) *Independence and Freedom from Dogma*: Such a treatment of *Anumāna*, further, is given with remarkable independence not only from influence of his predecessors from the Buddhist camp but also from that of *Nyāya*. Further still, especially since the theory under consideration is not worked out through modifications of theories of his predecessors in the Buddhist camp, it is free from dogma and philosophical fanaticism. In the *Prācīna-Nyāya* tradition, on the contrary, various aspects of its theory of *Anumāna* are not worked out by a single author, but rather through an elaborate process of refinement of the treatment of it at the hands of a predecessor. This has again been done in face of a challenge of Buddhist adversaries and with a single purpose of defending the *Nyāya* at any cost against the attacks of philosophical adversaries. The freedom from dogma enables Dharmakīrti to work out his theory of *Anumāna* in such a way that it is equidistant from both the Buddhist and the *Nyāya* camps. This has been frankly acknowledged by one of his commentators.[1] This sort of independence enables him to work out various aspects of the theory with sufficient clarity without pouring abuses on any of his predecessors.

(c) *Its Formulation within the Framework of the Regulative Conditions of Knowledge in General*—The theory under consideration has been worked out and elaborated in its various aspects within the framework and on the background of regulative conditions of knowledge in general, viz. *Avisaṁvādakatva, Avijñātārthaprakāśakatva* and *Vyavahartavyatva.* Treatment of no aspect of the theory is allowed to transgress the dictates of any regulative conditions of knowledge in general. And since *Anumāna* is the domain of *Parokṣa jñāna* its consideration, too, cannot disregard them or allow them to be sacrificed for some topically attractive suggestion. It is such features of regulative conditions of knowledge in general and their seminal importance in epistemic enterprise in particular that make him draw repeatedly upon them to ensure that the treatment of any aspect of *Anumāna* at his hands has not disregarded any of the above mentioned conditions of knowledge.

Having outlined general implications of Dharmakīrti's theory of *Hetu*-centrality of *Anumāna* we proceed in the next section to study its methodological implications.

II. Methodological Implications

Anumāna gives us inferential cognition and makes mode of its certification available. This is the domain of *Parokṣa jñāna.* Nonetheless, *Parokṣa jñāna* does not become available except through *Anumāna*—according to Dharmakīrti. Accordingly, the framework of *Parokṣa jñāna* would be determined by that of *Anumāna,* and the latter needs to be articulated within the jurisdiction of, and in accordance with, certain important methodological considerations which cannot be either ignored or violated without paving a way for serious consequences to the theory and its acceptability. The framework of the theory of *Hetu*-centrality of *Anumāna* which Dharmakīrti establishes in the *Hetu-bindu*,[2] seems to be determined by three methodologically significant considerations:

(i) *The Doctrine of Priority and Precedence*—Those considerations which need to be given priority and precedence over others have to be acknowledged to be so if our articulation and elaboration of the framework is not to turn out to be arbitrary and indefensible. Accordingly, cognitive epistemology is prior to justificatory one, or regulative conditions are prior to structural conditions, or structural aspects are prior to functional aspects, as being is prior to knowing, etc.

(ii) *Superiority of Explanation*—Distinctions with greater explanatory power cannot be allowed to be sacrificed for whatever other considerations. For example, such distinctions as those between context-free and contextual considerations, between validity and soundness of an argument and, correspondingly, between formal and material aspects of *Anumāna*, between necessary and sufficient conditions of something, between coherent possibility and actuality, etc. have to be carefully drawn and maintained. For, their being ignored and disregarded is more likely to bring in greater confusion and error.

(iii) *The Principle of Economy*—Whenever we can accomplish the same task with less number of entities, concepts, constituents, determinants, etc. at our disposal, it is needless and indefensible to have more of them.

In accordance with such methodologically strong considerations, Dharmakīrti proceeds to work out and articulate his theory of *Anumāna*. In the process, the whole exercise has given rise to certain important methodological implications, without taking which into account one would fail to comprehend its methodological relevance. We take a note of some of them in the sequel.

(a) It is on the basis of such methodologically important considerations that Dharmakīrti not only made careful distinctions among epistemic, structural and regulative conditions of *Anumāna* but also explained the range of their respective applications. This saved him from confusing *Trairūpya* with *Tridhātva*

(*Triprakārakatva*) of *Hetu*,[3] conducive, respectively, to the consideration of validity and classification of *Anumāna*.

(b) Secondly, since methodological considerations enjoy priority and precedence over extra-methodological ones, and since the distinction between methodological and extra-methodological considerations is in order, he never allows this distinction to be ignored or the boundaries of the demarcation of the applicability of their respective domains to be blurred.

(c) It is rationality and reasonableness along with methodological defensibility of anything rather than pragmatic purposiveness and priority of convenience that seems to weigh with him heavily. This, again, seems to be backed by methodological considerations. It is on such a ground that he rejects the view of *Nyāya* that there are five constitutive[4] or structural conditions of *Anumāna* or that classification of it springs from that of *Vyāpti* on the one hand,[5] as also the suggestion from Diṅnāga that structural constituents of *Svārthānumāna* and *Parārthānumāna* should be acknowledged to be different, on the other.

(d) Such methodological considerations enabled him to distinguish between his concerns with theory of *Anumāna*, *Parokṣa jñāna* as one important kind of knowledge and Buddha's philosophy and its significance which he wanted to explain. But, on the other hand, they also enabled him to relate and connect them with one another in such a way that no major consideration concerning the first two could be said to be exclusively and solely springing from and determined by the third and yet its treatment would be significantly important with reference to it.

(e) As the necessary and sufficient conditions of our being able to fashion and formulate an *Anumāna* have to be clearly articulated, so too those of its certification. Further, necessary and sufficient conditions of communication of *Anumāna*, too, would have to be formulated. But care will have to be taken that we do not mix them up, although inferential cognition must be communicable in principle. Further still, various contexts in which we employ arguments—say of debate, controversy etc.—and their rationale need to be explored into independently of the first two kinds of inquiries, and, conversely, those enquiries, too, should he explored independently of these contexts.

Having looked into some of the important methodological

implications of Dharmakīrti's theory of *Hetu*-centrality of *Anumāna*, we proceed to outline briefly some of its epistemological implications in the next section.

III. Epistemological Implications

Since, in Dharmakīrti's view, there are two domains of knowledge—direct and indirect—corresponding, respectively, to two important kinds of knowables—*Svalakṣaṇa* and *Sāmānya-lakṣaṇa*—enough care should be taken to ensure that we do not mix up or confuse the two. Likewise, insofar as the distinction between cognition and certification of knowledge or that between cognition and communication of indirect knowledge or inferential cognition is in order, we should ensure that their respective determinative conditions are spelt out in such a way that those of the former do not automatically turn out to be those of the latter. Otherwise, the very rationale and purpose of making such distinctions would be lost sight of and that would engender confusion and error. Although, further, the domains of two respective sorts of knowledges are different, in our analysis we should not disregard any of the regulative conditions of knowledge in general. For, otherwise, it would cease to be knowledge proper and hence would not be acceptable.

On the basis of these preliminary remarks, we give below some important epistemological implications of Dharmakīrti's theory of *Hetu*-centricity of *Anumāna*.

(a) Since *Anumāna* is the only mode of indirect cognition or cognition of *Sāmānya-lakṣaṇa*, and since the former is *Hetu*-centric in nature, it follows that the latter too should be so.

(b) Although the domains and modes of perceptual and inferential cognitions are different, possibility of the convergence of the resultant cognitions on the same object should not be ruled out in advance. Otherwise, that would mean undue compartmentalization of knowledge. Further, implication of this would be taken into account when we come to explore the implications of the theory of *Hetu*-centrality of *Anumāna* with special reference to Buddhism or, better still, Buddha's philosophy, explication of which is one of the major concerns in Dharmakīrti's philosophy.

(c) The conditions of occurrence of indirect cognition and those of its communication need to be demarcated in such a way that they do not come to get mixed up. It is these which are sought to be correlated, respectively, with those of *Svārthānumāna* and *Parārthānumāna* and preserve their bearing on *Hetu*-centricity of *Anumāna*. Conversely, *Hetu*-centricity of *Anumāna* has its bearings on these conditions especially because, as stated above, *Anumāna* is the only mode of having indirect cognition. If not understood in this way, the very distinction between *Svārthānumāna* and *Parārthānumāna* would cease to make any sense, epistemologically as well as methodologically.

(d) In our analysis of knowledge—direct as well as indirect—we should not dogmatically follow common sense, nor should we refuse, likewise, to give any credence to it. However, a philosopher or an epistemologist has a right to differ from common sense, although such a departure from it may turn out to be counter-intuitive, provided, of course, it remains defensible at least on methodologically warrantable grounds. Thus understood, methodological considerations have their bearing on epistemological considerations as well.

(e) Minimal and maximal conditions of viability of indirect cognition need carefully to be distinguished and demarcated in order that we do not mix up context-free viability with contextual viability. This, as one can understand, has a bearing upon the distinction between validity and soundness of an argument.

Having looked into some of the important epistemological implications of Dharmakīrti's theory of *Hetu*-centrality of *Anumāna*, we proceed, in the next section, to study its prominent implications with reference to interpretation of Buddha's Philosophy in its various aspects. For, this has remained one of his main concerns in all his philosophical inquiry. Accordingly, the theory of *Hetu*-centrality of *Anumāna* which he puts forth should also have some bearing on that aspect of his philosophy. We give below some implications of his above-mentioned theory from this perspective.

IV. Buddha's Philosophy

(a) To begin with, the Buddha is said to have explored two sorts of truths: *Paramārtha-sat* and (*Loka*) *Saṁvṛti-sat*, and the respective objects of *Pratyakṣa* and *Anumāna*, viz. *Svalakṣaṇa* and *Sāmānya-lakṣaṇa*, are said to be correspondingly connected with them. Accordingly, Dharmakīrti's *Hetu*-centric theory of *Anumāna* and an indirect cognition it makes available could be said to be a *Hetu*-centric theory of (*Loka*) *Saṁvṛti-sat*. If *Puruṣārthasiddhi* in our life could be said to be its major goal,[6] as Dharmakīrti acknowledges it to be, and if indirect cognition has any bearing upon it, then his theory of *Anumāna* as an enquiry into indirect knowledge too has to have bearing upon it.

(b) Now, these two truths may be understood in two different ways: (i) As truths pertaining to two different sorts of objects, in which case they would not be connected. Accordingly, they would remain compartmentalised and segregated. This view seems to have been favoured by Diṅnāga. Or (ii) they could be held to be two modes of comprehension of the features which objects have, given that objects may have sharable and/or non-sharable features. Dharmakīrti seems to favour this alternative. Accordingly, the possibility of convergence of direct and indirect cognitions on the same object, instead of being ruled out in advance, would have to be kept open. Dharmakīrti's theory of *Hetu*-centrality of *Anumāna*, which leaves such a possibility open, therefore, has a bearing on this aspect of his philosophy.

(c) We have seen that Dharmakīrti accepts *Avijñātārthaprakāśakatva* to be a regulative condition of knowledge in general. Hence it is applicable both to perceptual and inferential cognitions alike. Given this, hitherto undiscovered and unavailable aspects of the interpretation of *Paramārtha-sat* and *Lokasaṁvṛti-sat* may continue to be available, older ones may get refuted or rebutted and this sort of exploration into interpretation of Buddha's Philosophy may go on. However, no interpretation of them could be said to be final, indefeasible, uncontestable and irrevocable. Since the above mentioned criterion of knowledge is regulatively applicable to inferential cognition, since Dharmakīrti's theory of *Hetu*-centrality of *Anumāna* is a theory concerning such a cognition, and since such a cognition is an exploration into *Lokasaṁvṛti-sat*, the possibility, through the theory under consideration, of growth of knowledge with regard to such a truth at least seems to be accepted in principle. That is why, perhaps, he feels no compunction in differing from his predecessors and even in rejecting some of their views, whatever high esteem and regard he holds for them.

(d) Through *Avisaṁvādakatva*, as a regulative criterion of acceptability of knowledge applicable to inferential cognition, and through *Hetu*-centricity of *Anumāna* as a theory concerning it, he not only seems to demand consistency between perceptual and inferential cognitions, in spite of their convergence upon the same object, but also between three principal aspects of our life—thought, action and fellowship—on which the Buddha is said to have laid a great emphasis.

(e) Through the distinction between *Svabhāvānumāna* and *Kāryānumāna* he seems to have articulated, through his theory of *Hetu*-centrality of *Anumāna*, the need to make a distinction between being and becoming on the one hand, and continuity and change on the other. It goes without saying that these distinctions have an important role to play not only in the Philosophy of the Buddha but also in Dharmakīrti's interpretation of it.

(f) Lastly, through refusing to give credence to the consequential and purposive classification of *Anumāna* and through preferring instead a methodologically oriented classification, he seems to insist upon making a marked distinction between *Sakāraṇatā* and *Sahetukatā*. For, the Buddha warned people repeatedly not to confuse between the two, perhaps because it amounts to confusion between two sorts of truths, two sorts of orientations—cosmocentric and anthropocentric—, and also because it amounts to confusion between two principal modes of cognition available to us, viz. *Pratyakṣa* and *Anumāna*. Through his theory of *Hetu*-centrality of *Anumāna* Dharmakīrti seems to draw our attention to it in bolder relief.

So far we have outlined some of the prominent implications of Dharmakīrti's theory of *Hetu*-centrality of *Anumāna*. We cannot go into detailed investigation of them here, for our principal concern here has been to outline Dharmakīrti's theory of *Hetu*-centrality of *Anumāna* in its important aspects and show interconnections among them. Side by side, we also thought it proper to highlight some of its prominent implications.

Having accomplished our major task, we leave further exploration into any problem discussed above, or into those which seem to originate from it as its consequence, to some future consideration, either at our hands or of someone else. The question of judgement concerning the worth of the exercise we have done we leave humbly to the judicious discretion and expertise of the knowledgeable persons.

Notes and References

1. Prajñākara Gupta; *P.V.A.*; p. 648.
2. Arcaṭa; *H.B.T.*; pp. 10-11.
3. Dharmakīrti; *P.V.*; III.1, *Svārthānumāna-pariccheda*; pp. 1-7. M.N. *Vṛtti*; p. 257. Arcaṭa; *H.B.T.*; pp. 204-205.
4. Arcaṭa; *H.B.T.*; pp. 62-72. Durveka Miśra; *H.B.T.A.*; pp. 314-324.
5. Dharmakīrti; *H.B.*; p. 72. Durveka Miśra; *Dharmottara-pradīpa*; pp. 96-97, 168-170.
6. Arcaṭa; *H.B.T.*; p. 3. Dharmakīrti; *N.B.*; (also *N.B.T.* of Dharmottara) pp. 1-6.

BIBLIOGRAPHY

Anacker, Stefan, (ed.); *Seven Works of Vasubandhu*; Motilal Banarsidass, Delhi, 1984.

Annambhatta; *Tarka-Saṁgraha*; (with auto-commentary *Tarka-Dīpikā* and Govardhana's *Nyāya-Bodhinī*); Athalye and Bodas (eds.); Bhandarkar Oriental Research Institute; Poona, 1974.

Atreya, B.L.; *The Elements of Indian Logic*; Nalanda Pub. Dhannur, Sir P.M. Mehta Road, Bombay, (3rd ed.), 1948.

Aung, Shwe, Zam and Davids (Mrs.) Rhys; *Points of Controversy and Subject of Discourse*; Pali Text Society Publications, Humphrey Milford, 1915.

Bagchi, Sitansusekhar; *Inductive Reasoning: A Study of Tarka and its Role in Indian Logic*; Shree Munishchandra Publications; Oriental Press, Calcutta, 1953.

Bandopadhyaya, M.; *The Concept of Logical Fallacies*; Sanskrit Pustak Bhandar; Calcutta, 1977.

———"The Buddhist Theory of Relation Between *Pramā* and *Pramāṇa*"; *Journal of Indian Philosophy*; Vol. 7, No. 1, March 1979, pp. 43-78.

Banerjee, A.C.; *Sarvāstivāda-Literature*; Calcutta Oriental Press, Calcutta, 1957.

Bapat, Lata, S.; *Dharmakīrti's Philosophy: A Fresh Study*; a Ph.D. Thesis; University of Poona; 1984, (unpublished).

Bapat, P.V. (ed.); 2500 *Years of Buddhism*; Director, Publications Division, Ministry of Information and Broadcasting, Govt. of India, Delhi, 1976, (4th ed.).

Barlingay, S.S.; The Significance of *Pratītya-Samutpāda, Sāmānya-lakṣaṇa* and *Apoha* in Buddhism"; Buddha Jayanti Lecture, Indian Philosophical Congress, XLV Session, Dec. 1971, Osmania University, Hyderabad.

———*A Modern Introduction to Indian Logic*; National Publishing House; Delhi, 1976, (2nd ed.).

———*Beliefs, Reasons and Reflections*; Indian Philosophical Quarterly Publications; Poona; 1983.

Basu, Sarnath; "Some Consideration on *Nyāya-Vaiśeṣika* Ontology"; *The Visva-Bharati Journal of Philosophy*, Vo. 8, No. 1, Aug. 1971, pp. 31-34.

Bhaduri, Sadananda; *Studies in Nyāya-Vaiśesika Metaphysics*; Bhandarkar Oriental Research Institute, Poona, 1975.

Bharadwaj, V.K.; "*Tarka* and Implications"; *Indian Philosophical Quarterly*; Vol. 5, No. 1, Oct. 1977; pp. 91-103.

Bhāsarvajña; *Nyāyasāra* with *Nyāya-Bhūṣaṇa*; Swami, Yogindrananda; (ed.); Ṣaḍ-darshana Pratiṣṭhāna; Varanasi; 1968.

Bhate, G.C.; "Indian Logic"; *The Indian Philosophical Review*; Vol. 2, 1918-19, pp. 3-16.

Bhatt, S.R.; "On the Validity of Inferential Knowledge in Indian Philosophy"; *Indian Philosophical Quarterly*; Vol. X, No. 3; April 1983; pp. 323-327.

Bhattacarya, Tara Sankar; "The Five Provisional Definitions of *Vyāpti* (*Vyāpti*-pañcaka) in Gaṅgeśa"; *Journal of the Ganganath Jka Research Institute*, Vol. III No. 1-3, 1945-1946, pp. 67-88, 169-188, 315-348.

Bhattacharya, Gopika Mohan; "The Concept of *Pakṣatā* in *Navya-Nyāya*", Carudev Shastri Felicitation Volume; Delhi; 1974; pp. 337-343.

Bhattacharya, V.; "Evolution of *Vijñānavāda*"; *Indian Historical Quarterly*; Vol. 10, 1934.

Bodas, Mahadev Rajaram; "A Historical Survey of Indian Logic"; *The Journal of the Royal Asiatic Society* (Bombay Branch); Vol. XIX, No. LIII; 1897; pp. 306-347.

Chakraborty, Krishna; "Definition of *Vyāpti* (pervasion) in *Navya-Nyāya*: A Critical Survey"; *Journal of Indian Philosophy*; Vol. 5, No. 3; Jan. 1976, pp. 209-236.

———"Determination of Universal Concomitance (with special reference to Gaṅgeśa's *Vyāptigrahopāya* in *Tattvacintāmaṇi*); *Journal of Indian Philosophy*; Vol. 5, No. 4, Aug. 1978; pp. 291-310.

———"The *Nyāya* Concept of *Svābhāvika Saṁbandha*: A Historical Report"; *Journal of Indian Philosophy*; Vol. 5, No. 4; Aug. 1978; pp. 385-392.

Chakravartti, Vanamali; "The *Pramāṇas* of Hindu Logic"; *Journal of the Royal Asiatic Society*, London; Vol. 80; 1928; pp. 377-390.

Charpentier, Jarl; "On The Fragments From Diṅnāga"; *Journal of Royal Asiatic Society*; London; Vol. 80; 1928; pp. 377-390.

Chatterjee, A.K.; "Introduction to Yogācāra School"; *Maha Bodhi*; Vol. 64, 1956, pp. 11-14.

———"Logic and Ontology"; *The Visva-Bharati Journal of Philosophy*; Vol. 8, No. 1, August 1971, pp. 7-13.

———*The Yogācāra Idealism*; Motilal Banarsidass, Varanasi; (2nd ed.), 1975.

Chatterjee, S.C.; "The *Nyāya* Doctrine of *Pramāṇa*"; *Journal of the Department of Letters*; University of Calcutta; Vol. XVI; 1927, pp. 1-62.

———"The Theory of *Pakṣatā* in Indian Logic"; *The Philosophical Quarterly*; Vol. 14 No. 1, April, 1938; pp. 52-59.

———"The Theory of *Pakṣatā* in Indian Logic"; *The Calcutta Review*; Vol. 66, No. 3, March, 1938, pp. 287-292.

Chatterji, Durgacharana; "*Hetucakranirṇaya*"; *Indian Historical Quarterly*; Vol. 9; 1933, pp. 266-272.

———"Sources of Buddhist Logic (From the Traditional Point of View)"; *Indian Historical Quarterly*; Vol. 9; 1933; pp. 499-502.

———"The Doctrine of *Trirūpa-Hetu*"; *Indian Historical Quarterly*; Vol. 9; 1933; pp. 503-510.

———"Sources of Knowledge in Buddhist Logic"; *Indian Culture* (Calcutta); Vol. 1, No. 2, Oct. 1934, pp. 263-274.

———"*Hetucakranirṇaya* (*Hetucakrahamaru*)"; (Translation into English); *Indian Historical Quarterly*; Vol. 9, 1933; pp. 511-514.

Chattopadhyaya, D.P. and Gangopadhyaya, M.K.; *Nyāya-Philosophy*; (Gautama's *Nyāya-Sūtras* and Vātsyāyana's *Bhāṣya*); (ed. and trans. into English); Part I & II; Indian Studies, Past & Present; Calcutta; 1968.

Chi, Richard, S.Y.; "Topics on Being and Logical Reasoning", *Philosophy East-West*; Vol. 24, No. 1-4; 1974; pp. 293-300.

———*Buddhist Formal Logic* (A Study of Dinnāga's *Hetucakra* and K'uei-chi's Great Commentary on the *Nyāya-praveśa*); Motilal Banarsidass; Delhi; 1984.

Chinchore, Mangala R.; *Vādanyāya: A Glimpse of Nyāya-Buddhist Controversy*; Sri Sadguru Publications, Delhi, 1988.

——"Some Epistemological and Social Implications of *Kṣaṇikatā*"; *Annals of the Bhandarkar Oriental Research Institute*, Poona, LXVII; (1986); pp. 57-76.

——"Some Thoughts on Significant Contribution of Buddhist Logicians"; *Journal of Indian Philosophy*, Oxford; Vol. 15 No. 2, June 1987; pp. 155-171.

Croce, Benedetto; "On Indian Logic", *East and West* (Roma); Vol. 4, 1953; pp. 1-30.

Das, Rasvihary; "Relations in Modern Indian Logic"; *The Calcutta Review*; Vol. 45, No. 2, Nov. 1932; pp. 143-160.

Dasgupta, S.N.; *A History of Indian Philosophy*, 5 Vols., Cambridge University Press; Cambridge, 1951.

Dharmakīrti; *Hetu-bindu*; (with *Ṭīkā* by Arcaṭa and *Āloka* by Durveka Miśra); Sanghavi, Sukhalalji, and Jinavinayaji, (eds.); Gaekwad's Oriental Series, No. CXIII; Oriental Institute, Baroda; 1949.

——*Nyāya-bindu*, (with Dharmottara's *ṭikā*) Shastri; Acharya, Chandrasekhara, (ed.); Chowkhamba (The Chowkhamba Sanskrit Series, No. 22), Banaras, 1954.

——*Pramāṇa-vārtika*; (with Manorathanandi's *Vṛtti*). Shastri, Swami Dwarikadas, (ed.) Bauddha Bharati, Varanasi, 1968.

——*Vādanyāya* (with Śāntarakṣita's *Vipañcitārthā*); Sānkṛtyāyana, Rahula (ed.); Appendix to *Journal of Bihar and Orissa Research Society*, Vols. XXI-XXII, 1949.

——*Santānāntarasiddhi*; Kitagawa, Hidenori (tr.); *Journal of Greater India Society*; Calcutta; Vol. XIV, No. 1 & 2 (1955), pp. 407-429.

——*Vāda-nyāya*; (with Śāntarakṣita's *Vipañcitārthā* and *Saṁbandhaparīkṣā*) Shastri, Swami Dwarikadas, (ed.); Bauddha Bharati Series; Varanasi; 1972. (In the text I have used this edition).

——*Svārthānumāna-pariccheda*, Malavaniya, Dalasukhabhai—(ed.); Hindu Vishvavidyalaya Nepal Rajya Sanskrit Series, Publication Board (Pub.); Varanasi, 1959.

——*Pramāṇa-viniścaya*; (Teil-I) Steinkellner, Ernst, (ed.); Verlag Der Östereichischen Akademe Der Vissenschaften, Wien, 1973.

Dhruva, A.B.; "*Trividhaṁ Anumānam*—A Study in *Nyāya Sūtra*

I.i.5"; *Proceedings of All India Oriental Conference*; 1919; Poona; Vol. I & II; pp. 251-280.

Diṅnāga; *Pramāṇa-samuccaya*; (Ch. I only *Pratyakṣa Khaṇḍa*) (Sva-*vṛtti* sahita) Iyengar, H.R. Rangaswamy, (ed.); Mysore Govt. Press, Mysore, 1930.

———*The Nyāya-mukha*; Tucci Guiseppe, (ed.); Jabuch des Institutes für Buddhismus-kunde Vol. I, Heidelberg, 1930.

———*Hetu-cakra-hamaru* (*Hetu-cakra-nirṇaya*); Chatterjee, Durgacharana (ed.); *Indian Historical Quarterly*; Vol. 9, 1933, pp. 266-272.

———*Ālaṁbana-parīkṣā* & *Vṛtti*; Shastri, Aiyaswami, N. (ed.); The Adyar Library, Adyar, 1942.

———*Nyāya-Praveśa*; Part I, Sandesara, B.J. (ed.) Gaekwad's Oriental Series, No. 38, Oriental Institute, Baroda, 1968.

———*Nyāyāvatāra*; Vidyabhusana, S.C. (ed.); Indian Research Society, Calcutta.

Dixit, Shrinivas; "The Redundance of the *Vyatirekī-Vyāpti* of the *Nyāya*-system;" *The Philosophical Quarterly*, Amalner, Vol. 23 No. 1, April 1950., pp. 13-15.

Dravid, Raja Ram; *The Problem of Universals in Indian Philosophy*; Motilal Banarsidass, Varanasi, 1972.

Durveka Miśra; *Dharmottara-pradīpa*; Malvania, Dalsukhabhai, (ed.); Kashi Prasad Jayaswal Research Institute, Patna, (2nd ed.), 1971.

Empson, W.; *Seven Types of Ambiguities*; Chatto and Windus, London, 1947.

Frauwallner, E.; "Vasubandhu's *Vādavidhiḥ*"; *Wiener Zeitschrift für die kunde Sud-und Östasiens*; Band I; 1957, pp. 104-146.

———"Landmarks in the History of Indian Logic"; *Wiener Zeitschrift Für die kunde Sud Und Östasiens*, Band V; 1961, pp. 125-148 & 470-550.

Ganguli, H.K.; *Philosophy of Logical Construction*; Sanskrit Pustak Bhandar, Calcutta, 1963.

Gautama, *Nyāya-Sūtras* (with *Nyāya-Bhāṣya* of Vātsyāyana) Shastri, Swami, Dwarikadas (ed.); Bauddha Bharati, Varanasi, 1976.

Geshelobsang, Tharchin; *The Logic and Debate Tradition of India, Tibet and Mangolia: History, Reader, Resources*;

Rashi Gampil Ling, First Kalmuk Buddhist Temple, Howell, U.S.A., 1979.

Gokhale, P.P.; *An Investigation in Fallacies Discussed in Indian Logic with Special Reference to Ancient Nyāya and Buddhism.* A Ph.D. Thesis; (unpublished); University of Poona, Poona, 1980.

Guha, D.C.; *Navya-Nyāya System of Logic*; Bharatiya Vidya Prakashana, Varanasi, 1968.

Gupta, Bina; "Are *Hetvābhāsas* Formal Fallacies?"; *Journal of Indian Philosophy*; Vol. 8 No. 2; June 1980, pp. 135-147.

Gupta, Prajñākara, *Pramāṇa-vārtikālaṅkāra* (also known as *Pramāṇa-vārtika-bhāṣya*); Sankrityayana, Rahul Bhadra; (ed.); Kashi Prasad Jayaswal Research Institute, Patna, 1953.

Gupta, Rita; "The Buddhist Doctrine of Momentariness and its Pre-suppositions"; *Journal of Indian Philosophy*; Vol. 8, No. 1, March 1980.

Hattori, Masaki; "Fragments From *Pramāṇa-samuccaya*"; *Journal of Indian Buddhist Studies*, Vol. VII; No. 1, 1958, pp. 330-335.

——— "*Pratyakṣābhāsa* (Diṅnāga's view and Dharmakīrti's Interpretation)", *Miscellanea Indologica Kiotiensa* Vol. 6-7, March 1965, pp. 122-128.

——— *Diṅnāga on Perception*; (*Pratyakṣa-pariccheda* of Diṅnāga's *Pramāṇa-samuccaya*); Harvard Oriental Series, Massachusetts, 1968.

——— "*Apoha* and *Pratibhā*", *Sanskrit and Indian Studies*, (Essays in Honour of Daniel H. H. Ingalls) D. Reidel Publishing Company, Holland, 1980, pp. 61-73.

Hayes, Richard, p.; "Diṅnāga's Views on Reasoning (First half of the 2nd Ch. *Svārthānumāna Pariccheda* of *Pramāṇa-samuccaya*) translated into English"; *Journal of Indian Philosophy* Vol. 8, No. 3, Sept. 1980, pp. 219-277.

Heimann, Betty; "Opposites: Contrasts & Complements in Early Greek and Indian Philosophy"; *Brahmavidyā*, (The Adyar Library Bulletin); Vol. XXV, No. 1 to 4, (Jubilee Volume); Adyar, 1961, pp. 216-228.

Herzberger, H. G.; "Double Negation in Buddhist Logic", *Journal of Indian Philosophy*, Vol. 3, No. 1 & 2, March/April 1975, pp. 3-16.

Ingalls, D. H.; *Materials for the Study of Navya-Nyāya Logic*; Harvard Oriental Series; Reprinted by MLBD, Delhi.

Iyengar, Rangaswami; "Vasubandhu and *Vādavidhi*"; *Indian Historical Quarterly*; Vol. V, No. 1, 1929, pp. 81-86.

——— (ed.); *Pramāṇa-samuccaya* of Diṅnāga (*Pratyakṣa khaṇda* only); Mysore University Publications; Mysore, 1930.

Iyengar, H. R. R.; "Some theories of Buddhist Logic in the *Kāvyālaṅkāra* of Bhāmaha"; *Proceedings of All India Oriental Conference*, No. VIII, 1935, Mysore, pp. 419-425.

——— "The *Vādavidhi* and the *Vādavidhāna* of Vasubandhu", *Brahmavidyā*, The Adyar Library Bulletin, Vol. XVII, Part I, Feb. 1953, pp. 9-19.

Jagadīśa Tarkālaṅkāra; *Pakṣatā-prakaraṇa*; Chowkhamba Sanskrit Samsthan; Varanasi, (2nd ed.), 1980.

Jayanta Bhaṭṭa; *Nyāya-Mañjarī*; (Part I & II) Śukla, Surya Narayana, (ed.); Chowkhamba, (The Chowkhamba Sanskrit Series) Varanasi, 1971.

Jayatilleke, K. N.; *Early Buddhist Theory of Knowledge*, George Allen and Unwin Pvt. Ltd., London, 1963.

Jha, Ganganath; (ed.); *The Nyāya-Sūtras of Gautama*, (tr. into English); 4 Vols. Motilal Banarsidass, Delhi, 1984.

Jhalakīkar, Bhīmācārya; *Nyāya-koṣa*; The Bhandarkar Oriental Research Institute, Poona, 1978.

Jitāri; *Hetutattvopadeśa*; Chattopadhyaya, Durgacarana (ed.) University of Calcutta, Calcutta, 1939.

Joad, C.E.M.; "Indian Logicians: A Study in Indian and Western Philosophizing", *The Aryan Path*; Vol. X No. 10, Oct. 1939, pp. 495-497.

Joshi, Rasik Vihari; "Treatment of Fallacy in Indian Logic"; *Dr. V.V. Mirashi Felicitation Volume*; Vidarbha Samshodhan Mandal, Nagpur; 1965; pp. 270-301.

Junankar, N.S.; *Gautama: The Nyāya Philosophy*; Motilal Banarsidass; Delhi, 1978.

Kajiyama, Yuichi; "On the Theory of Intrinsic Determination of Universal Concomitance in Buddhist Logic", *Journal of Indian Buddhist Studies*: Vol. VII, No. 1, Dec. 1958; pp. 354-360.

Kajiyama, Yuichi; "The *Avayavī-Nirākaraṇa* of Paṇḍita Aśoka", *Journal of Indian Buddhist Studies*; Vol. 9, No. 1, 1961, pp. 371-376.

——— "Buddhist Solipsism—A Free Translation of Ratnakīrti's *Santānāntara-dūṣaṇa*"; *Journal of Indian Buddhist Studies*; Vol. 13, No. 1, Jan. 1965; pp. 420-435.

Karṇakagomin; *Pramāṇa-vārtika-ṭīkā*; (*Svārthānumāna pariccheda* only). Sankrityayana, Rahul Bhadra, (ed.), Kitab Mahal, Allahabad, 1943.

Katsura, Shoryu; "New Sanskrit Fragments of the *Pramāṇa-samuccaya*;" *Journal of Indian Philosophy*; Vol. 3 No. 1 & 2; March & April 1975, pp. 67-78.

——— "Diṅnāga on *Trairūpya*"; *Journal of Indian Buddhist Studies*; Vol. XXXII, No. 1, Dec. 1983, pp. 540-544.

——— "Dharmakīrti's Theory of Truth"; *Journal of Indian Philosophy*, Vol. XII. 3, Sept. 1984, pp. 215-237.

Keith, A.B.; "Vasubandhu and his *Vādavidhi*"; *Indian Historical Quarterly*; Vol. IV, 1928; pp. 221-227.

——— *Indian Logic and Atomism*; Oriental Reprint Corporation, New Delhi, 1977.

Kenneth, K.I.; "Some Basic Misconceptions of Buddhism"; *International Philosophical Quarterly*; Vol. 10, No. 1, March 1969.

Kher, Chitrarekha; "The Concept of *Pramāṇa* According to Diṅnāga and Dharmakīrti"; *Journal of the Oriental Institute*, Baroda; Vol. XXII; No. 3, March 1973, pp. 256-264.

Kimura, Ryukan; *A Historical Study of the Terms Hīnayāna and Mahāyāna and the Origin of Mahāyāna Buddhism*; University of Calcutta, Calcutta, 1927.

Kitagawa, Hidenori (ed. & trns. into English) "A Refutation of Solipsism, (An annotated translation of the *Santānāntara-siddhi*)", *Journal of Greater India Society*; Vol. XIV, No. 1 & 2, Calcutta, 1955, pp. 407-429.

———"A Note on the Methodology in the Study of Indian Logic"; *Journal of Indian Buddhist Studies*; Vol. VIII, No. 1, 1960, pp. 380-390.

Kitagawa, Hindori: "On *Upādhi*", *Journal of Indian Buddhist Studies*; Vol. 14, No. 1, Dec. 1965; pp. 430-436.

Koros, Alexander, Csoma, de: *Analysis of the Kanjur*; Sri Satguru Publications, Delhi, (2nd ed.), 1982.

Kunst, Arnold, "The Two-membered Syllogism"; *Rocznik Orientalistyczny*; Vol. 15, (1939-40), pp. 72-83.

——— "An Overlooked Type of Inference"; *Bulletin of the School of Oriental and African Studies*; Vol. 10, 1940; pp. 976-991.

Law, N.M. (ed.); *Winternitz Memorial Volume*, Calcutta Oriental Press, Calcutta, 1968.

Malvania, Dalsukhbhai; "Review of D.N. Shastri's Critique of Indian Realism"; *Journal of the Oriental Institute*; M. S. University of Baroda; Vol. 16, 1967, pp. 389-391.

Mallişeṇasūri, *Syādvāda-mañjarī*; Dhruva, A. B. (ed.); Bombay Sanskrit and Prakrit Series, No. LXXXIII; Bhandarkar Oriental Institute, Pune, 1933.

Matilal, B.K.; "Diṅnāga's Remarks on the Concept of *Anumeya*"; *The Journal of the Ganganatha Jha Research Institute*, Vol. XXIV; No. 1-4, Jan.-Oct. 1968, pp. 151-159.

———"Gaṅgeśa on the Concept of Universal Property (*Kevalānvayin*)"; *Journal of the American Oriental Society*; Vol. XVIII, No. 3, July 1968, pp. 151-163.

———*The Navya-Nyāya Doctrine of Negation*, Harvard Oriental Series, No. 46, Harvard University Press, Cambridge, Massachusetts, 1968.

———*Epistemology, Logic and Grammar in Indian Philosophical Analysis*, Mouton, The Hague, 1971.

———"Ontological Problems in *Nyāya*, Buddhism and Jainism—A Comparative Analysis"; *Journal of Indian Philosophy*; Vol. V, No. 1 & 2, Sept. & Dec. 1977, pp. 91-105.

———"Problem Concerning 'Self-awareness' in Indian Philosophy"; *Studies in the History of Indian Thought*, Japan; No. 3, Feb. 1985, pp. 1-12.

———"A Note on *Nyāya* Fallacies"; *Journal of Indian Philosophy*; Vol. 2, No. 3 & 4, p. 215.

Matilal, B.K. and Robert D. Evans (eds.); *Buddhist Logic and*

Epistemology: Studies in the Buddhist Analysis of Inference and Language; D. Reidel, Dordrecht, 1986.

Matsumoto, Shiro, "*Svabhāvapratibandha*"; *Journal of Indian Buddhist Studies*, (Indogaku Bukkyogaku Kenkyu); Vol. XXX, No. 1, Dec. 1981, pp. 494-498.

Mikogami, Esho; "Some Remarks on the Concept of *Arthakriyā*"; *Journal of Indian Philosophy*; Vol. 7, No. 1, March 1979, pp. 179-194.

Miśra, Durveka, Paṇḍita; *Dharmottara-pradīpa*; (ed.) Malvania, Dalsukhabhai, Pandita; Kashi Prasad Jayaswal Research Institute, Patna, 1971.

Misra, G. S. P.; "Logical and Scientific Methods in Early Buddhist Texts"; *Journal of Royal Asiatic Society* (G. B. & I), 1968, pp. 54-64.

Miśra, Vācaspati; *Nyāya-vārtika-tātparya-ṭikā*; Vol. I & II; Dravid Shastri R., (ed.); Kashi Sanskrit Series No. 24, Chowkhamba Sanskrit Samsthana, Varanasi, 1926.

Miyasaka, Yusho; "Fragments from Vasubandhu and Diṅnāga" *Journal of Indian Buddhist Studies*; Vol. VI, No. 1, Jan. 1958, pp. 23-34.

Mookerjee, Jatilkumar; "*Vitaṇḍā* or Wrangling" *Gopinath Kaviraj Abhinandana Grantha*; Akhila Bharatiya Saṁskrit Parishad (pub.); Lucknow, 1967, pp. 146-150.

Mookerjee, Satkari, (ed.); *The Nava-Nalanda Mahavihara Research Publications*, Patna; Vol. I & II; 1937.

———"The Grounds of Inference as Classified by Dharmakīrti" *Siddha-Bharati*, (The Rosary of Indology), Vishveshvarananda Indological Series No. 2, (Dr. Siddheshwar Varma Felicitation Volume); Part II, Section IV; 1950, pp. 63-67.

———*Buddhist Philosophy of Universal Flux*; Motilal Banarsidass, Delhi, 1975, (2nd ed.)

———"The Grounds of Inference as Classified by Diṅnāga", *Studies in Buddhism*, No. 2, pp. 63-67.

Mukherjee, A.K.; "The Definition of Pervasion in *Navya-Nyāya*"; *Journal of Indian Philosophy*, Vol. 4, No. 1, 1976, pp. 1-50.

Murti, T.R.V.; "The Theory of Judgement in the Indian Systems", *The Philosophical Quarterly*, Amalner; Vol. 8, No. 4, Jan. 1932; pp. 381-393.

Murti, T.R.V.; *The Central Philosophy of Buddhism*; George Allen & Unwin Ltd., London, 4th ed., 1974.

Nāgārjuna, *Madhyamakaśāstra*; (with Chandrakīrti's *Prasannapadā* & *Vigrahavyāvartanī* as an Appendix); Vaidya, P.L., (ed.) Buddhist Sanskrit Text No. 10; Mithila Institute, Darbhanga; 1960.

Nagatomi, Masatoshi; "The Framework of the *Pramāṇa-vārtika* book I"; *Journal of the American Oriental Society*, Vol. 79, No. 4, Dec. 1959, pp. 263-266.

———"*Mānasa-Pratyakṣa*: A Conundrum in the Buddhist *Pramāṇa-system*", *Sanskrit and Indian Studies*, (Essays in Honour of Daniel H. H. Ingalls), D. Reidel Publishing Company, Holland, 1980, pp. 243-260.

Nakada, Naomichi: "Three Kinds of Inferences in the Commentaries of *Sāṁkhya-kārikā*"; (Part II) *Journal of Indian Buddhist Studies*; Vol. 14, No. 2, March 1966; pp. 875-828. continued in Vol. 15, No. 1, Dec. 1966, pp. 427-437.

——— "*Vyākhyāṅga* and *Parapratipādanāṅga* in *Yuktidīpikā*"; *Journal of Indian Buddhist Studies*; Vol. 13, No. 2, March, 1965; pp. 729-805.

———"Word and Inference in the *Yuktidīpikā*"; (Part I) *Journal of Indian Buddhist Studies*; Vol. 18, No. 2, March 1970, pp. 1018-1022.

Nakamura, Hajime; "Buddhist Logic Expounded by Means of Symbolic Logic"; *Journal of Indian Buddhist Studies*; Vol. VII, No. 1, Dec. 1958; pp. 375-395.

———*Indian Buddhism: A Survey With Bibliographical Notes*; pp. 274-395. Kufs Publications; Japan, 1980.

Narendra Deo, Acharya; *Bauddha-Dharma-Darshan*; Bihar Rashtrabhasha Parishad, Patna, (2nd ed.), 1971.

Nariman, J.K.; *Literary History of Sanskrit Buddhism*; Motilal Banarsidass, Delhi, (2nd ed.), 1972.

Oliver, J.W.; "Formal Fallacies and Other Indvalid Arguments;" *Mind*; (new series), Vol. 76, 1967.

Pande, G.C.; *Studies in the Origins of Buddhism*; Motilal Banarsidass, Delhi, (3rd ed.), 1983.

Pandeya, R.C.; "Ontological Basis of the Buddhist Theory of Inference", *The Visva-Bharati Journal of Philosophy*, Santiniketan, No. 5.2 (1969), pp. 26-33.

Pandeya, R.C.; *Buddhist Studies in India*; Motilal Banarsidass, Delhi, 1975.

Pathak, K.B.; "Dharmakīrti and Śaṅkarāchārya"; *Journal of Royal Asiatic Society*, (Bombay Branch); No. 18, 1894, pp. 88-96.

———"Dharmakīrti's *Trilakṣaṇa-hetu*—attacked by Pātrakesarī and Defended by Śāntarakṣita"; *Annals of the Bhandarkar Oriental Research Institute*, Pune, Vol. XII, 1930-31.

Perrett, Roy, W.; "The Problem of Induction in Indian Philosophy"; *Philosophy East & West*; Vol. 34, No. 2, April 1984, pp. 161-175.

Perszuk, Kenneth, J.; "The *Nyāya* and Russell on Empty-terms", *Philosophy East & West*, Vol. 34, No. 2, April 1984, pp. 131-147.

Potter, Karl; "Logic and *Nyāya*"; *The Aryan Path*; Vol. XXVI, No. 1, Jan. 1955, pp. 9-15.

———(ed); *Encyclopaedia of Indian Philosophies*; (*Nyāya-Vaiṣesika*), Vol. II, Motilal Banarsidass, Delhi, 1977.

Pranaraj, D.M.; "A Note on the Ascertainment of *Vyāpti*"; *Darshana International*; Vol. XIII, No. 4; Oct. 1973; pp. 35-40.

Prasad, Someshwar; "Nature of Knowledge According to Dharmakīrti"; *Nagpur University Journal* (Humanities); Vol. XV, No. 1, Oct. 1964, pp. 68-75.

Randle, H.N.; "A Note on the Indian Syllogism"; *Mind*; Vol. 33, 1924, pp. 398-414.

———*Indian Logic in the Early Schools*; Oriental Books Reprint Corporation, New Delhi, 1976 (1st ed.)

———*Fragments from Diṅnāga*; Motilal Banarsidass, Delhi, 1981.

Rao, Krishna, A.S.; "Inference in Indian Logic"; *Journal of the Oriental Research*; Madras; Vol. I, Oct. 1927, pp. 375-379.

———"The Place of Praśastapāda and Diṅnāga in the Evolution of *Vyāpti*"; *Journal of the Oriental Research Institute*, Madras; Vol. I, 1927; pp. 77-86.

Rao, P. Nagaraja; "Logic and Intuition in Indian Philosophy"; *The Aryan Path*; Vol. XXI, No. 11, Nov. 1950; pp. 511-514.

Rastogi, M.N.; "Study of Logic in India"; *Prabuddha Bharat* (or Awakened India); Vol. LXII, Sept. 1957; pp. 383-387.

Rao, S.K. Ramchandra; "Foundations of Indian Logic", *Bharatiya Vīdya*; Bombay; Vol. 16, No. 1, pp. 41-51.

Sankrtyayana, Rahul; *Darshan-Digdarshan*; Kitab Mahal, Pvt. Ltd., Allahabad, (3rd ed.), 1961.

Saradchandra, E.R.; "From Vasubandhu to Śāntarakṣita"; *Journal of Indian Philosophy*; Vol. 4, No. 1; 1976, pp. 67-107.

Sasaki, Genjun, H.; "The Three Aspects of Truth in Buddhist Epistemology"; *Journal of the Oriental Institute*; Baroda; Vol. XIV, No. 3 & 4, March-June 1965; pp. 236-251.

Sen, Saileswar; "The Historical Origin and the Distinction between *Svārthānumāna* and *Parārthānumāna*"; *Journal of Indian Philosophy*; Vol. X, Part II, Aug. 1931, pp. 29-39 and 187-190.

Shah, K.J.; "Logic and Ontology: Some Preliminary Considerations"; *The Visva-Bharati Journal of Philosophy*; Vol. 8, No. 1, Aug. 1971, pp. 24-30.

Shah, Nagin, J.; *Akalaṅka's Criticism of Dharmakīrti's Philosophy*; L.D. Institute of Indology, Ahmedabad, 1967.

———"Essentials of Dharmakīrti's Theory of Knowledge (Based on the *Pramāṇa-vārtika*)", *Studien zum Jainismus und Buddhismus*, Wiesbaden, 1981, pp. 251-259.

Sharma, B.L.; "*Pakṣatā*—The Motivational Conditions of Inference According to the *Navya-Nyāya*"; *Darshana International*; Vol. 6, No. 1, Jan. 1966; pp. 103-107.

Sharma, Brajanarayana; *Bhāratīya Darshan men Anumāna*; M.P. Hindi Granth Academy, Bhopal; 1973.

Sharma, C.: *A Critical Survey of Indian Philosophy*; Motilal Banarsidass, Delhi (4th ed.), 1976.

Shastri, D.N., *The Philosophy of Nyāya-Vaiśeṣika and its Conflict with the Buddhist, Diṅnāga School*, (Critique of Indian Realism), Bharatiya Vidya Prakashana, New Delhi, (2nd ed.), 1976.

———*Uddyotakara kā Nyāya-vārtika—eka Adhyayana*; Bharatiya Prakashana, Kanpur, 1974.

Shastri, H.P., "An Examination of the *Nyāya-Sūtras*", *Journal*

of the Asiatic Society of Bengal (New series); Vol. I, No. 10, 1905, pp. 245-250.
(Reprinted in)
Studies in the History of Indian Philosophy (ed.) D. P. Chattopadhyaya, Calcutta, 1978, Vol. II, pp. 88-96.

Shastri, Harprasad; "History of *Nyāya-śāstra* from Japanese Sources"; *Journal of Royal Asiatic Society of Bengal* (new series); Vol. 1.8, 1905; pp. 177-180.

Shastri, Kuppuswami, S.; *A Primer of Indian Logic*; The Kuppuswami Shastri Research Institute, Mylapore, Madras, (3rd ed.), 1961.

Shastri, P.S.; "Theory of Inference in Indian Philosophy"; *Bhāratiya Vidyā*; Vol. 18, No. 3 & 4, 1958; pp. 1-23.

Shastri, S.; "Syllogistic Reasoning: A Comparative Study of Indian Logic with European Logic"; *Journal of Shri Venkatesvara Oriental Institute*, Tirupati; Vol. III, 1942, pp. 191-203.

———"The Conception of External Object in the School of Diṅnāga", *Darshana International*, Vol. V, No. 2, April 1965; pp. 91-95.

———(ed. and tr. into Hindi) *Nyāya Darshanam*; Bauddha Bharati Grantha Mala No. 11; Bauddha Bharati; Varanasi; 1976.

Shukla, Balirama; *Anumāna-Pramāṇa*; Eastern Book Linkers, Delhi, 1986.

Singh, Amar; *Heart of Buddhist Philosophy*: *Diṅnāga and Dharmakīrti*; Munshiram Manoharlal, New Delhi, 1984.

Stall, J.F., "Correlations Between Language and Logic in Indian Thought"; *Bulletin of the School of the Oriental and African Studies*; Vol. XXIII (23.1), 1960; pp. 109-122.

———"The Concept of *Pakṣa* in Indian Logic"; *Journal of Indian Philosophy*; Vol. 2, No. 2, 1973.

Stasiak, Stefan; "Fallacies and their Classification According to the Early Hindu Logicians"; *Rocznik Orientalistyezny*; Vol. 6, 1928, pp. 191-198.

Stcherbatsky, Th.; *Buddhist Logic*, Two Vols; Dover Publications, Inc, New York, 1962.

Steinkellner, Ernst, "On the Interpretation of the *Svabhāva-Hetu*"; *Wiener Zeitschrift für die Kunde Sudasians und*

Archiv für Indische Philosophie; Wien; Band XVIII, 1974, pp. 117-129.

———"Philological Remarks on Śākyamati's *Pramāṇa-vārtika-ṭīkā*"; *Studien zum Jainismus und Buddhismus*, Wiesbaden; 1981.

———"The Spiritual Place of the Epistemological Tradition in Buddhism"; *Nanto Bukkyo or Journal of the Nanto Society for Buddhist Studies*, Japan, No. 49, Dec. 1982, pp. 1-15.

———"*Svabhāvapratibandha* Again", *Acta Indologica*, VI, 1984, pp. 457-476.

Sugiura, Sadajiro; *Hindu Logic as Preserved in China and Japan*; Pennsilvania University Publication; Pennsilvania, 1900.

Swami Agehananda Bharati; "The Place of Inductive Reasoning in *Navya-Nyāya* Logic", *Journal of Indian and Buddhist Studies*; Vol. V No. 1, 1957, pp. 311-315.

Tamura, Kwansei; "Some Developments of the Buddhist Approach to Reality;" *International Philosophical Quarterly*; Vol. IV, No. 4, 1964.

Thakur, Anantalal; (ed.); *Nyāya-Darshanam*; Vol. I; Ch. I; *The Nyāya Sūtras of Gautam, with the Bhāṣya of Vātsyāyana, the Vārtika of Uddyotakara, the Tātpāryaṭīkā of Vācaspati and the Pariśuddhi of Udayana*. Mithila Institute Series No. 20, Prakrit Jain Institute, Vaisali, Muzaffarpur, 1967.

Thomas, K.; *A Study of the Buddhist Epistemology According to Dharmakīrti's Nyāya-bindu*; Motilal Banarsidass, Delhi, 1982.

Tripathi, C.L.; "The Nature of Reality in Yogācāra Buddhism"; *Philosophy East-West*; No. 19, 1969, pp. 474-84.

———"The Idealistic Theory of Inference"; *Annals of the Bhandarkar Oriental Research Institute*, Pune, Vol. LI, 1970, pp. 175-188.

———"The Problem of *Svalakṣaṇa* in *Sautrāntika* Epistemology"; *Journal of the Oriental Institute*, Baroda; Vol. 20, 1970-71, pp. 216-225.

———"Knowledge and its Validity"; *Journal of the Oriental Institute*, Baroda; Vol. XXI, No. 1 & 2, Sept. Dec. 1971, pp. 71-89.

Tripathi. C. L., *The Problem of Knowledge in Yogācāra Buddhism*; Bharat Bharati, Oriental Pub. & Booksellers, B 28/15, Durgakund, Varanasi-5 (India), 1972.

Tucci, G., "On The Fragments From Diṅnāga", *Journal of Royal Asiatic Society*, Vol. 80, 1928, pp. 377-390, 905-906.

———"Is the *Nyāya-praveśa* by Diṅnāga ?" *Journal of Royal Asiatic Society*; (G.B & I), Vol. 82, 1928, pp. 7-13.

———"*Vādavidhi*", *Indian Historical Quarterly*, Vol. IV, 1928, pp. 630-636.

———"Buddhist Logic Before Diṅnāga (Asaṅga, Vasubandhu, *Tarka-śāstras*)", *Journal of the Royal Asiatic Society* (Great Britain and Ireland), Vol. 81, 1929, pp. 451-488.

———*On Some Aspects of the Doctrines of Maitreyanātha and Asaṅga*; Calcutta University, Calcutta, 1930.

——— (tr. & ed.); "The *Jātinirākṛti* of Jitārī"; *Annals of the Bhandarkar Oriental Research Institute*, Poona, Vol. 11, 1937, pp. 54-58.

———*Pre-Diṅnāga Buddhist Texts on Logic from Chinese Sources*; Vesta Publications; Madras, 1981; (2nd ed.)

Uddyotakara; *Nyāya-vārtika*; Dvivedi Vindyeswari Prasad (ed.) Vārāṇasī Rājakīya Sanskrit Pāṭhaśālā; Chowkhamba Sanskrit Series, Varanasi, 1916.

Uno, Atsushi; "One Aspect of Extraordinary Perception"; *Journal of Indian Buddhist Studies*; Vol. 8, No. 2, 1960; pp. 740-735.

———"The Concept of *Vyāpti* in the *Nyāya*-School"; *Acta Asiatica*; Vol. 3, 1962, pp. 16-29.

———"*Satpratipakṣa* as a Fallacy in the *Navya-Nyāya*", *Journal of Indian Buddhist Studies*; Vol. 18, No. II; March 1970, pp. 1035-1023.

Upadhyay, B.; *Bauddha Darśana Mīmāṁsā*, Chaukhamba Vidya Bhavan, Varanasi (3rd ed.), 1978.

Uryuzu, Ryushin; "A Note on Bhavaviveka's Logic"; *Journal of Indian Buddhist Studies*; Vol. 18, No. 2, March 1970; pp. 1017-1009.

Varadachari, K.C.; "A Critique of the *Pramāṇas*"; *Journal of the Ganganath Jha Research Institute*; Vol. V, No. 2, Feb. 1947; pp. 93-119.

Varadachari, K. C.; "Logic of Sāṁkhya"; *Sri Venkatesvara University Oriental Journal*, Tirupati; Vol. 3, Part I, 1960; pp. 27-34.

———"Requisites of a Good *Hetu*"; *Annals of the Bhandarkar Oriental Research Institute*, Pune, Vol. XLVI, 1965; pp. 43-48.

Varadarāja; *Tārkika-rakṣā*; Mallinaga (ed.); Varanasi; Rajakiya Sanskrit Pathasala; 1903.

Vassiliev, Boris; "Ju-Shih-Lun—a Logical Treatise Ascribed to Vasubandhu"; *Bulletin of the School of Oriental Studies*; Vol. 8 No. 4, 1935; pp. 1013-1037.

Verma, Roop Rekha; "Logic and Ontology", *The Visva-Bharati Journal of Philosophy*; Vol. 8, No. 1, Aug. 1971, pp. 14-23.

Vidyabhusana, S.C.; "Dinnāga and his *Pramāṇa-samuccaya*" *Journal of Royal Asiatic Society* (Bengal) (new series); Vol. 1, No. 9, 1905; pp. 217-227.

———"Indian Logic as Preserved in Tibet"; *Journal and Proceedings of the Asiatic Society of Bengal* (new series), Vol. 3, 1907, pp. 95-102, 241-255, 541-551.

———"Vātsyāyana: the Author of *Nyāya-Bhāṣya*"; *Indian Antiquary*; Vol. 44, 1915, pp. 82-88.

———"Ancient Indian Logic: An Outline"; *Commemorative Essays presented to Sir R.G. Bhandarkar*; Bhandarkar Oriental Research Institute; Pune, 1917, pp. 155-166.

———"Influence of Aristotle in the Development of the Syllogism in Indian Logic"; *Journal of Royal Asiatic Society*; (Great Britain and Ireland); Vol. 70, 1918; pp. 469-488. (also in *History of Indian Logic* as an Appendix).

———*A History of Indian Logic*; Motilal Banarsidass, Delhi; (3rd ed.); 1978.

Vijaya Rani; *Buddhist Philosophy as Presented in Mīmāṁsā-śloka-vārtika*; Parimal Publications, Delhi, 1982.

Vinītaveda; *Nyāya-bindu-ṭīkā*; Gangopadhyaya, Mrinalakanti; (ed.); Indian Studies, Past and Present, Delhi, 1971.

Vostrikov, A; "The *Nyāya-Vārtika* of Uddyotakara and the *Vādanyāya* of Dharmakīrti"; *Indian Historical Quarterly*, Vol. XI.1; March 1935, pp. 1-35.

Watanabe, F.; "The Principles of Reasoning and Forms of Argument in Early Buddhistic Canons"; *Journal of Indian Buddhist Studies*; Vol. 19, No. I, Dec. 1970, pp. 476-469.

Watanabe, F.; "Logical Arguments in the Dialogues (*Sutias*)"; *Journal of Indian Buddhist Studies*; Vol. 20, No. II, March 1972, pp. 988-976.

Wayman, Alex; "The Rules of Debate According to Asaṅga"; *Journal of the American Oriental Society*, Vol. 78, No. 1, Jan. 1958, pp. 29-40.

———"A Reconsideration of Dharmakīrti's 'Deviation' from Diṅnāga on *Pratyakṣābhāsa*"; *Annals of the Bhandarkar Oriental Research Institute*, Pune; Vol. LVIII and LIX (Diamond Jubilee Volume); 1977-78.

Winternitz, Maurice; *A History of Indian Literature* (Vol. II); Oriental Books Reprint Corporation, New Delhi, 2nd ed., 1977.

AUTHOR INDEX

SUBJECT INDEX

TITLE INDEX

ERRATA

Page Number	*Line from Above*	*Incorrect*	*Correct*
54	7	thc	the
133	32	fy	by
158	25-26	dogmatic the	dogmatic mode of defending the